Jung's Philosophy

Jung's Philosophy explores some of the controversial philosophical ideas that are both explicit and implicit within Carl Jung's psychology, comparing the philosophical assumptions that underlie this and other psychotherapeutic traditions.

Within this book, Corbett provides a useful introduction to the philosophical issues relevant to the practice of analytical psychology, showing how these are viewed by different psychotherapeutic traditions. Most of the disagreement between schools of psychotherapy, and much of the comparative literature, concerns differences in theory and technique. This book takes a different, more fundamental approach by comparing schools of thought based on their underlying philosophical commitments. The author discusses the philosophical basis of various worldviews such as idealism and realism, beliefs about the nature of the psyche and the unconscious, and the mind–brain relationship, and focuses on the way in which Jung's psychology addresses these and related issues, including the possible relevance of quantum mechanics to depth psychology.

This text will be of value to practicing psychotherapists and Jungian analysts, individuals undertaking the relevant training, and students in depth psychology.

Lionel Corbett is a psychiatrist and Jungian analyst. He is the author of six books and four volumes of collected papers. His primary interest is in Jung's concept of the religious function of the psyche.

Jung's Philosophy

Controversies, Quantum Mechanics, and the Self

Lionel Corbett

Routledge
Taylor & Francis Group

LONDON AND NEW YORK

Designed cover image: Getty Images

First published 2024
by Routledge
4 Park Square, Milton Park, Abingdon, Oxon OX14 4RN

and by Routledge
605 Third Avenue, New York, NY 10158

Routledge is an imprint of the Taylor & Francis Group, an informa business

© 2024 Lionel Corbett

British Library Cataloguing in Publication Data
A catalogue record for this book is available from the British Library

ISBN: 978-1-032-61844-9 (hbk)
ISBN: 978-1-032-61843-2 (pbk)
ISBN: 978-1-032-61845-6 (ebk)

DOI: 10.4324/9781032618456

Typeset in Times New Roman
by Taylor & Francis Books

Contents

Preface

This book describes some of the controversial philosophical issues that are explicit or implicit in Carl Jung's psychology. The book shows the contrasts between the philosophical assumptions of his approach and the assumptions that underly other psychotherapeutic traditions. I hope this approach will enable psychotherapists to place Jung's thinking about the psyche in the larger context of psychology as a discipline.

I believe it is important for students and practitioners of any form of psychotherapy to be familiar with the philosophical ground that underlies their particular theoretical orientation. It is also valuable to understand the limitations and strengths of the intellectual heritage on which one's practice is based. Without some knowledge of that background, the psychotherapist trained in a particular school of thought may unwittingly subscribe to a view of humanity that he or she does not really hold. This book will help students and practitioners to choose a way of working that is truly in keeping with their beliefs and values.

Most of the disagreements between schools of psychotherapy have been focused on differences in theory and technique. However, it is also useful to compare schools of thought based on their underlying philosophical commitments, their views of humanity, their beliefs about the nature of the psyche, their approach to the unconscious, and their approach to mental health. In this context, Jung is still marginalized or ignored in most university departments of psychology, because his interests are seen as too metaphysical or too close to spirituality, and his view of the unconscious is seen as unprovable. This critique ignores the evidence Jung provides for his theories, which are nevertheless seen as difficult to test or quantify. His ideas are too holistic for academic specialists; Jung's work bridges disciplines in a manner that cannot be confined within traditional academic silos. Furthermore, he focuses on subjectivity and self-knowledge rather than the current emphasis on rationalism, objectivity, and behavior. Jung's primary philosophical assumptions, such as the reality of the psyche and the irreducible importance of numinous experience, challenge mainstream approaches to psychology.

For historical reasons, mainstream psychology has modelled itself after Newtonian physics, whereas the discoveries of quantum mechanics offer new potentials for our understanding of reality. Quantum mechanics raises questions about the role that the psyche or consciousness might play in this understanding. The philosophical problems raised by quantum mechanics are therefore very relevant to psychology. Jung and Wolfgang Pauli were pioneers in the attempt to bridge these disciplines. Jung's discovery of synchronicity, and discoveries such as indeterminacy, non-locality, and acausality at the quantum level, mean that we must reappraise some of our approaches to psychology, which can no longer be based on the philosophical assumptions of traditional Newtonian science. Quantum mechanics has opened up a new horizon for psychology as well as physics. However, many psychologists are intimidated by the mathematical aspects of quantum mechanics, which are essential for the precise description of quantum phenomena. Fortunately, however, thanks to many texts by physicists who explain quantum mechanics without entering into its mathematics, it is possible to describe some important issues using ordinary language, metaphors, and analogies. This is the most a psychologist can hope for, and this is the approach I have adopted. The caveat is that physicists are understandably irritated by the misappropriation of quantum mechanical findings by other disciplines in the attempt to bolster personal metaphysical beliefs and pet theories, so this pitfall must be avoided by psychologists.

A further challenge for the non-physicist is that there is considerable disagreement within the physics community about the interpretation of quantum mechanics, which psychologists are not competent to evaluate. I have tried to find a balance between these conflicting opinions by presenting the debate from various points of view. To make the discussion relevant to psychology, I particularly focus on the contentious issue of the relevance of consciousness to quantum mechanics. At the moment, of the major interpretations of quantum mechanics, only about half of them take consciousness or the importance of the observer into account.

The term "consciousness" has a range of meanings. At the personal, human level, consciousness is generally taken to mean the subjective quality of experience, or the awareness that one is aware. In some non-dual spiritual traditions such as Advaita Vedānta, Pure Consciousness is seen as the ultimate ground of reality. When that level is implied, I capitalize the word to maintain the distinction between these personal and transpersonal levels. I also follow the convention in much of the Jungian literature of using an upper-case letter "S" to indicate the transpersonal Self as described by Jung and the Upaniṣadic tradition. I use the lower case "s" to refer to the personal self or one's sense of self, roughly synonymous with the empirical personality and the ego in Jung's sense.

The abbreviation 'CW' is used for citations from the English-language edition of Jung's *Collected works*, edited by Herbert Read, Michael Fordham, and Gerhard Adler (translated by R.F.C. Hull from the original German-language *Gesammelte Werke*), published between 1954 and 1990 by Princeton University Press in the US and by Routledge in the UK, in 20 volumes (with volume 9 in two parts). The number following CW gives the volume number, with the two parts of volume 9 cited as CW 9i and CW 9ii. Wherever possible I have cited these volumes using paragraph numbers rather than page numbers, to avoid any pagination differences between US and UK editions.

Chapter 1

Philosophical issues in psychology and psychotherapy

Psychotherapy, psychology, and philosophy

Many of the disputes between different schools of psychotherapy are based on fundamentally different worldviews and different beliefs about human nature and the nature of the psyche. Theories of psychotherapy are grounded in attitudes and assumptions that reflect important themes in Western philosophy, so a knowledge of the philosophical basis of these theories is relevant to psychotherapeutic practice (Orange, 2010; Downing, 2000; Erwin, 1997; Raabe, 2014). Important philosophical questions relevant to the psychotherapist are those such as the nature of the self, problems such as the mind–body relationship, questions about the sources of human motivation, whether we can know objective truth about reality or about another person, and the extent to which we can accurately know or reasonably infer the mental states of other people. Like philosophers, psychotherapists wonder whether our sense that we have free will is an illusion, which is argued by many neuroscientists (Carter, 2010) who believe that the field of psychology can be reduced to brain science.[1]

Schools of psychotherapy always have underlying pre-commitments, including assumptions about the nature of the psyche that they cannot prove. Thus, some take for granted that the psyche is generated by the brain, while Jung sees the psyche as a domain in its own right, not simply a product of the brain. Some psychotherapists prefer to approach people purely naturalistically, assuming that reality can be explained in purely physical terms without invoking the existence of a spiritual dimension. Many psychotherapists ignore or deny the existence of a dynamic unconscious, not to mention Jung's collective or transpersonal level of the psyche and the Self, which for Jungians are crucial. Most schools of psychotherapy do not acknowledge the existence of synchronicity.

Although philosophical concerns are relevant to psychotherapy, they are often ignored and seen as speculative and pragmatically unimportant. However, a degree of convergence between philosophy and psychotherapy has developed in recent decades, partly because of advances within neuroscience

DOI: 10.4324/9781032618456-1

that highlight the ancient question of the relationship between mind and brain. Neuroscientific findings now recognize the importance of emotions, intersubjectivity, and empathy as well as rational thought. The caveat in this area is that for many psychotherapists who engage with the depths of the psyche, a neuroscientific approach to the profound human questions and dilemmas that arise in psychotherapy, such as whether life is meaningful and worth living, is about as useful as is the chemical analysis of paint to the appreciation of a great painting.

Implicit or explicit assumptions about human nature and beliefs about the best way to understand people are built into all models of psychotherapy. It is preferable for the therapist to be conscious of these assumptions, partly because they act as a lens through which we see others, partly because they may clash with the patient's beliefs, and partly because it is important not to unconsciously impose these beliefs onto others (Willig, 2019). The practice of psychotherapy inevitably expresses the practitioner's assumptions, be they the biological drives of Freud at the root of human nature, the nonexistent mind of behaviorism, Jung's Self as the God within, or the self-actualizing urge of humanistic psychology. These assumptions operate in the background of the therapist's interventions, and conscious or not, they color his or her style of practice.

Philosophical issues relevant to psychotherapy

Ontological questions

Ontology is a branch of philosophy that studies our ideas about what exists, or the real nature of things, or what it means to say that something is real. Ontological questions are those such as whether the psyche exists independently of the brain, as it seems to do during near-death experiences, and whether consciousness is a fundamental, irreducible property of the universe, somehow woven into the fabric of reality. The nature of phenomena such as dreams, spiritual experiences, and other aspects of human subjectivity are ontological questions important to psychology. Jung's idea of the Self, the archetypes, and the collective unconscious is such an ontological claim. If the ontological assumptions that are the axiomatic foundations of a particular branch of psychotherapy are incorrect, that entire field is called into question.

There is a wide range of ontological beliefs about reality. Physicalism insists that only matter and energy exist. Realist philosophers and scientific realism hold to an objectivist ontology, the idea that material reality exists independently of our perceptions and thoughts about it. For realists, objects have properties such as mass and shape that can be measured. Psychologists with a realist orientation believe that there are psychological features common to all human beings, and these aspects of the mind can be reduced to their constituents and measured in a way analogous to the way we measure physical objects. Depth psychologists tend to believe that the psyche must be treated as a whole and cannot be measured.

Cognitive psychologists and neuroscientists usually adhere to various forms of philosophical naturalism, the idea that only phenomena that the natural sciences can objectively detect and study are ontologically real. In this view, mental events can or will be explained neurologically. This approach requires adherence to a physicalist ontology. It assumes that any psychological theory that is incompatible with physicalism, or any concept of non-physical entities such as a soul or an immaterial psyche, can be ruled out a priori. All psychological theories must be consistent with the rest of the natural sciences.

An objectivist ontology is often seen as a commonsense view of reality, especially given the success of science. However, as Klein (2015) points out, devices such as neuroimaging and electroencephalography are useless in the absence of an experiencing subject. An objectivist ontology raises questions such as how well we know the nature of the relationship between the way the world is and the way we observe it. Can we be sure that science accurately portrays the way the world is? Subjectivist ontologies point out that the outer world is experienced differently by different subjects.

In contrast to naturalism, constructivism is a relativistic ontology, often adopted by social psychologists. In this view, reality does not exist independently of the way we construct or think about it. Our experience of reality is based on our interactions with the social, linguistic, and historical environment in which we live. Constructivism assumes that what we take to be material reality is a product of the descriptions we have developed to describe particular situations. We make meaning by constructing our knowledge of the world, or even by creating our reality rather than discovering it. These constructed realities are not necessarily true in any absolute sense, because it is difficult to know how much our personal perspective is affecting the way we experience the world. The objects we perceive may not exist independently of our descriptions of them. Accordingly, some constructivists believe that ontological questions are in principle unanswerable. These philosophers tend to be either antirealist or suspicious of realist ontologies and they do not trust foundationalist approaches based on fundamental beliefs that seem to be self-evident and do not need to be justified.[2] Relativists see the many features of human psychology as simply individual perspectives rather than being ontologically fundamental.

For pragmatic constructivists, truth does not necessarily mean correspondence with an underlying objective reality, but the extent to which an idea works successfully in a particular context. Constructivists believe that all data is subject to interpretation; they reject the idea that there is an objective truth waiting to be discovered; rather, we generate truth and meaning, which we impose on the world by interpreting it in a way that makes sense to us.

Post-modern psychotherapists often believe that the truths arrived at in psychotherapy are creations of the therapeutic dyad, and do not necessarily correspond to reality because there are a variety of ways to understand the individual.

Praetorius (2003) points out that naturalism and constructivism fail to see that we need a notion of true and false prior to deciding how to apply these terms, and the assumption that the notion of truth is purely relative renders accounts of anything merely relatively true, so the assumption itself is inherently self-defeating. If we doubt the independent existence of reality, we doubt our own objective existence and the truth of our descriptions of ourselves. She believes that we cannot talk about ourselves or our reality without presupposing that things exist, and we cannot describe things without assuming that they exist independently of our descriptions.

Realist ontology: scientific realism

Based on Enlightenment values, the Western intellectual tradition and much of its science has been formed by the idea that we can discover the absolute truth about reality with increasingly sophisticated technology. Much mainstream psychological research is based on an ontology of scientific realism, which assumes that what is known through the senses and by experiment corresponds to the nature of the world. In this view, there is a material, objective world "out there," independent of our perception of it, independent of our minds, and our observations are not contaminated by pre-existing theory or by the language we use to describe it. The success of science is said to be good evidence that science describes the world as it actually is, although it is also argued that the way science studies the world depends on the preconceived ideas that scientists bring to their research, so that the questions they ask may not simply reflect the way the world actually is. Scientific theories are instruments that make predictions based on the method of observation.

Psychotherapists with a realist orientation, such as behaviorists and even some traditional psychoanalysts, assume that it is possible to discover objective truth about a person.[3] Many empirically oriented, "scientist-practitioner" psychotherapists subscribe to a realist ontology. Realism is sometimes associated with determinism, the belief that each event is the result of past causes in an inexorable chain of cause and effect.[4] Often realism shades into or is accompanied by materialism.

Some contemporary thinkers are somewhat skeptical about the project to describe reality entirely objectively, since some of what we think we have discovered may be influenced by pre-existing commitments, history, language, and culture. Critics of scientific realism point out that the data of empirical observation can be interpreted in different ways by different theories. Furthermore, the relationship between the nature of the world and our knowledge and perception of it is not clear. Human beings have evolved sensory systems that allow us to survive, but they do not necessarily tell us about many aspects of the world, such as magnetic fields, whose existence was unimportant to the survival of our early hominin ancestors. Quantum mechanics offers some support to antirealists who insist that reality cannot be said to have properties independent of the mind, because the outcome of quantum mechanical experiments is affected by choices made by the experimenter. Critics of scientific realism also point to the historical fact that the history of science is full of theories that are now known to be false. The recent suggestion that we are living in a computer-generated virtual reality tends towards an antirealist perspective.

Epistemological questions

Epistemology concerns the processes by which we acquire knowledge, the nature of knowledge, how we assess its truth, its limits, and its origins. How do we justify what we think we know? How can we be sure we have valid knowledge and not just ungrounded belief? How do our assumptions influence our findings? If we ask for evidence to support a psychological theory, we are asking an epistemological question. Theories of psychotherapy adopt characteristic epistemological approaches, ways in which we can know about the psyche, which are derived from their theory. Examples are approaches to the study of the unconscious by means of attention to dreams and the analysis of the transference.

Claims to knowledge are based on assumptions about how valid knowledge can be obtained. Empiricists believe we achieve knowledge by experiment and observation, and this is the default assumption for most research psychologists. This approach tends to assume that reality is the same for all people, and reality is objective, value neutral, and quantifiable. In contrast, the constructivist view is that reality can be different for different people, and the observer can only interpret what he or she imagines the subject is experiencing, using qualitative approaches. In contrast to empiricists, rationalists believe there are other ways to achieve knowledge besides empirical research, such as by means of reason, intuition, deduction, logic, and our human response to a situation. Certain types of knowledge are innate aspects of human nature, such as the acquisition of language.

The "linguistic turn" in epistemology made it apparent that our language and concepts help to constitute our knowledge claims. The "social turn" explained that what we know and what we believe to be rational is often a function of our socio-cultural context and practices. Epistemological claims often have an element of belief attached to them, even when they are claimed to be empirically based.

The epistemological problem for traditional realism is how and to what extent we can know the world and how much we can rely on the truth of our findings. Naïve realism has given way to critical realism, the idea that although the world exists independently of our observation of it, we cannot be sure that we perceive it accurately or completely. We can only approximate our understanding of reality. Anti-realist approaches suggest that what we call reality is inextricably entangled with our pre-existing concepts and linguistic descriptions of it. For anti-realists, there is no such thing as an independent, objective reality beyond our descriptions of it; we only know the world within a particular frame of reference. Therefore, there are many constructed versions of the world and many perspectives on it (Goodman, 1984). This view is held by many social psychologists and postmodern constructivists, who believe that ideas of truth and knowledge are products of socially and historically derived practices, and the way we think is partly a function of the language we use. In these approaches, truth is not well defined; it is often a matter of convention.

The limitations of rational and logical thought as a means to knowing truth are straightforward; this approach is based on axiomatic assumptions or premises whose truth is itself difficult to prove. As an instrument of inquiry into knowledge and truth, reason has important limits. The project of increasing knowledge by psychological means, using intuition, imagination, and attention to dreams, which was Jung's approach, offers the possibility of a different kind of science that considers the value of our inner life. The imagination has played an important role in the scientific discoveries made by people such as Einstein, Kekulé, and others.[5]

Many scientists use a correspondence model of truth, which is a commonsense approach that compares a statement with the thing it is describing; a statement is true if it accurately describes a particular aspect of the world. This view presupposes that there is an objective reality, one true description of the world, and truth is singular. However, the correspondence theory leads to the problem of what exactly constitutes a fact, because all facts are laden with presuppositions and theory that is assumed to be true, so this theory of truth can produce a circular argument.

The exact nature of the distinction between ontology and epistemology is much debated; they are clearly interdependent, and it is not clear which is primary. We need some form of epistemology to gain knowledge of what exists, and the researcher's ontology can be seen as a function of her epistemological stance. That is, what we think exists depends on how we study it. Other authors believe that ontology is prior to epistemology because there has to be a world before we try to know it. Some writers collapse the distinction and see them as inseparable. Post-structuralists conflate the two, denying the value of any distinction between them, although for most people they refer to different things and cannot be reduced to each other. In quantum mechanics, it seems that measurement acts as a bridge between the physicist's epistemology and his ontology, since the way he measures an experiment affects what he observes to exist. There does seem to be a relationship between what we think exists and what we believe we can know about it. We see this very clearly in the case of the Self; Jung believes that our knowledge of its manifestations is evidence that it exists. However, it is important to remember that given the human capacity for self-deception and the limitations of our sensory systems, what we believe we observe or know is not necessarily ontologically real, and reality consists of more than we can observe.

Can we know a mental state by measuring it?

The emphasis on measurement in psychology has historical roots (Michell, 1999). Beginning in the mid-nineteenth and early twentieth centuries, the development of psychophysics and psychological testing seemed to provide a mathematical or quantitative basis for psychological phenomena, offering hope that psychology could become a respectable science. Although qualitative research was carried out by figures such as William James, quantification and empiricism seemed to provide the most valid forms of knowledge. These approaches were very much in keeping with the tenor of the times (Morawski, 1988). The fundamental question of whether psychological phenomena or lived experiences are really measurable in a meaningful way was avoided. This question was highlighted by Michell (1999), who pointed out that the mere act of measuring a psychological state does not confirm that what is being measured is actually measurable in the same way as physical phenomena can be measured. It is not necessarily true that scientific research must involve measurement. He argued that "in psychology, the quantitative imperative is an egregious, potentially self-perpetuating form of methodological error" (Michell, 2003, p. 5).

The quantitative approach to the mind was challenged by proponents of qualitative methods such as humanistic psychologists, existentialists, phenomenologists, depth psychologists, and feminists. These critics pointed out the limited value of quantitative methods for clinical practice (Hunsley, 2007). Today, however, quantitative methods are almost synonymous with evidence-based practice, despite the fact that they cannot allow access to the individual's subjectivity, which is most important to the psychotherapist. Subjective mental states, or the private quality of one's experience, cannot be measured in ways comparable to the ways physics measures objects, yet mainstream quantitative psychological research often tries to exclude subjectivity in the service of objective results. The result is information from a third person point of view that sometimes seems sterile or unimportant. Attempts to quantify psychological distress produced by problems of living only give the illusion of objectivity and may distance the therapist from the patient's subjectivity. A measurement on a psychometric test does not tell us what it feels like for the sufferer to have a particular experience, which the psychotherapist can better sense empathically or by means of inference from the patient's overall demeanor. It is true that empathy and inference about another's state of mind are not always reliable, but at the same time people are not always reliable when competing psychometric instruments. It is impossible to meaningfully measure experiences of anguish, sorrow, alienation, states of affliction and oppression, despair, and other forms of mental pain. Many voices have complained that the psychological laboratory yields little information that is useful to everyday life because its results are so decontextualized. The results of large-scale statistical research may be irrelevant to the individual in the psychotherapist's office.

Self-report scales that purport to measure mental states quantitatively are intended to describe conscious levels of the personality, but they are notoriously unreliable and subjectively colored. Subjects can manipulate tests, conceal their feelings, and deny problems such as excessive alcohol use. Self-report scales cannot tell us about the unconscious. Objective tests such as fMRI studies may not correlate with the patient's subjective experience. Natural science of the quantitative type is the wrong model for psychologists interested in human individuality and subjectivity. Many aspects of our lives are not subject to the methods of natural science because life events are often unrepeatable, unpredictable, entirely private, immeasurable, and experienced in the context of a specific developmental history and culture. What it means to be human, what it means to be happy, or what it means to live a good life, are not questions that can be addressed by measurement.

Whether human subjectivity can indeed be objectified, quantified, and studied from a third person, objective point of view is doubtful; giving a subjective experience a number on a rating scale strips the experience of its rich, essential nature, and tells the researcher or the psychotherapist nothing about what it is like to have the experience.[6] The number gives an appearance of objectivity and scientific respectability, but two depressed people with the same score on a rating scale may be having entirely different experiences. For many psychotherapists the psyche is not material and so cannot be quantified. If a psychotherapist wants to understand a mental state such as depression, depth psychologists believe that the best approaches are empathic immersion in the individual's experience and the study of his dreams and relational dynamics. The attempt at the objectification of subjectivity is not necessary and not sufficient; states of mind can be studied phenomenologically but they cannot be meaningfully reduced to numbers in a manner that is helpful to the psychotherapist. First person and third person ontologies are conceptually distinct (Klein, 2015) and have to be studied on their own terms. Intuitive, non-verbal, unconscious, and spiritual experiences are very important in terms of their psychological effects, but they are notoriously difficult to study from an external, third person perspective. Observable behavior is not a good guide to subjective experience, which is why terms such as "behavioral health" are misleading.

Ontological and epistemological attitudes in psychotherapy

Different ontological and epistemological assumptions underpin different psychotherapeutic theories and practice, but there is little discussion of the philosophical foundations of different schools of psychotherapy in standard textbooks. Consequently, psychotherapists do not necessarily study the philosophical basis of the theory with which they work. In training programs, the theory is often presented as a self-contained body of knowledge without being subject to epistemological questioning. For example, we may ask the adherent of any theory a series of questions, such as: what justifies your theory's claim to be valid? What makes it plausible? To what extent is your adherence to the theory based on faith? If your theory seems to work in practice, does that mean it is true? Do you have any criticisms of your theory? What convincing evidence warrants the theory's claim to be better than competing theories? Is your theory relevant to Western cultures only? How complete a theory of the human mind is your theory?

Jung's claim of the existence of an objective, transpersonal level of the psyche is an ontological claim, as is Freud's idea of an instinctually driven unconscious. Psychotherapists use epistemological methods to get to know their patients, for example by looking at dreams and the transference as a way to know what is in the unconscious. Some of the conviction about the value of these approaches found among psychotherapists of different orientations is reminiscent of a religious attitude, as if belief in a particular theory is sufficient. Such attachment to a theory is understandable. It takes considerable psychological and material resources to train in any school of psychotherapy, especially analytic schools, and it may be disconcerting to question it too closely if doing so would undermine the practitioner's confidence in his theory. The emotional power of belonging to a group of like-minded colleagues is considerable; Kohut pointed out that psychotherapeutic theory acts as a selfobject that helps to sustain the practitioner's sense of self. These factors may be sources of the resistance to scrutinizing the epistemological basis of one's favorite theory, but doing so is essential for the sake of intellectual and professional honesty. In the long history of mental health (and medical) treatments, the enthusiasm of advocates of various therapies has often overridden evidence of their ineffectiveness.

All psychotherapeutic theories have ontological assumptions about the ego or the personal self. Some see it purely as a social construct, a product of development. Others, like Kohut, assume the presence of a set of inborn potentials. Jung's ontology includes an innate Self that provides a set of archetypal potentials for the development of the personality. The reality of the Self or the personal self as ontological entities is questioned by some psychological theorists and by Buddhist psychology (this question is discussed on p. 185).

Narrative psychotherapists and many psychoanalysts with an intersubjectivist perspective believe that truth is not so much discovered as mutually created in the psychotherapeutic relationship. The debate is partly about whether the personality has an intrinsic truth that can be recovered in therapy, and if so whether the discovery of that truth is important in the outcome of psychotherapy. It can be argued that a satisfying narrative is as helpful as objective truth. Neo-pragmatic psychotherapists are content with whatever truths appear in therapy if they are useful to their clients. These practitioners are not bound by positivist or foundationalist approaches to psychotherapy that are based on fundamental beliefs that are said to not need justification. These practitioners emphasize practicality and consensus. They do not believe there is any single approach to psychotherapy that is universally effective. Instead of asking whether a belief accurately represents reality, neo-pragmatists ask, "For what purpose would it be useful to hold that belief?" (Rorty, 1999, p. xxiv). In this view, the most we can hope for is an approach that is effective for the individual and has the support of other colleagues. This attitude does not lend itself to a rigid, evidence-based approach, but these practitioners believe that the field has to extricate itself from a purely scientific, positivist, or bio-medical approach.

Many contemporary psychotherapists and psychoanalysts see their work not as a scientific endeavor but as a hermeneutic or interpretive discipline that is inescapably subjective and meaning based. A central tenet of the hermeneutic approach to psychotherapy is that the therapist always interprets what he or she hears in terms of the therapist's personal history, personal psychology, preferred theory, and cultural context. The therapist brings a set of preconceptions, or what Gadamer (1982) calls "prejudices," to the data. These preconceptions act as a kind of filter through which the therapist organizes and understands what she perceives. There can be no neutral or objective interpretation. This means that in psychotherapy the interpreter of a patient's material always contributes to the interpretation and the meaning derived from it. The therapist can interpret a patient's story in terms of a particular theoretical frame of reference, such as Jungian or Freudian theory, or the patient's material can be interpreted in terms of the patient's own frame of reference and personal situation. In the latter case, which many contemporary practitioners prefer, the validity of the psychotherapist's interpretation depends on the patient's acceptance or rejection of it. This means it must be congruent with his experience and emotionally resonant. Interpretation has to be based on mutually agreed-upon understanding of the individual's psychology. Meaning is mutually created by the therapeutic dyad rather than discovered. We arrive at meaning through listening and dialog, through a hermeneutic circle of questions and answers that tries to reveal what was hidden.

Jung's approach to psychotherapy is largely dialectic, a form of dialog between two people, between consciousness and the unconscious and between different aspects of the personality. He saw psychotherapy as two psychic systems in a reciprocal relationship, whose outcome might be entirely unpredictable. Jung was opposed to efforts to convert people in therapy to "some kind of system" (CW 16, para. 11). He was very tolerant of the ambiguities and apparent contradictions that inevitably emerge when studying the unconscious. He did not believe that "the validity of any statement about unconscious states or processes will ever be verified scientifically" (CW 8, para. 417). In support of this approach to the psyche, Jung appealed to the fact that the quantum physicist has to simultaneously view his system with contradictory but complementary properties. The dialectic approach is very different than natural science methods of investigation, in which a neutral observer tries to find objective facts. For the hermeneutic approach to psychotherapy, there is no such objective, verifiable truth independent of those in dialog. Kohut's emphasis on understanding by means of empathy (which was not Gadamer's approach[7]) is a hermeneutic process that is not empirical by the standards of natural science, because it cannot be verified. However, the validity of empathic understanding is usually made obvious by means of the patient's emotional response to it.

Hermeneutic approaches to psychotherapy have their critics, especially among those who see hermeneutic approaches as unscientific, not grounded in testable, objective, empirical evidence, therefore really a form of mythology (Holowchak, 2014). Some people believe this approach tries to locate meaning within a circle that is too closed, as if we could understand the Bible by only staying within the Bible without any external evidence of its truth. If truth derived hermeneutically is only a product of its own cultural and personal setting, it cannot claim to be universally applicable in the way that is true of findings in the physical sciences. Critics of the hermeneutic approach therefore see it as a retreat from the search for truth and objective knowledge. These critics believe it makes truth too relative, or even faith-based because of its lack of an evidential base. Nevertheless, the hermeneutic approach has become important to depth psychologists, even though it has little influence in mainstream psychology because of the hegemony of empirical approaches.

Debates about the validity of empirically supported or manualized therapies compared to meaning-based or hermeneutic approaches are common within psychotherapy circles (Shean, 2013). Some psychotherapists believe that the best way to help suffering people is to correct dysfunctional beliefs or pathological cognitive schemas, while others prefer to examine intrapsychic or relational dynamics. Although many psychotherapists acknowledge that some of their practice is a craft or a skill-based art, many training programs stress the use of empirically supported or evidence-based approaches in their work, which they see as the scientific ground of their practice.[8] However, it is debatable whether psychotherapy can or should attempt to attain the level of scientific rigor found in the natural sciences. Value-laden questions, societal views of exactly what constitutes psychopathology, spiritual beliefs, cultural issues such as gay marriage and abortion, and moral questions such as euthanasia arise within the practice of psychotherapy, but they are not amenable to resolution in terms of "evidence-based" methods. No amount of statistically derived evidence will suffice in some of these situations. Theories that are generalizable may not help the suffering individual. The therapist's capacity for relationships, her capacity for empathy, her innate therapeutic intelligence, and her level of personality development are far more important than her knowledge of empirically derived treatment methods and techniques.

Many psychotherapists are not aware that they implicitly subscribe to a philosophical ideology by virtue of their approach to the person. Thus, there are "objective" approaches that basically tried to study human beings as if they were mechanisms that could be fixed with the right kind of adjustments. These kinds of behavioral approaches ignore issues of existential meaning and do not do justice to human subjectivity. That attitude led to a reaction from humanistic psychologists who had a very different view of human beings. These practitioners wanted to make psychotherapy more humane and related. Humanistic therapists such as Carl Rogers and Abraham Maslow objected to both psychoanalysis and behaviorist psychology. Humanistic psychologists did not like the psychoanalytic idea that childhood determines so much of our life course, and they also objected to the idea that our behavior is determined by a set of conditioned responses, so that we have little autonomy. Humanistic psychologists stressed our ability to choose how we behave and insisted that we have power over our fate. To alleviate emotional distress, they preferred to focus on current problems rather than exploring the past. They stressed that human beings are self-aware, that we have an innate urge to fulfill ourselves, and that we possess inner resources for self-healing, creativity, and growth into our full potential. The therapist's job is to enable the client to make full use of these resources, by providing a safe space to facilitate this process. Growth, authenticity, intuition, and the expression and sharing of genuine human feelings are given a very high value in this way of working. This tradition was therefore an attempt to bring romantic values, which tend to be anti-materialist, back into psychotherapy. The humanistic movement is still viable, but it has faded in importance. It does not consider the unconscious, and it can be a little too Pollyannaish when it ignores the dark side of human nature. This approach was criticized by psychologists who thought that humanistic psychology is too speculative and not scientifically rigorous enough.

Transpersonal psychology tries to blend techniques and ideas from the world's spiritual traditions with current western psychology. These practitioners are interested in the ways in which we might deal with or get beyond the problems of the personal self by means of spiritual techniques. Therefore, they value altered states of consciousness, esoteric practices such as shamanism, and meditation. Transpersonal psychologists take into account phenomena such as para-psychological and near-death experiences and other events that tend to be ignored by mainstream psychologists who have no room for these kinds of phenomena within their professional framework. By affirming the therapeutic value of spiritual practices, which the mainstream tends to ignore, transpersonal psychologists radically depart from the Newtonian–Cartesian framework of academic psychology. The main problems of the transpersonal approach are that the turn to the transcendent may avoid personal material that needs attention, or, encouraging a spiritual technique such as meditation or mindfulness may influence the transference in an artificial manner. For some very fragile people, encouraging the induction of altered states of consciousness is potentially dangerous. Many mainstream psychologists are reluctant to admit that transpersonal psychologies are valid, because doing so would require a radical change in their worldview and style of practice. This reluctance persists even as the evidence of a transpersonal dimension accumulates from psychedelic research, shamanism, and other types of consciousness research.

In the last few decades, the growing (and heavily marketed) field of positive psychology has claimed to create a science that supports human well-being, strengths, and happiness while cultivating virtues such as wisdom, resilience, and transcendence. All this is said to be an alternative to the traditional focus on psychopathology. However, positive psychology has been criticized for promoting particular ethical values and advancing a type of neo-liberal, Western, ethnocentric individualism that ignores social factors such as discrimination and poverty. Positive psychology's vision of the good life, and its values, are not necessarily universally valid. Critics say this field blames the victim by assuming one can be happy by simply thinking in the correct manner, ignoring the fact that optimism, positive thinking, and the cultivation of positive emotions do not necessarily help people struggling to survive difficult social conditions. Positive psychologists stress setting and achieving goals, but goal-directedness is not necessarily a marker of mental health. Where people do have goals, an optimistic attitude is not an essential ingredient in their fulfillment. A meaningful life is not necessarily a happy one. Research in the area of positive psychology is currently controversial. This field has many devotees but is often criticized for being a naïve self-help approach to emotional distress.

The psychotherapist's responses to these issues have significant implications for his or her approach to practice. It is preferable to make one's assumptions and beliefs about reality and about the psyche conscious, rather than only implicit and unexamined, which may lead to significant blind spots. It may seem that fundamental questions of ontology and epistemology are remote from psychotherapeutic practice, but these underlying assumptions are so much like the air we breathe that they are often ignored, even though they unconsciously shape our work (Babbage et al., 2000).

What kind of evidence is valid?

Different schools of psychology and psychotherapy accept different types of data as valid evidence for their approach. Hayes (1993) points out that all scientists bring such assumptions to their work "because no symbolic or analytic system can function without assumptions that lie outside of the system itself." Many empirically oriented psychotherapists prefer data limited to observable or quantifiable phenomena, although the claim that quantitative approaches are objective and value-neutral is now widely questioned (Parker, 2015), and as discussed above, it is not clear that mental states can legitimately be quantified. These methods sometimes produce results that have limited clinical value. As well as empirical evidence based on observation, experiment, quantification, and conceptual thought, there are also types of knowledge and evidence based on material that emerges from the unconscious, on the intuitive perception of others, on the psychotherapist's empathy, his or her lived experience of human nature, clinical experience, and the study of the humanities. These latter approaches do not seem rigorous, but they provide information that is otherwise inaccessible to the clinician. The tension between the importance of immeasurable aspects of human subjectivity and the need for good science remains an issue in the field.

Our worldview, and our view of humanity, affect what we think it is important to study and the approaches we use to do so. Different theories of psychotherapy have different visions of reality, different ideologies, and a range of ideas about the human condition (Messer & Winokur, 1984; Marcus & Rosenberg, 1998). These issues, which are philosophical as well as psychological questions, remain hotly debated.

Much mainstream psychology adopts the philosophical stance of naturalism, which insists that human beings are biological organisms, part of the natural order, and governed by the same physical laws that govern the behavior of matter. In this view, nothing exists that is not material, and this includes the human mind. There is no need to invoke anything spiritual or supernatural. For these practitioners, psychologists should use the same empirical methods to study the psyche as natural scientists use, since only what is observable and measurable gives reliable, objective data. Observations have to be translated into measurable quantities. This is a positivist approach, which is often the unspoken basis of research-supported psychotherapy. It assumes that people can be studied from an objective point of view. Many mainstream psychotherapists adopt a medical model approach to psychological distress, using diagnostic classifications such as the Diagnostic and Statistical Manual, discussed further below. This model is grounded in positivism.

Positivism, empiricism, and the scientific approach to psychotherapy

The twentieth-century philosophers who referred to themselves as logical positivists rejected knowledge derived from any means other than rigorous scientific methods. Logical positivism evolved into a movement known as logical empiricism, which tried to find a way to justify or confirm a scientific hypothesis by insisting on a purely empirical approach to research, based on experimental evidence. Positivism is typically associated with a rejection of metaphysics and a commitment to physicalism. In the view of the positivists, only knowledge based on systematic observation, experiment, and measurement allows valid claims to truth. They try to explain human behavior in terms of specific causes, looking for generalizations that are free of any context. Positivism is neutral about values and does not accept the existence of entities (such as a spiritual dimension) that cannot be proven to exist.

Positivism depends on the realist assumption that there is an objective reality whose organizing principles and mechanisms can be discovered. Subjectivity is seen as an unwanted intrusion into the objective observation of reality. Positivism is often associated with the foundational belief that our senses give us valid, direct awareness of objects as they actually are, a philosophy of naïve realism, although later positivists acknowledged that we cannot be sure how well we understand reality because of the limitations of our sensory and cognitive abilities (Lincoln et al., 2017).

Scientists with a positivist orientation believe they can know the world objectively without the experimenters' subjectivity influencing their results; they use strategies such as double-blind studies to reduce the possibility of observer contamination of their research. This is a deeply entrenched, dualistic position that tries to radically separate the observer from the observed. Early positivists believed that they could divorce their values from their impartial, empirical observations by the use of the correct methodology and controls. Later, it was realized that all observations are laden with values and the possibility of subjective bias, if only because the researcher's values determine what he or she chooses to study and even how the results are interpreted. Cultural, personal, and historical biases and expectations affect scientific research, but researchers who believe in a mind-independent reality that can be known objectively believe these biases can be minimized, especially if the research can be replicated by other workers. Many quantum physicists believe that there is no entirely objective position from which to study a quantum level phenomenon; they see the observer as an active participant in the observation.

Positivism became a dominant philosophy of science until it was largely refuted in the later twentieth century (Tolman, 1992). For a range of reasons contemporary philosophers of science see positivism as outdated (Gupta, 2014; Westen et al., 2004). Positivism has several flaws. The positivist claim that only scientific knowledge is reliable is widely decried; there are other approaches to the world, such as humanistic perspectives. The humanities are important sources of knowledge about human nature. Positivism ignores the importance of the subjective interpretation of data and the fact that the same data can often be interpreted in different ways. Furthermore, because inductively[9] acquired scientific data can potentially be falsified by new observations, claims to absolute certainty are not reasonable. Philosophers of science pointed out that throughout the history of science, good ideas were not always arrived at rationally, and several hypotheses based on good reasoning turned out to be incorrect. Observable sensory experience cannot explain ideas such as democracy, nor can it explain abstract reasoning such as mathematics. Positivism ignores aspects of life that cannot be verified or proven scientifically; it regards subjectivity, emotions, meaning, and ethical factors as unimportant sources of knowledge, although in fact these are important to many people. Also, scientific creativity has artistic as well as logical aspects. Another objection to positivism is that it restricts access to forms of knowledge not amenable to direct observation and measurement, such as intuition and empathy, which are important in psychotherapy although they cannot be measured empirically. Today, some philosophers are suspicious of foundational "master narratives" that try to account for reality as a whole. Scientific theories must remain tentative and be open to re-evaluation.

Post-empirical philosophers of science have made it clear that empirical research always has an a priori starting point and a tacit set of assumptions and suppositions that pre-exist investigation. What seems to be a self-evident fact is often embedded within a conceptual framework that is not itself empirically based and is not always explicit. Facts and their theoretical background are often not separable; often a pre-existing theory determines what constitutes a fact and what can be ignored.

Psychological phenomena are always contextual and dynamic, not static, and not independent of each other. Many psychological phenomena, such as dreams, are not repeatable and are embedded in the complexity of the subject's entire psychology, cultural context, and personal history. A complex whole such as a dream cannot be meaningfully studied as if it consists of disparate elements with no connections to each other. As Ratner (1997, p. 25) put it: "Positivists assume that variables and their components are inherently simple, uniform, and discrete. However, these features are imposed on psychological phenomena by methodological procedures; they are not characteristic of the phenomena themselves." In spite of such difficulties with positivism, this view has been an underlying or tacit assumption in many academic departments of psychology that teach only evidence-based approaches, although the underlying positivist philosophy is not always taught consciously.

It is now understood that all researchers have values and subjective biases that affect their observations. The current fashion for evidence-based treatment in psychotherapy is an example; the background philosophical assumption of this approach is that quantitative empirical science is the most rational way to understand reality, and questions that are not amenable to the scientific method are meaningless or unimportant. But this is surely not so; this kind of scientific method has presuppositions and assumptions that cannot themselves be analyzed scientifically but rest on metaphysical grounds such as materialism and positivism. Many contemporary psychotherapists and researchers claim to focus on evidence derived from empirical data and observation, perhaps not realizing that this point of view has these philosophical underpinnings. Empiricism is valuable in the physical sciences, but it is not true that complete reliance on empiricism in psychotherapy can be justified except as a matter of faith and personal values. The development of chaotic, nonlinear[10] dynamic systems and quantum mechanics all challenge strict empiricism. It may also be mentioned that the thesis that truth has to be empirically verifiable is not itself empirically verifiable. Empiricism is now seen to be only one approach to research, albeit a valuable one if applied to the right type of problem. There are no grounds for insisting that empirical research is the best approach to all questions (Indick, 2002).

To say that science can answer all our questions is to take a naturalist metaphysical position. In this view, nothing exists apart from the physical order, and there is no room for anything supernatural such as a spiritual dimension. However, although the value of science arises from its rigorous methodology, science cannot tell us about the nature of existence itself, where it came from, and why it is ordered as it is. It is not necessarily true that ultimate reality is in principle knowable by the human mind. Perhaps there are deeper truths about reality than science can detect or that our minds can conceive of.

Hibberd (2014) points out that scientists have always wanted to restrict their claims to those that can be justified by experience, and they are averse to "meta-issues" such as the philosophical questions raised by quantum mechanics. However, she believes that psychology must develop a metaphysics of its own, in part because questions of ontology are inescapable, even though many psychologists believe that philosophical or foundational issues are irrelevant to their research. Hibberd points out that in its attempt to be scientific, psychology has focused on methods, such as experiment and measurement, while ignoring ontology, or what it is to be, which is "the metaphysical 'ground' of Psychology's ontology" (p. 162). In her view, "methodology can only emerge from an understanding of metaphysical conditions" (p. 162). She agrees with Robinson's (2007) view that the discipline of psychology needs to accept the existence of something foundational whose nature is a metaphysical question.

Although current mainstream psychology purports to be a science, it makes several unprovable metaphysical assumptions (Dafermos, 2021) such as ontological mind–body dualism, the study of the mind as if it were the sum of independent elements and processes, and the belief that the mind can be studied from a third person, objective point of view. Arguments about free will vs. determinism are unresolved but relevant to psychology, since this question affects the possibility of achieving invariable, universal laws of behavior. In the physical sciences, the assumption has been that there is a reality independent of human ideas about it, combined with the hope that theories refer to realities that are independent of the theories themselves. Scientific theories based on classical realism claim to discover ontic truth, not simply epistemic truth that allows the understanding and prediction of empirical data. This is a form of foundationalism, which contemporary philosophers often question because of the recognition that observations are laden with theoretical knowledge and an underlying set of assumptions that influence research. Verification and falsification are more complex than previously recognized (Lakoff & Johnson, 1999). It may be impossible to absolutely prove or falsify the truth of a useful scientific theory. Furthermore, different theories may explain the same set of observations equally well. Accordingly, theories can only be evaluated on the basis of their effectiveness, their range of explanation, their dependability, and their capacity to explain particular phenomena.

Multiple competing frameworks to study the psyche coexist, each claiming to be true, but although they often contradict each other they are difficult to categorically refute or prove. It is arguable that the attempt to apply empirical approaches to the psyche becomes too reductionist, and the results are difficult to generalize because they do not include the unpredictable, first person, creative dimension of being human and the wide range of possible responses to life situations. The touchstones of empirical research and the scientific method are observation and experiment, but by themselves these are never enough for the development of general laws in any discipline, much less psychology. Empirical research is only one type of approach to the psyche. Sometimes a preoccupation with rigorous methods of research excludes subjectivity and so leads to research without meaningful content. Problems like depression and anxiety are inordinately complex and not homogeneous. The focus by many mainstream researchers on isolated aspects of the mind or on measurable variables may not consider the complicated context of our lives. It is therefore arguable that psychology cannot be treated as a science in the sense of the physical sciences.

Whether it is possible to develop a rigorous science of human nature, if there is such a thing, is a metaphysical question that asks what it means to be human and how we are to understand ourselves. If there is a spiritual dimension of reality, another metaphysical question, psychotherapy would have no purchase on aspects of our psychological life that are affected by that level, which is not reducible to the effects of family, learning, psychodynamics, genetics, and culture. Science traditionally requires control of variables, and good theories offer predictions, but to what extent can psychology predict or control human values, ethics, religious beliefs, aesthetics, the discovery of meaning in life, and creativity, all of which may radically affect behavior? These and several metaphysical questions, such as the existence of a soul or the mind–body relationship, impinge on the field of psychology in practical ways. One example is the question of whether psychology (or social science) can eliminate evil by understanding and controlling human behavior, or whether there is a source of evil that is not purely human such as the mythical Devil or the dark side of God.

Psychoanalysts and Jungians who are criticized for not being scientific often respond that their criteria of success are developments such as broadened self-understanding, relationship to the unconscious, fostering the individuation process, and the discovery of meaning, rather than symptom removal. Some emphasize the idea that new perspectives are mutually created by the therapeutic dyad. However, this kind of work is difficult to evaluate because it is not clear how one can judge the validity of the individual's self-understanding or the process of individuation.

Defenders of depth psychology point out that the empirical approach is only one of several ways to study the psyche, and empiricism itself is not entirely objective because research is much affected by the researcher's ideology, choices, methods, preconceptions, and interpretations of data. This critique is relatively weak in the face of the successes of empirical methods in the physical sciences, which suggests they attain a good deal of objectivity. However, they study objects, and the psyche and psychological phenomena are not objects with discrete boundaries.

The view that empirical science is the only valid path to truth is known as scientism. This approach sees philosophy and metaphysics as useless, producing ideas that cannot be tested. The problem with this argument is that it is circular; it holds that if science cannot tell us about something it cannot exist, and it does not exist if science cannot tell us about it. This attitude implies that science has no limits to its explanatory power, as long as we stay within its purview, which is material reality. However, although science is the best way to study the physical world, it is of little value in the face of spiritual or non-material reality. Furthermore, if we only allow scientific approaches to reality, we risk collapsing ontology into epistemology; we only know what exists in terms of the way we know it. Then: "Reality seems to recede or, at least, becomes a mere reflection of what we can know" (Trigg, 2015, p. 32). Epistemology need not dictate our ontology. As Trigg points out, if human observation alone determines what exists, existence "appears anthropocentric," since all knowledge is human knowledge, and "what counts as the universe is limited by the limits of human knowledge" (p. 35). Trigg notes that to say that science can answer all questions requires that we stand outside science to make such a claim. Trigg believes that "all science collapses without metaphysical support," (p. 148) and it is a mistake to ignore the philosophy that undergirds scientific exploration.

It seems likely that there are realms of reality, both psychological, physical, and spiritual, that are currently beyond the reach of empirical study, except in terms of their manifestations. If empirical evidence is to be the only criterion of belief, all our religious traditions would be called into question. If we insist on purely empirical approaches to understand the world, we confine ourselves to naturalism and physicalism, approaches that see matter as the only reality, and reality as only that which is amenable to study by science. Physicalism wants to make consciousness, and indeed all human experiences, explicable in terms of material processes and ultimately explained by the laws of physics. Naturalism does not allow any kind of "supernatural" explanations; the physical world is a closed system with no possibility of spiritual intervention. This is an unprovable metaphysical position that has no way of approaching phenomena such as religious experiences that do not seem to be explicable by materialistic science, except by dismissing them as unreal. The need to validate psychotherapy scientifically has ideological, political, financial, and even narcissistic roots when the prestige and authority of the field is in question.

Behavioral and cognitive approaches to psychotherapy are largely based on positivism. For psychotherapists interested in depth psychology, these approaches are unsatisfactory because much of what depth psychology deals with, in particular the unconscious, is private, subjective, unobservable, and not always amenable to rational understanding. A more humanistic or anti-naturalism approach denies that human beings can be treated as if they were comparable to material objects. This approach doubts the positivist claim that human beings can be completely understood through empirical observation. Therapists with a humanist or depth psychological orientation believe that we need a different, qualitative approach to study people that considers the unconscious and factors such as subjectivity, meaning, values, intentionality, and the like. Relational psychotherapists stress that our understanding and interpretation of experience always occurs in a relational field, and these dynamics may have unconscious—hence not directly unobservable—underpinnings. Whereas natural science tries to find publicly verifiable, general descriptions of humanity, humanistic and depth psychologists are more interested in unique individual situations. The extent to which humanistic and naturalist approaches are compatible, integratable, or incommensurable is debatable. The tension between positivist and hermeneutic or purely interpretive approaches to psychotherapy continues. The difference between practitioners on either side of this divide may in part be the result of temperamental factors.

Positivist approaches contrast starkly with Jung's emphasis on what he refers to as the "personal equation," a subjective bias in psychotherapy that is inevitable: "The demand that [the therapist] should see only objectively ... is impossible" (CW 6, para. 10). Other irreconcilable philosophical questions abound between schools of psychotherapy. Essentialist theories such as Jung, who postulates the Self as an a priori, transcendental given, are radically different than constructivist theories that stress that there is only a personal self, which is built up by human cognitive and social systems. Jung's notion that the psyche has a collective, spiritual dimension is radically and irreconcilably different than purely brain-based theories of the psyche.

Every intervention the therapist makes has philosophical strings attached, even if they are difficult to detect. To be effective, it is important that the psychotherapist works with a theoretical orientation that is consistent with his or her personal philosophy. If the practitioner works with a type of psychotherapy that is not consistent with her own belief system and values or is trained to work in a manner that is inconsistent with her own therapeutic intelligence, she is particularly likely to suffer a career crisis (Fear & Woolfe, 1999).

Physicalism and idealism in psychology

The relationship between the human mind and its knowledge of physical reality is much debated in the history of ideas. The philosophy of idealism holds either that the material world has no existence independent of the mind, or that the perceived qualities of matter depend on the mind. Idealists point out that what we experience as the physical world consists of ideas and impressions within our minds, so the existence of an outer world is an inference based on our interpretation of sensory data. For idealists, the idea of an objective world independent of the mind is an explanatory model that cannot be empirically verified. In some accounts of idealism, such as Advaita Vedānta, physical reality is the result of the activity of consciousness, which is the primary reality. This kind of idealism has to explain how consciousness can produce our experience of a solid reality. It is supported by the fact that the dream world seems very solid, although its reality is clearly the activity of consciousness.

Idealism is not fashionable today because of the success of the physical sciences, which seems to depend on the independent reality of the outer world. Another question raised by idealism is how we can be sure of the existence of minds other than our own. Nevertheless, idealism has some vigorous supporters (Kastrup, 2019). By stressing the primacy and reality of the psyche as our only means of experience, Jung often expresses a view of reality suggestive of metaphysical idealism, for example by saying that: "Psychic existence is the only category of existence of which we have immediate knowledge, since nothing can be known unless it first appears as a psychic image. Only psychic existence is immediately verifiable" (CW 11, para. 769).

Idealism gains some support from those interpretations of quantum mechanics that suggest that consciousness is in some way responsible for the creation of reality, because quantum level phenomena only become either a wave or particle when they are observed or measured. These quantum theorists adopt an anti-realist position that denies the existence of an objective quantum level of reality prior to our observation of it; in this view, the world we describe is a product of our perceptions and the way we order them. It seemed to early quantum physicists that their observation collapsed the wave function into a definite state, suggesting that physical reality is not entirely independent of the mind that observes it. The proposed role of consciousness was an admission that the process of collapse was not understood. Today the role of consciousness in quantum mechanics is largely discounted by physicists who believe the collapse of the wave function occurs when the wave function interacts with a macroscopic measuring instrument, with no need for the consciousness of an observer.

Idealism is a minority position today, when the dominant view in the academic world and among most scientists is an ontology of physicalism combined with empiricism. This approach insists that scientific methods discover what there actually is in the world, which can be completely reduced to its material properties. This ideology is usually associated with the idea of the causal closure of the physical, meaning that all events have purely physical causes.[11] In this view, all mental events, and consciousness itself, are the result of brain processes. This metaphysical view remains unproven even though it is widely held by scientists, although some discount the materialist worldview (Beauregard et al., 2018; Kelly et al., 2009). Physicalism is taken for granted by a large segment of psychologists and neuroscientists who assume that the mind is purely a function of brain activity. This doctrine of eliminative materialism asserts that there are only brain states; our everyday belief in a mind is mere folk psychology.[12] Either all mental events are the result of brain events, or brain events and mental events are identical. The assumption is that to conceive of the mind as non-material is tantamount to mysticism. In this view, a rational view of reality can only be equated with the discovery of natural laws and the mathematical equations derived from them. Contemporary materialism is alive and well, but as yet the assertion that the mind is reducible to the brain is unproven, and for many philosophers it seems like an impossible task. Physicalism cannot explain meaning, values, beliefs, intentionality, and desires, and cannot explain how consciousness and the quality of experience arises from neural activity. Typically, physicalism ignores or explains away evidence for the spiritual dimension, which is often seen as illusory.

Adherents to a physicalist view of consciousness do not always acknowledge that they are adopting a metaphysical position that is currently as unprovable as an opposing view that the brain is an instrument used by consciousness, not its source. Instead, physicalists decry what *they* think is metaphysics, which is any opinion contrary to the materialist one. Some psychologists deny the reality of phenomena such as near-death experiences or psi phenomena that are not compatible with theories of brain-based consciousness, and they assume that the problem of the neural basis of consciousness will be solved in the future. Popper (1977) referred to this attitude as promissory materialism, calling it a baseless prophecy, and indeed decades of effort in neuroscience have discovered which parts of the brain correlate with particular psychological functions but nothing about how consciousness itself emerges from brain activity. Neither do we know what consciousness is in its own nature, or its purpose in the evolution of our species.

Many psychotherapy training programs have a distinct if implicit physicalist bias, even though the limitations of physicalist approaches to the mind are now well known (Kelly et al., 2009, 2019). Various authors have pointed out that neuronal activity cannot explain the arising of the qualitative aspects of consciousness, known as qualia, or the subjective feel of an experience or what it is like to perceive a certain quality (Chalmers, 2010). Thomas Nagel (2012) pointed out that even if we knew all about the brain of a bat and how it navigates by sonar, we would still not know what it is like to experience the world from a bat's point of view. The physicalist counters that the subjective feel of the experience *is* the way the objective neuronal events manifest themselves subjectively. Nevertheless, the sense of "I am" does not seem amenable to scientific observation because, like consciousness, it is intrinsically subjective and private and cannot be observed as an object.

A major critique of physicalism is its circularity. Everything not reducible to physicality is said to be mysticism and irrational; all rational explanations must be explicable in quantitative terms because that is true in physics, and what's true in physics must be true of the rest of reality because physics explains all reality. So, nothing non-material can exist by definition. Therefore, materialism is true because it must be true. However, the methods of the physical sciences are inapplicable in the realm of the psyche, which is not material.

Kastrup (2019) has provocatively suggested that physicalism is partly a defensive maneuver designed to allow one to avoid confronting painful aspects of the inner life. This is especially so, he believes, when our behavior is reduced to nothing but the result of brain events over which we have no control, at the same time as physicalism seems to have the potential for control over nature. One can also see physicalism as a defense against unconscious spiritual beliefs that, if made conscious, might require a radical change of worldview.

Problems with common philosophical assumptions in psychotherapeutic practice and research

The wide range of philosophical and cultural assumptions that underpin psychotherapeutic practice and research are often taken at face value. The assumptions themselves are rarely questioned. Neither are their origins within power structures in the profession such as guild interests, licensing requirements, or theoretical dogmatism among the leaders of professional organizations.

Training in some schools of psychology and psychotherapy is still implicitly based on positivism. Psychologists trained with positivist assumptions have tried since the beginning of the field to develop verifiable, law-like statements about human behavior, beginning with hypotheses that are operationally defined and can be tested by observation under controlled conditions. Ideally, the results are subject to measurement by psychometric instruments or rating scales. This approach asserts the principle of objectivism, which insists on the importance of consensual validation by multiple observers. Objectivism assumes the existence of a reality that is independent of the mind that observes it and is not dependent on the context of observation. This perspective tends to be reductionist, assuming that complex events can be completely understood in terms of the interaction of their constituent components, which are best studied in isolation. Many researchers subscribe to a philosophy of naturalism, which denies the existence of non-physical realities. In this view, everything that happens, including consciousness, arises in accord with the laws of matter. This reductionist view of the mind and reality in general is often accompanied by an assumption of determinism, which holds that if we know the initial conditions of a system, we can predict its subsequent behavior. The resulting mechanistic, reductionist, and determinist attitude, which characterized classical (pre-quantum mechanics) physics, became identified with the scientific method among many research psychologists as if it could be applied whole cloth to the psyche. The reductionist approach tries to separate individual psychological processes as if they can be decontextualized and studied in isolation. It ignores the fact that the psyche operates as a whole, and the different aspects of the psyche interact with each other in complex ways, leading to emergent properties that are greater than the sum of their constituent parts. Reductionist approaches often ignore creativity and human free will, which cannot be reduced to causal mechanisms. Reductionism leads to the monomodal treatment of problems such as depression that actually have many levels. Only a wholistic approach does justice to our study of the psyche.

Determinism is incompatible with interpretations of quantum mechanics that point to irreducible randomness at the quantum level. Some quantum level events, such as the decay of a radioactive atom, occur for no known reason, which means that the universe may be fundamentally not deterministic. Some philosophers have claimed that the indeterminism of quantum mechanics, or Heisenberg's uncertainty principle, lead to necessary belief in free will. This opinion has been challenged on the grounds that randomness is not the same as free choice and may only lead to chance events, thus ruling out free will. Also, quantum-level indeterminacies may be irrelevant to causality at the macroscopic level. Indeterminism has also been linked to creativity. It is not clear if indeterminism and randomness are also intrinsic features of the psyche or of the unconscious, but this often seems to be the case.

A residue of positivist thinking is found in the current emphasis on empirical ("evidence-based") forms of therapy. The idea that psychotherapy should be evidence-based is derived from evidence-based medicine, which asserts that medical practice should be based on randomized clinical trials to exclude ineffective treatments. These trials are valuable in medicine, but the extent to which assumptions from medical research can be applied to psychotherapy is dubious. Psychotherapy does not lend itself to the kind of randomized double-blind study used in medicine to test the efficacy of med-ications. Symptoms and syndromes seen in psychotherapy are less definitive than they are in medicine and are not measurable biologically. Psychother-apeutic techniques are much less specific than medications. The complexity of the therapeutic relationship cannot be compared with trials of medication efficacy where there is only one major variable, the choice between two medications or between a medication and a placebo. Medication trials rarely consider the effects of the transference to the researcher in the result of the trial, although this is probably a factor in the placebo response. The outcome of many medical treatments, such as surgical procedures, do not depend very much on factors such as empathy, the therapeutic relationship, the discovery of meaning, or other qualities essential to psychotherapy.

The reality is that the results of randomized controlled trials, which are highly valued for the purposes of scientific research, are not always general-izable to the realities of psychotherapeutic practice. The psychotherapist has to consider factors such as ethnicity, sexual identity, and socio-economic problems, which may not be part of the eligibility criteria required for clinical trials. For the practitioner, evidence may be derived from intuition and clin-ical experience as well as from controlled trials, and at times these latter factors may override empirically derived treatment methods. Objectivity, which is valued in medical science, is impossible in psychotherapy, where the psychotherapist's subjectivity, feelings, and values are inevitably present. Jung refers to these factors as the "personal equation," which is integral to the work of psychotherapy.

Jonathan Shedler (2015) demonstrates the weakness of research practices that attempt (but he believes fail) to show the value of evidence-based prac-tice. He points out that the term "evidence-based" has often been appro-priated to promote a particular ideology and agenda. Sometimes this phrase is a code word for manualized treatment, especially brief, highly structured cognitive behavioral therapy (CBT). Behind this ideology, Shedler sees a "master narrative" that justifies attacks on psychodynamic psychotherapy, implying that only CBT is scientifically proven to be effective. In fact, he demonstrates that evidence-based therapies are "ineffective for most people most of the time," and there is a "yawning chasm between what we are told research shows and what research actually shows." He believes that the ben-efits of evidence-based approaches are often trivial. In fact, "most patients do not get well. Even the trivial benefits do not last" (ibid., p. 48). In con-trast, Shedler (2010) has documented evidence for the efficacy of psychody-namic psychotherapy in the setting of a meaningful therapeutic relationship.

The insistence on evidence-based approaches in psychotherapy is an attempt to impose positivist criteria of truth on the field, ignoring the fact that we are now in a skeptical era that prefers pluralism. Postmodernism[13] is not fashionable today, but its critique of positivism is still relevant. Post-modernism revealed the hidden assumptions and unequal power structures underlying purportedly objective, value-free research that ignored diversity and marginalized certain groups. Postmodern philosophers point out that there are as many versions of the world as there are perspectives or frames of reference on it (Goodman, 1984). Social psychologists are particularly taken with this view since they stress the influences of culture and language in the construction of our knowledge of the world. This point of view is anti-essentialist and anti-realist; it denies that what we know is the result of the direct perception of reality and insists that our knowledge is always histori-cally and culturally specific. The nature of what we consider to be true is a product of social forces and the language we use to construct meaning (Burr, 1995). From this viewpoint, it is difficult to find criteria to determine truth, since truth becomes a matter of conventional agreement. However, psycho-logical research informed by postmodern approaches has a limited range of methods. This approach is too intellectually relative in denying that there are verifiable truths about the psyche. It sometimes discounts important empiri-cal evidence, it overvalues uncertainty, and it often cannot determine causal relationships between psychological phenomena. Postmodernism as a philo-sophy has largely been rejected because it provides no firm grounds for knowledge, and it is seen as sterile.

The research approach used in the physical sciences captures a great deal in its net, but it is unable to capture many subtle, non-material levels of rea-lity. For example, at the moment physical science has no mechanism that would explain synchronistic events or anomalous parapsychological phe-nomena such as psi events or near-death experiences, but for many observers their reality cannot be denied. There are a range of other phenomena to which scientific methods of proof cannot be applied, such as issues of mor-ality and spiritual experience. Indick (2002) has pointed out that the methods of evolutionary psychology and moral psychology[14] do not conform to the empirical standards of systematic observation, but they make valuable con-tributions. Empirical science is not the only route to knowledge. In spite of these difficulties, empiricism is accepted as foundational in much of today's mainstream psychological research, which assumes it achieves objective perception of reality.

An important critique of empiricism as a method of inquiry is that there is no way to verify or validate it unless we use another method to do so, and this method in turn would be subject to the same problem of validation, and so on ad infinitum, so it is difficult to absolutely validate the knowledge or truth obtained by empirical methods. In the end however, for pragmatic reasons, many research psychologists accept empiricism as the best method we have, in spite of the doubts it raises. One approach to this dilemma pre-ferred by depth psychologists is to use qualitative and phenomenological approaches that simply study experience from a first-person point of view, since this is self-evidently important, and we live from day to day in terms of our own subjectivity. These approaches also recognize the role of the psychotherapist or the researcher in the co-construction of the patient's reality. However, these approaches are open to skeptical objections about the trustworthiness of subjective reports. In the end, perhaps the method we prefer to use to study the psyche is a matter of opinion. Many researchers now embrace epistemological and methodological pluralism.

If we look for theories about the psyche that can be generalized, we must do so in a way that does not lose track of the individual human being. Research has to choose between a stress on first person accounts, individual subjectivity and individual psychological structures, or third person observations in the positivist, empiricist or realist traditions that purport to be objective. The former has its roots in humanism, depth psychology, and idealism, the latter in physicalism and naturalism. Each approach has strengths and limitations. Even among practitioners who adopt evidence-based approaches to psychotherapy, there are debates about which types of research give the best quality of information. One can make a case that mainstream psychology's attempt to insist on the implementation of evidence-based, empirical approaches by all psychotherapy training programs is largely based on the interests of those in power. Jungian and psychoanalytic thought, which are largely in the romantic tradition, are marginalized in part because they do not fit with positivist, empiricist approaches to knowledge.

For practitioners interested in depth psychology and in humanistic approaches, the traditional positivist scientific paradigm, which purports to offer certainty, has no appeal. Depth psychologists are searching for different types of validation to affirm their approach, which allows a different perspective on the psyche than that restricted by evidence-based approaches. Given the temper of our times, many therapists are suspicious of claims that any single approach to psychotherapy can be the absolute truth, in part because they recognize the complexity of the psyche and the therapeutic relationship.

The approach to psychotherapy preferred by a particular practitioner is partly determined by her or his academic background and personal therapy, which may be a matter of chance or circumstance. The practitioner's preference is also affected by the individual's temperament and personal psychology (Arthur, 2001). Various studies indicate that specific psychological traits are associated with opinions about controversies such as free will (reviewed by Yaden & Anderson, 2021). William James (2003 [1907]) for example distinguished between tender-minded and tough-minded individuals. Tender minded people are idealistic, religious, optimistic, and tend to be dogmatic; tough-minded people are empirical, materialistic, irreligious, and tend to be pessimistic or skeptical. The psychotherapist's temperament understood in terms of Jung's typology (King, 1999), his or her capacity for empathy and relationship, tolerance of ambiguity, need for emotional distance or closeness, predilection for action, passivity, and practicality, all seem to be important in deciding the practitioner's theoretical preference.

In the face of so many philosophical positions, Drob (2017) makes a strong case for the idea that there is "a single world that must be understood from opposing yet interdependent perspectives." He suggests that a reasonable approach to the wide range of theories in psychology is that, rather than being mutually exclusive, a "'hidden' unity lies at the foundation of all opposites" (p. 38). The division of this original unity into apparently separate entities or oppositions is brought about by language, conceptual thought, human sensory systems, and the ways in which our mind represents reality. Using the overarching archetypal principle of the *coincidentia oppositorum*, he makes a case for approaching the psyche in terms of multiple, opposing but complementary ideas. Bohr's principle of complementarity (see Chapter 3) tells us that sometimes we need apparently incompatible truths to fully describe a situation.

Psychology and the move from classical to quantum physics

The fundamental assumptions of a particular generation of scientists are often taken for granted, but typically these assumptions are called into question by subsequent generations. Such was the situation with the transition from classical Newtonian physics to the quantum era in the early twentieth century. However, mainstream psychology has not been much influenced by this development. In order to develop psychology as a scientific discipline in its own right, beginning in the early twentieth century, psychology tried to model itself on the worldview of the pre-quantum physical sciences, adopting a similar ontology and epistemology (Walsh et al., 2014). Psychologists suffered from "physics envy," assuming that their work had to match that standard. Objectivity was the goal. The hope for a physics of the mind remains alive (Perlovsky, 2016).

Newtonian physics assumed it was independent of factors such as human subjectivity, language, and our mental representations of the world. This doctrine, known as metaphysical realism, is partly a residue of Descartes' radical separation of mind and matter. It required the idea of a detached observer who could measure the objective properties of matter without interfering with them, producing factual results that can be replicated. Classical mechanics treated the material world and the mind of the experimenter as two separate, distinct realms. This model was at the heart of physics until the advent of quantum mechanics. However, for some (but definitely not all) scientists, quantum mechanics has taken us beyond metaphysical realism. In part this is because of the possible (but disputed) role of consciousness (Barzegar et al., 2021), since in some accounts of quantum physics the act of conscious observation affects the outcome of a quantum experiment. This is the antithesis of traditional scientific assumptions in which subject and object are sharply separated. In classical Newtonian mechanics the observer was detached from his experiments and had no subjective effect on them.

However, for some quantum theorists, at least those who adhere to the original Copenhagen interpretation, human subjectivity has become an essential part of science because conscious free choices made by the experimenter, such as the decision to view a photon as either a wave or a particle, affect the outcome of his experiments. For these physicists the role of consciousness in quantum experiments has called into question the existence of an objective, mind-independent world because we cannot measure the quantum system without affecting it. This observation led to the controversial idea of observer created reality (discussed further on p. 137). The important caveat here is that the idea that the role of consciousness is increasingly discounted (see p. 125 et seq.) and there are various approaches to quantum mechanics, such as hidden variables theories or the many worlds theory, which postulate a reality independent of consciousness.[15] For people who do accept the central role of consciousness in quantum experiments, quantum mechanics undermines purely physicalist explanations of reality, and the relationship between the nature of the world and the way we experience it is more complicated than has ever been imagined.

Some interpretations of quantum mechanics make the nature of matter itself very uncertain, even calling into question whether matter exists as we believe it does. At its submicroscopic levels, matter is not as solid as it was traditionally assumed to be. If observation affects the properties of the object being observed, and chance as well as natural law operate at a fundamental quantum level, it may be that our ability to understand that reality is intrinsically limited. Although it is not clear to what extent these considerations apply to the study of the psyche, the indeterminism of quantum processes, which presumably occur in the brain, may affect our psychology in unknown ways. This possibility is ignored by mainstream psychology, which largely adopts a mechanistic, realist, and physicalist worldview. Perhaps this is because quantum mechanical ideas tend to be abstract, difficult to visualize, and remote from our usual ways of experiencing the world. As Mansfield and Spiegelman (1989) point out, Newtonian mechanics allows us to visualize the universe as a mechanism analogous to a great clock, but there is no equivalent image or metaphor that easily fits the quantum mechanical picture. Scientists in many fields other than physics are still operating with a Newtonian world view because quantum phenomena are only visible with sophisticated means of observation and can usually be ignored when studying macroscopic events. However, some of the difficulties replicating psychological research may be due to randomness or indeterminism within the psyche.

Classical or Newtonian physics assumed that reality is largely determined (highly predictable), based on immutable laws.[16] This means that every event is necessitated by preceding events. Because Newtonian physics became an ideal for various branches of science, scientifically oriented psychologists also assumed that human nature and human behavior can also be accounted for in terms of uniform laws that are deterministic, attributable to known causes. The hope was to find psychological principles that are universally applicable, analogous to the laws of physics. However, human behavior is much more unpredictable than early theorists imagined. Classical mechanics found that identical experimental conditions lead to identical results, but quantum mechanics teaches that nature is fundamentally random at the quantum level. Identical quantum level experiments may have different results. If randomness is also a feature of human psychology, and if we consider the complexity of human values, creativity, imagination, and spirituality, the possibility of finding deterministic laws of the psyche recedes even further. Within the practice of psychotherapy, the notion of an objective observer is no longer tenable.

Newtonian science was based on locality, the idea that an object can only be influenced by direct contact with it. In this realist view, there can be no unmediated action at a distance, an idea that was anathema to many physicists because it smacks of occultism. However, the discovery of entanglement[17] between quantum connected particles disconfirmed the importance of locality. Because of entanglement, quantum mechanics is often thought to imply an inherent holism, the notion that nature is non-separable and the whole is more than the sum of its parts. Quantum constituents are not always separable, calling into question a reductionist approach to reality. Bohm (1989 [1951]) believed that quantum mechanics implies that reality is a whole that cannot be analyzed into discrete parts, as if each of which has a separate existence.

Classical physics assumed that cause–effect sequences are fixed in one direction, and that a moving object would have a continuous, precisely defined trajectory. It also assumed continuity, the idea that there are no discontinuous jumps in nature. The subsequent discoveries of quantum physics undermined all these assumptions. At the quantum level, motion, for example of the electron, is described in terms of a series of indivisible transitions or tiny, discrete jumps. Whereas it used to be assumed that elementary particles have an essential nature that cannot change, quantum mechanics shows that they may act either as waves or particles depending on how they are observed. This means that the nature of a quantum object depends on its context. At the quantum level of observation, the result of an experiment is affected by the apparatus used, so that different experimental conditions produce different views of quantum levels of reality. The nature of a quantum level object therefore depends on its relationship to its environment. There is an obvious parallel to psychotherapy, in which different observers with different theoretical approaches see the psyche very differently, resulting in very different effects on their patients.

When the theory of relativity and quantum mechanics appeared, Newtonian physics was shown to be incomplete although applicable within limits. In part, its limitations were revealed because in some (but not all) approaches to quantum mechanics, subatomic particles do not obey deterministic laws.[18] Many quantum processes seem to be random, not attributable to any known cause. Heisenberg's uncertainty principle says that it is impossible to simultaneously know both the position and the momentum of a quantum-level particle, and this is often said to undermine the determinism of classical physics. This uncertainty may only be the result of our lack of knowledge about the complete state of a quantum level system, but for some investigators causal explanations cannot be found in principle for quantum level events, which is a very disturbing notion for Western rationalism, which always seeks deterministic explanations for events. Causality seems to protect us from chaos, which is one reason for resistance to Jung's notion that synchronistic events are acausal.

Although a great deal of behavior and many psychological processes occur in local reality at the macroscopic level, observations at that level do not tell us anything about the underlying ontic reality or common ground from which these processes emerge. For heuristic purposes, this deep level of reality can be described in terms of Jung's postulate of a psychoid level, a neutral reality such as that postulated in dual-aspect monism or it might be the Pure Consciousness of the non-dual traditions. Whatever this deep reality is, it is inaccessible to the psychologist. It may be a quantum level of reality, which is why acausal, non-deterministic, apparently random synchronistic events are such a tantalizing connection between depth psychology and quantum theory.

A psychology that considers the application of quantum mechanical ideas to the psyche would be non-mechanistic, recognizing the place of uncertainty, contradictory or complementary descriptions of the same phenomenon. It would forgo exclusively causal explanations in favor of synchronicity, and it would acknowledge the importance of randomness and indeterminacy. However, mainstream psychology has not modified its thinking in accord with the new physics. DeRobertis (2005) points out that mainstream psychology has remained attached to the "metaphysical assumptions implicit in causal-empirical thought" (p. 102).

If quantum mechanical principles such as randomness and indeterminacy apply to human psychology and brain functioning, they would call into question the possibility of finding invariably uniform or universal psychological laws that will definitively predict or explain behavior, much less control it.

The mind–brain question

One of philosophy's long-standing and most contentious debates concerns the question of whether the mind is a function of the brain's activity or whether the mind or consciousness is somehow independent of the brain. The brain-based view of consciousness ultimately means that the mind and consciousness are generated by the interaction of material particles.

Consciousness might be nothing more than a product of the evolution of the complexity of the brain. However, from the point of view of evolution it is difficult to know where to draw the line between organisms that are conscious and those that are not. The emergence of consciousness seems to violate the principle of the gradual continuity of evolution by producing an entirely new quality.

If the mind is made by the brain, the problem is to explain how inert matter can produce subjective experience. This contrasts with the view that consciousness is a fundamental, irreducible property of the universe. This view insists that consciousness is so radically different from the material brain that it could not have emerged from neural activity (Koch, 2014).

For many mainstream psychologists, because material reality is the only reality, everything that seems to be mental is actually a derivative of brain processes (Damasio, 2000). This physicalist attitude is often adopted unconsciously, absorbed from the psychologist's academic milieu. However, it is based on a series of unprovable assumptions, such as the idea that life and consciousness are products of complex physical processes that in principle can be understood by reducing them to the interaction of their component parts.

The mind–brain question has an important history. Dualism, or the idea of the absolute separation of mind and matter or body and soul, has been at the heart of Western thinking since the time of the ancient Greek philosophers. From them we have inherited the idea that everything can be divided into these two contrasting, mutually exclusive aspects of reality. (There were also philosophers in the Greek tradition who were not dualists.) Contemporary mainstream psychology ignores the ancient idea of a soul, partly because of the influence of figures such as William James. James wanted the new psychology to be a science of the mind and the brain, suggesting that psychology does not need the concept of soul, which he saw as a metaphysical notion that people might believe in if they wish but was superfluous for science. Most subsequent psychologists followed James' lead, except for Jung, who had the courage to write *Modern man in search of a soul* in 1933.[19] This book was very much against the tenor of the psychology of that time, since in this book Jung describes the importance of human spiritual needs, and he critiques materialism and materialistic psychology by saying it offers us only a psychology without the psyche.

Dualism

Modern dualism is associated with the seventeenth-century philosopher René Descartes, for whom soul and mind were equivalent. Descartes inherited a traditional distinction between the soul, which was divine, and the body, which was mortal. He turned this split into a radical distinction between body and mind, which has become an everyday, commonsense way of looking at things, although it is misleadingly simple. Descartes believed that mind and body are two different substances with different properties. Like other physical objects, the body takes up space, but the mind only thinks and occupies no physical space. For Descartes, this meant that the Church could take care of the soul and science could focus on the body. Descartes was an interactionist; this attitude says that mental events cause physical events, as we see in volitional movements, and physical events cause mental events, as we see in sensation.

Dualists point out that mind states and brain states are essentially different, and brain processes can never fully explain mental states. The pain of toothache is radically different than the chemistry of transmission along the facial nerve. We can only know what it feels like to have toothache from personal experience. However, one of the problems with dualism that Descartes struggled with was the riddle of how mind and matter can interact with each other if they are so different in quality—how can something that is not material interact with matter? The mind consists of thoughts and ideas, whereas matter is about molecules. How can a non-material mental state cause something physical to happen? The interaction problem is a major reason that dualism is unpopular today.

Dualists support their point of view by pointing out that the properties of mental states and physical entities are very different; physical objects do not possess subjectivity. Mental states have intentions, they are about something, but physical objects are not intentional. Dualists believe that there are mental processes that cannot be brought about by the brain alone, such as beliefs and values. The kinds of mental processes that produce creative or abstract works of art and literature seem to be based on more than brain functioning. Some dualists believe that the brain is a kind of antenna that receives consciousness rather than generates it, analogous to the way a radio receives sound. Aberrations in the equipment lead to aberrant sound, which is why impairment of the brain affects our mental states.

Dualism seems to violate the principle of the conservation of energy if there is an interaction between mind and brain, because physical energy is required to do work, and we cannot imagine how anything mental can be converted into physical energy. A few mainstream scientists, such as the neurophysiologist John Eccles (1994), have espoused the dualist view, but this is very much a minority opinion among contemporary thinkers. Incidentally, dualism of the kind found in religious traditions, which distinguish between the body and the soul, offers the possibility of the survival of consciousness after biological death.

A form of dualism known as property dualism maintains that although only matter exists, matter has both physical and mental properties. The brain has different types of properties, including mind and consciousness as well as its neurological mechanisms. This gets rid of the idea that mind and brain are two different types of substances and denies the idea of an immaterial mental substance. Since there are only physical events going on, and physical events produce mental events, this is a physicalist form of monism. The mind is causally dependent on the brain and can only exist as long as the brain exists. As the brain changes, so the mind changes, but the mind is not entirely reducible to the brain. This is a supervenience relationship, meaning that the mind appears on top of the brain, which is more basic. Mental characteristics are dependent on the properties of the brain, but there is no explanation for how brain states give rise to non-physical minds. Property dualism offers a middle path between radical materialism, which denies mind altogether, and substance dualism which postulates an immaterial mind (and even a soul) as well as a material brain.

The related idea of psychophysical parallelism suggests that each event has a mental component and a physical component, and neither is an explanation of the other; they correlate with each other, since they occur at the same time, but they are causally independent of each other. Leibniz believed that mind and matter run along constantly parallel lines that do not actually meet, but they are perfectly in tune, like two identical clocks, so my wish to move my arm occurs at the same instant as I move it. God has created a pre-established harmony between mind and matter, so it looks like one seems to influence the other but there is really no interaction.

Dual aspect monism and neutral monism

In contrast to Descartes' insistence on the radical distinction between mind and matter, the seventeenth-century philosopher Baruch Spinoza believed that there is only one infinite substance, God, which includes all of reality. For Spinoza, mind and matter are two attributes or different expressions of the same underlying unity of nature, which has an infinite number of attributes. Whatever happens in the body also occurs in the mind; these are two ways of looking at the same event. This idea is often interpreted today in terms of neutral monism, which suggests that mind and matter are two components of the same underlying neutral domain, which consists of elements that combine to form either mind or matter. These elements are themselves neither mental nor physical. Neutral monism has to explain how the mental and physical levels are combined within the more primary level, and what that level might consist of.

A different view known as dual aspect monism also sees matter and mind as two equally primordial aspects of the same underlying ontic reality that is itself neither mental nor physical. The mental and physical are two sides of the same coin, inseparable, each of which is real from its own perspective. The difference is that while neutral monism says that mind and matter are both reducible to the neutral domain and are dependent on it, dual-aspect monism holds that the mental and the physical cannot be reduced to the underlying domain; they are co-primary, distinct things. The underlying domain is wholistic and splits into mental or physical aspects as it emerges. Dual aspect monism says that we see reality either in its mental or its material aspects, depending on our focus; the mental or physical are thus epistemically dual perceptions of an underlying ontic unity. Reality is both material and experiential, but since these are two aspects of one neutral reality, one does not cause the other. We only have knowledge of the underlying domain when it is manifested as either mind or matter. One can only speculate about the nature of the background domain; it may be inaccessible to us. Speculatively, the fundamental reality might be a quantum level of reality. In a letter, Jung (1975, p. 43f) speculates about the existence of a single energy that may appear in lower frequencies as matter and as more intense frequencies as psyche.

A more radical form of idealistic monism is seen in the tradition of Advaita Vedānta, which sees Pure Consciousness as the primary and sole reality. Here, the material world is the result of the activity of Consciousness. From this non-dual point of view, dual aspect monism is based on an artificial distinction since Consciousness and matter are never separate entities, except as an appearance within the ego. There is no need for a theory to unite them because only Consciousness is ultimately real. The separateness and distinctions we see in our consensual reality are the result of the ways in which human brains and sensory systems experience reality, combined with the superimposition of language and conceptual thought on an undivided totality. Vedānta suggests that rather than correlations between mind and matter (Atmanspacher & Fach, 2013), reality does not consist of separate parts. Pure Consciousness is the sole existent. Pure Consciousness manifests itself as subject and object, the knower and the known, which are inseparable. From this point of view, synchronicity is a manifestation of pure Consciousness experienced as both matter and psyche. Just as materialistic monism cannot explain how consciousness could arise from matter, so the idea of the primacy of Consciousness has to explain how matter could arise from it.

Physicalist theories of consciousness and the mind

The question of the nature and source of consciousness is one of the most challenging problems facing contemporary science. There is a wide range of responses to this question; one recent review of 68 papers (Sattin et al., 2021) describes 29 neurological theories. Materialistic monism, the doctrine that only matter and energy exist, insists that consciousness is brain-based. This reductionist view is currently the reigning paradigm in mainstream neuroscience and cognitive science (e.g., Dennett, 1991; Edelman 2004). John Searle (2005) refers to this approach as biological naturalism. A typical physicalist explanation of consciousness is given by Crick and Koch (1990), who proposed that phenomenal consciousness is the result of semi-synchronized 40–75-hertz neural oscillations in the sensory cortex of the brain. Solms (2021) believes that consciousness evolved with the development of feelings, which are the "foundational form of consciousness, its prerequisite" (p. 265). For him, consciousness is fundamentally affective.

In the physicalist view, all mental events, including thoughts, feelings, and consciousness itself, are the result of brain processes. The mind is often described as an epiphenomenon or byproduct of the activity of the brain, just as foam on the ocean is an epiphenomenon of wave action. Epiphenomenalism implies that the mind has no causal effect on the world and the mind cannot bring about other mental states. Everyday experience seems to render this theory implausible, given the obviously creative effect of the mind on our behavior and the world.

Some theorists have tried to eliminate the mind–brain question altogether by denying the existence of anything mental, claiming that there are only brain states, which are identical to mental states. We only imagine ourselves having thoughts, memories, and other mental operations, which are derisively dismissed as "folk psychology." For the strict physicalist therefore, there is no mind–body problem. The mind–brain identity theory is a straightforward solution, and it seems plausible to many people. This idea gets rid of the problem of understanding how two different things can interact with each other, because for the materialist only matter exists. States of the mind can only be states of the brain. However, the same mental state, such as pain, may be brought about in different ways in different animal species; mental states may not have a one-to-one correlation with physical states. Another difficulty with the mind–brain identity theory is that there are no one-to-one correspondences between a psychological state and a type of body movement. There are many ways of expressing pain, for example. One could be in pain with no outward behavioral signs of pain, and sometimes body movements do not express a mental state, as we see in the case of a muscle spasm. Mind–brain identity theorists agree that talking about mental states is different than talking about brain states, but they point out that this does not mean they are different in kind. We can experience saltiness without knowing anything about the chemistry of NaCl that underlies it. Only a knowledge of chemistry tells us that we are talking about the same thing using two different vocabularies. However, it is equally possible that the same type of thought can be produced by means of various neurological processes, so brain states and mental states are not necessarily identical the way salt and NaCl are the same. A further problem for the strict materialist is the mind's ability to represent or imagine events or states of affairs that are not themselves mental and may not actually exist. In spite of these difficulties, the doctrine of eliminative materialism insists that we should completely give up talking about mental states, because they are in fact brain states. In this view, mental states are in the same category as unicorns; once we realize they do not exist, we do not mention them anymore—they are folklore. To many people this idea seems over-simplified. Our subjectivity is not a mythic fantasy like belief in unicorns; it is very real to us.

The main problem for the materialist is to explain *how* neural events in the brain produce subjective experience, what it is like to experience the world, and how intentionality and consciousness arise from brain mechanisms. David Chalmers (1996) refers to this as the "hard problem" of consciousness.[20] The hard problem is how to account for qualia, or the quality of experience, what it is like to see red or feel pain, while the "easy" problem is the attempt to correlate brain mechanisms with cognitive functions such as perception, discrimination, attention, and behavior. These functions may go on even when we are not fully conscious of them; in fact, consciousness of some complex physical activities actually inhibits our ability to perform them well. Thinking and problem solving obviously go on at an unconscious level and creative solutions suddenly erupt into awareness. Cognitive functions may eventually be explicable in terms of brain functioning, but many philosophers doubt that consciousness can be entirely reduced to brain states. There is an as-yet-unbridgeable explanatory gap between physical processes in the brain and conscious experiences. A neuroscientist might be able to describe the neurological mechanisms associated with cognitive functions without explaining why we experience them consciously. Knowing that the occipital lobe of the brain is correlated with sight does not tell us how we become aware of what we see. Neurological patterns in the brain correlate with or correspond to psychological states but it is not clear whether neural activity causes these psychological states. For many theorists, the sense of subjectivity and metacognitive awareness, the ability to interpret and think about one's experiences, mark the distinction between humans and machines. The brain is obviously necessary for human consciousness, but at this point in our knowledge the brain is not a sufficient explanation. It requires faith in materialist science to believe that subjectivity will eventually be explained in terms of neuronal activity. At present, the dedicated materialist assumes there is a connection between the brain and consciousness but cannot explain the gap between them. We could in principle observe electro-chemical events in the brain at a finer and finer level of magnification, down to the behavior of molecules, as the subject describes his subjective experience. We might then be seeing the same phenomenon from different perspectives, but still without explaining how consciousness emerges from brain chemistry. We would have two levels or types of description, but not necessarily an explanation.

Chalmers does not believe that phenomenal consciousness is necessarily a function of brain activity, in part because we can conceive of an artificial intelligence that is physically identical to a human being but does not experience subjectivity or consciousness. The famous philosophical zombie is a robotic structure that behaves in a way that mimics human behavior but has no subjective self-awareness or sentience. It would be impossible to discern from the outside whether such a machine is conscious or not since the presence or absence of consciousness would not affect its behavior. Complex behavior alone does not tell us whether such a system would have the capacity for self-reflection or a felt experience of what it was doing. Chalmers points out that even if we could explain the neurological basis of cognitive and behavioral functions, there is no explanation for why these should be accompanied by conscious awareness of them. He suggests that consciousness could be recognized to be a fundamental property of the universe, alongside features such as space-time, and that would require a new kind of physics.

It is much more important to the depth psychologist to know what it is like to have our experiences than it is to know how the brain works when we have them. Modern instruments such as PET and fMRI scans tell us which areas of a person's brain are active, but we still have to ask the person what she is thinking or feeling, because the instruments do not tell us—they only show a correlation between brain activity and mental processing. It is interesting to understand the neurological correlates of dreaming, such as rapid eye movements, but each dream has its own content and its own meaning to the person, which cannot be gleaned from observation of the dreaming brain. The phenomenology of near-death experiences has never been adequately explained in terms of brain functioning, even though many biological explanations have been suggested. Near-death experiences are characterized by mental clarity even in the absence of neuronal activity (Parnia et al., 2007), suggesting that consciousness is independent of the brain.

Materialism has difficulty explaining the effect of the mind on the body, for example in meditation, which is known to produce physical changes in the brain (Hölzel et al., 2011). There is good evidence that with training and effort, people can alter brain circuitry associated with psychopathology (Schwartz & Begley, 2002). Mental effort such as mindfulness assists in self-regulation. The placebo effect and the "voodoo death" or psychogenic death[21] are other examples of the influence of the mind over physical functioning. In short, one cannot explain all human behavior in terms of brain mechanisms.

Not only is phenomenal consciousness, or what-it-is-like to be aware, impossible to explain in terms of neuronal activity alone, so also is intentionality. Intentionality here refers to the idea that mental states such as hopes and fears are always about something; they point to something else beyond themselves. Only mental states exhibit intentionality; physical states cannot show it. There seem to be unconscious intentional states that drive behavior, such as complexes, and not all conscious states are intentional; anxiety is one example. The question of how intentionality and phenomenal consciousness are related to each other is much debated.

Emergentism is a less reductive forms of physicalism; it assumes that new properties, such as consciousness, emerge from brain activity but these emergent properties cannot be understood purely on the basis of physical laws operating in the brain (Chibbaro et al., 2014). Mental events emerge from lower-level neural functions but cannot be entirely reduced to them. The organizing principles and properties of each higher level are absent from the lower levels from which they emerge. Emergent mental events can causally affect the lower-level brain functions that produced them. Emergentism suggests that consciousness emerged during the evolution of biological organisms as a property of the increasing complexity of the nervous system. This complexity allowed something—mind—to appear that is new and different, and greater than the sum of its physical parts. However, no explanation has appeared that explains *how* the mind appears.

Another proposed solution to the mind–body problem is the philosophy of functionalism, which says that what makes something count as an inner experience or a mental state is not its origin in brain mechanisms but the role it plays in our psychological life and our behavior. Functionalism sees mental states only in terms of what they do, and in terms of their purpose, rather than what they are made of. Mental states can only be understood in terms of other mental states within a causal network. A mental state such as pain can be identified with the causal role it plays, such as avoidant behavior. The nature of the mind is its functional role. This idea is attractive because it describes the mind, including purpose and behavior, without recourse to specific brain mechanisms.[22] Most functionalists are materialists who reject dualism and avoid reference to anything nonphysical.

Functionalism is widely used by cognitive psychologists to describe psychological processes such as language and emotion. It avoids the issue of the origin of a mental state by limiting description of it to its function. However, it is not clear that a functionalist explanation of a mental state is a causal explanation of that state. Functionalism also does not solve the problem of qualia, or subjectivity, or what it feels like to have an experience, and it is debatable whether it can explain intentionality, or the fact that our beliefs and attitudes are about something.

Psychologists and philosophers who adhere to physicalism deny the existence of immaterial spirit or a soul, on the grounds that the existence of these dimensions is not empirically testable. Such belief is typically dismissed as pre-scientific superstition. These theorists either tacitly ignore or deny the reality of phenomena that do not fit theories of brain-based consciousness, such as psi phenomena and near-death experiences. Physicalists do not consider near-death experiences as evidence of spiritual identity independent of the body, because they consider the evidence for these events to be unconvincing and no mechanism is available to explain them. However, these experiences have been validated sufficiently often to challenge reductionist materialism (Kelly et al., 2009, 2019; Tart, 2009). Near death experiences cannot be explained in terms of brain mechanisms, and there are no reductionist explanations for some features of near-death experiences such as the ability of the blind to see during the experience and the subsequent acquisition of spiritual gifts or healing.

Ironically, the physicalists' belief that materialist science will ultimately explain consciousness, which is an ideology that pervades all their research, is actually a form of faith, since there is no incontrovertible evidence for it. The question of the source of consciousness is still debatable, and a strong case can be made against the materialist hypothesis (Kelly et al., 2009). The hard problem of consciousness remains unsolved, in spite of considerable research efforts.

Panpsychism

Panpsychism is the view that all matter, living or nonliving, possesses some mind-like quality. The idea has several variants, but basically posits that even the simplest forms of matter, such as elementary sub-atomic particles, possess a rudimentary form of consciousness, something it is like to be one of them. A primitive form of consciousness is therefore present in the simple forms of matter that make up more complex forms such as brains (Nagel, 1979b, 1998). Thomas Nagel believes that unless there is no explanation for mental properties in complex systems such as brains, we have to accept the possibility that primitive levels of consciousness, or what he calls "proto-mental properties," are a basic property of matter. He suggests that these properties and the matter with which they are associated may emerge from a more fundamental level of reality that has the potential to become both mental and material. This view is reminiscent of the theory of dual aspect monism.

Panpsychism suggests that consciousness and matter are both fundamental; consciousness is an intrinsic property of matter, and consciousness is irreducible. Panpsychism is one approach to the problem of the possible interaction of consciousness and matter at the quantum level, and it is also seen as a possible solution to the mind–body problem and the question of how consciousness could emerge from non-conscious matter. Non-conscious material in the brain could just produce a very complex but non-conscious system, but if the ultimate material constituents of the brain are themselves conscious, this problem is less mysterious because consciousness was present all along and there is no concern about how it emerged. This view can be seen to be a disguised form of materialism because it says that matter *has* consciousness, as if matter were primary. It also has a dualistic flavor although it is not quite dualism or pure physicalism, especially if consciousness is seen as constituting matter, which is the Vedāntic view. The attraction of panpsychism is that it is unifying and does not deny the reality of either mind or matter. However, there is not much evidence for this idea. A major difficulty with panpsychism is to explain how the elementary consciousness within these elements of matter combines into the complex, rich, and unified consciousness we experience (Seager, 1997). It is difficult to explain how the subatomic particles that make up the body, each of which in this theory is a miniature conscious subject, could add together to make another conscious subject such a person. This combination problem is one of the most difficult aspects of panpsychism. It may be resolved by assuming emergentism, in which case new properties appear with increasing complexity of the system. If the panpsychist insists on adding consciousness to matter as if they were different, the problem of how consciousness initially arose remains. Many people reject panpsychism on the grounds that it is slightly absurd or counterintuitive to think that a physical object could be conscious, but this objection is not an adequate refutation. Many philosophers have avoided this theory because it seems to involve metaphysical speculation and it cannot be tested experimentally.

The philosopher Galen Strawson (2006, 2008) believes that the universe and all the events in it, including experiential phenomena, are physical, but physics cannot fully capture the nature or essence of subjective experience. He embraces panpsychism because he believes that experience cannot emerge out of that which is non-experiential; in his view, only panpsychism can account for the mind–body relationship. As well, in his words, "we have no good reason to think that we know anything about the physical that gives us any reason to find any problem in the idea that experiential phenomena are physical phenomena" (Strawson, 2006, p. 4). In his view the intrinsic nature of matter is experiential.

Strawson (2016) also pointed out that we know what consciousness is because we have it, but we don't know the intrinsic nature of matter, except what we experience of it consciously. Strawson believes that although reality is entirely physical, physics tells us the structure and mechanics of the physical world but not about its nature, what matter *is*. [23] There is a limit to what physics can say about reality. Accordingly, according to Strawson, the really hard problem is the nature of matter, the same matter that makes up the brain.

Some quantum physicists adopt a view that suggests panpsychism; David Bohm (1986, p. 275) writes that a "mind-like quality of matter reveals itself strongly at the quantum level." Furthermore: "in some sense a rudimentary mind-like quality is present even at the level of particle physics, and that as we go to subtler levels, this mind-like quality becomes stronger and more developed." Bohm (ibid., p. 129) also writes that "the mental and the material are two sides of one overall process ... separated only in thought and not in actually."

The philosopher David Skrbina (2017) prefers the theory of panpsychism to the notion of "strong emergence," the idea that consciousness emerged as a new property out of non-conscious matter, since emergence does not explain *how* consciousness emerges. Emergent phenomena, such as the flocking of birds or the schooling of fish, are observations of matter from the outside, but tell us nothing about whether any kind of internal experience occurs.

Giulio Tononi's integrated information theory of consciousness has become a major theory within modern neuroscience. This theory states that any mechanism or system that integrates information in the right way exhibits some form of consciousness; consciousness *is* integrated information. The level or amount of consciousness in a system depends on the amount of integrated information, which is a property known as ⊠ or *phi*. Examples of such systems are neurons or a collection of neurons, but the idea applies to all forms of matter, not just biological systems. In principle therefore, a mobile phone would have a measurable amount of *phi*. This theory is claimed to provide a mathematically rigorous theory of consciousness. It suggests that consciousness is a unity or a field that exists independently of external observers (Tononi et al., 2016). This theory has been a major boost for panpsychism because it suggests that consciousness can emerge from any system of integrated information, even if we cannot imagine what its consciousness is like, so even a subatomic particle might possess *phi*. It is not clear if this theory explains qualia or the hard problem of consciousness, or whether it deals with the question of whether consciousness is truly metaphysically fundamental.

Challenges to physicalism

The physicalist solution to the mind–brain question and the origin of consciousness is very popular in academic circles, but it has been trenchantly questioned. Physicalism insists that there is nothing besides energy and matter, but that position is impossible to prove. Materialistic theories of mind have to discount phenomena such as near-death experiences. These theories cannot account for intentionality, the fact that consciousness is characteristically directed towards something, because a physical event in the brain could not be about something such as a belief. If the materialist theory were true, the theory itself would only be the result of a set of brain events, and other theories would be other sets of brain events. How then could one set of brain events be truer than any other set? They would all have equal validity with no possibility of independent validation. A materialistic theory of mind might lead to a completely deterministic account of human behavior, to simplistic cause and effect thinking, and even to stimulus-response psychology. This implies that there would be little room for creativity, ethics, moral choices, or personal responsibility. However, if consciousness is indeed primary and irreducible as the Vedantic tradition and some Western philosophers believe, science will never penetrate its nature because science studies objects, but consciousness is never an object; it is the ultimate subject of all experience.

The physicalist credo is still defended vigorously, apparently due to an emotional attachment to materialism. There are philosophers who deny that there really is a hard problem of consciousness. Patricia Churchland (1996) points out that what Chalmers calls the easy and hard problems are not really any different in terms of difficulty; in both cases we don't know what a solution would look like, but the solution will one day be revealed by understanding the neurobiology involved. She notes that many phenomena that we now understand were incapable of explanation at an earlier time. Daniel Dennett (1991) also believes there is no explanatory gap between consciousness and brain activity that cannot be solved by understanding the necessary brain science. Another view is that even if we were to find definite neurological correlates of consciousness, we would still not know why or how consciousness emerges from these neuronal processes. Colin McGinn (1999) adopts a mysterian position by arguing that the human mind has evolved to the point that it can deal with scientific and mathematical problems, but our brains are not equipped to solve the hard problem of consciousness. There is an unbridgeable gap between the felt qualities of experience and the underlying neural events, even if these brain states are producing subjectivity. He has been criticized on the grounds that this attitude might inhibit inquiry into the brain mechanisms involved, but he is not alone in thinking that consciousness is irredeemably mysterious.

The astrophysicist Adam Frank (2017) makes the point that physicalists are clinging to classical physics, ignoring the problems raised by quantum physics. Frank notes that all interpretations of quantum mechanics force us to step away from the naïve realism of Newtonian physics and dispel any hope that materialism will explain consciousness. If we have to put the consciousness of the experimenter back into quantum physics, materialism is no longer on solid ground. At the quantum level, our observations of matter are no longer entirely objective. However, physicists tend to ignore the problem of the true nature of matter raised by the measurement problem in quantum physics, which some physicists believe includes a role for consciousness. This blurs the materialist conviction of the nature of reality. At the moment, there is no agreed-upon scientific solution to this problem, and the role of consciousness remains controversial.

The mind in behaviorism and cognitive science

The tradition of behaviorism began in the early twentieth century. Behaviorists either ignored the existence of mind and consciousness or they thought that consciousness was unnecessary to the study of psychology. In order to be scientific, they believed that psychology should be restricted to the study of behavior that can be quantitatively analyzed and objectively observed. They saw no need to postulate an immaterial mind. For behaviorists, statements about the mind are equivalent to statements about a person's behavior. Whatever can be said about beliefs, thoughts, and sensations can be better said by describing the behavior to which they correspond. This approach avoids the problem of mind–brain interaction, since the mind is really just how the body behaves. There are no mysterious mental processes to explain. According to Gilbert Ryle (1949), when we talk about the mind, we are really talking about a disposition to behave in a certain way, and we can know the minds of others by studying their behavioral dispositions.

Psychologists such as John Watson and B.F. Skinner saw consciousness as not only inaccessible but also possibly nonexistent. Skinner's *Beyond freedom and dignity* even argued that our notions of freedom, dignity, and free will are simply attempts to glorify the individual and have actually retarded human development. He believed that people can be shaped by positive and negative reinforcement into the kind of people we want, in order to achieve human happiness. This author did not address the question of who should determine what happiness and human advancement should look like or who would ensure compliance with correct behavior.

Behaviorism is a radically objectivist approach to knowledge. It developed partly because subjectivity was too difficult to study mechanically. This movement partly had its roots in the scientific revolution, because the scientific method was producing increasingly impressive results. Another important influence on the field was logical positivism, which developed the criterion of cognitive significance; only entities or ideas for which there is empirical evidence can be considered to be meaningful. In the first part of the twentieth century, the new empiricism seemed better than trying to understand the inner life, which was too vague to study, so that the baby of subjectivity was thrown out with the bath water of superstition and demonology. Direct measurement seemed to be superior to the old armchair methods of inquiry, so to keep up with the new frontier, psychology had to develop a scientific persona. Behaviorism seemed to answer that call.

For many people the most problematic aspect of behaviorism is its radical denial of human subjectivity, or what it is like to have experiences such as pain, which may not be reflected in behavior. There seems to be no way, using this theory, to account for the imagination, which is purely mental, private, and subjective, and also may not appear as outer behavior. We have sudden inspirations and ideas that are not dispositional, and we have long-standing knowledge and beliefs that are more complex than mere dispositions to specific behavior. Radical behaviorists have to assume that the person has no inner life, and they ignore the facts of lived experience such as our existential framework and our capacity for self-reflection. Behaviorism also ignores the fact that the baby is born with an enormous reservoir of information—for Jung, this includes the archetypal dimension of the psyche.

The story of the rise and fall of behaviorism is instructive because it repeats an important lesson in the history of ideas. When the academic establishment embraces or repudiates a psychological theory, this really means little in terms of the ultimate value of that theory, or how it will be viewed by later generations. For decades, behaviorism was the dominant ideology in major universities. Such was the strength of the commitment to this approach that for many years a large group of influential psychologists continuously denied the importance of consciousness. Currently, most psychologists think that behaviorism is a useful way of understanding relatively simple forms of behavior that make up only a small part of the entire repertoire of human behavior. Otherwise, behaviorism has proven to be of relatively limited application, given the enormous investment of effort that went into it. A similar fate befell classical psychoanalysis, which at one time dominated psychiatry and is now marginalized.

As the majority of psychologists became disenchanted with traditional behaviorism, in the 1960's it gave way to a new discipline called cognitive science, which brought the mind back into psychology. Whereas behaviorists thought that there is no such thing as a mind that intervenes between a stimulus and a response, cognitive psychologists believe that the mind does process the information that we receive before we respond to a stimulus. This discipline treats people as "information processors" whose minds are essentially analogous to computer programs or connected computer modules. Cognitive scientists have turned their focus away from rats in mazes towards higher mental processes such as memory, intelligence, and thinking.

Many cognitive scientists believe that they have explained consciousness when they explain abilities such as perception. But the "hard" problem of consciousness is to explain why we are *aware* of these functions going on. It is one thing to explain behavior, but this does not explain why we are conscious of the behavior. When I burn my finger, the neuroscientists can tell me the pathway that the nerve impulses take from my finger to my brain, but that does not account for my subjective experience of pain. As far as my purely biological survival is concerned, it would be enough to learn to avoid fire.

The computational model of mind

Cognitive scientists focus on a model of thinking that is called "computational," meaning that information processing in the brain is thought of as if the brain were a kind of computer. Like computers, the mind contains symbols and internal logic, but whereas computers use hardware to compute, people use "wetware," or brain cells, to do basically the same thing. What we call the mind is a program run by the brain the way a computer runs a software program. So great is the enthusiasm for this approach that some of its proponents believe that knowledge about the brain will soon replace a purely psychological approach to the mind. However, we cannot explain the psychological importance of a home by understanding the engineering principles behind its construction and the chemistry of its bricks and mortar.

The extreme version of the computational model of the mind is seen among artificial intelligence scientists who try to reproduce psychological processes in computers; some of these researchers believe that eventually computers will have consciousness, self-reflexive subjectivity, and intentionality. In principle, therefore, according to the computer model, once the brain's wiring diagram has been fully mapped, it could be replicated in silicon, which would recreate consciousness.

The attempt to liken the mind to a computer does not work very well. A computer can mimic some aspects of the way the human mind works, but the philosopher John Searle (2005) pointed out that, although a computer can manipulate symbols, the computer does not understand what the symbols mean or what they imply. The computer use syntax (the rules and patterns that govern the proper use of words and symbols), but the computer cannot grasp the larger context of the problem it is "thinking" about, or the implications of the answer—only the mind understands semantics (the meaning of these words and symbols). When the computer recognizes the color red, does it have the same experience as we do when we see red? Although some scientists hope that sentience will eventually emerge within artificial intelligence, at the moment, a computer is not conscious of itself as a subjective entity; it cannot think about what it is computing and change its mind about its conclusions. It does not have anything like free will, and emotions do not affect its thinking. It is ironic that, rather than thinking of the computer as a model for understanding the mind, some artificial intelligence researchers are beginning to use the mind as a model for building better computers.

Tallis (2004) believes that the weakness of the computational model of the mind is the result of the misuse of language, "machinising" the mind and anthropomorphizing the brain. He notes that words such as "information" and "memory" have a range of meanings; they can be applied to human beings and also used metaphorically to describe aspects of computers, but when their metaphorical use is lost or forgotten, machines are described in human terms. Memory in a computer operates in an entirely different manner than human memory. Tallis refers to the computer model of the brain as a form of "neuromythology" that cannot account for what makes human beings distinctively human.

The linguist Noam Chomsky provides an important critique of the notion that artificial intelligence might one day surpass human intelligence and creativity (Chomsky, 2023). He points out that machine learning programs differ profoundly from the ways in which humans reason and use language, and these differences "place significant limitations on what these programs can do, encoding them with ineradicable defects." The human mind creates causal explanations and can imaginatively conjure counterfactual possibilities and creative criticisms, but the machine only describes, correlates, and predicts from the available data. Chomsky points out that the machine cannot distinguish the possible from the impossible, but human thinking can discover meaningful but improbable insights. Therefore, he believes that machine predictions "will always be superficial and dubious." Machines are unable to reason from moral principles, so they endorse both ethical and unethical decisions.

The implications of the physicalist theory of mind for psychotherapy

The physicalist philosophy of the mind has major implications for the way we treat people suffering from psychological disorders. A medical model approach to these disorders based on neurobiology gives psychiatry a respectable place amidst the biological sciences and rationalizes modern psychiatry's lack of interest in psychotherapy, which is more time consuming and less remunerative than medication management. The assumption that the brain explains consciousness is partly driven by the economics of our health care system, the preferences of insurance companies, and the stream of new pharmaceutical agents. It is cheaper and quicker to treat people with medication than with psychotherapy, and medication avoids emotional entanglements with the sufferer. The medical model partially insulates the psychiatrist from his own vulnerability reflected in the patient.

The relationship between science, politics, power, money, and values is noticeable in the corporate-influenced aspects of the *Diagnostic and statistical manual of mental disorders* (DSM) (American Psychiatric Association, 2022).[24] Insurance companies and pharmaceutical manufacturers have a powerful influence on mental health practice, controlling much mental health treatment and making suspect claims of scientific objectivity. For example, there is an enormous vested interest in brain-based explanations for a problem such as depression, because this means it can be treated purely chemically. However, depression is not simply a problem of brain chemistry. Depression often originates in the circumstances of the individual's life and relationships, losses, and disappointments, but many biologically oriented practitioners see these problems as irrelevant to their treatment with antidepressants. These practitioners hold an implicitly physicalist approach to the mind, which they see as purely a function of brain activity. Yet the fact that antidepressants may alleviate severe depression does not mean that the problem was initially caused by a primary biochemical disturbance, which may be secondary to psychosocial factors such as loss. When antidepressants are effective, the psychosocial origin of the person's depression may remain untouched because there is then no necessity to deal with the psychosocial problem. It is true however that sometimes that level of the problem cannot be helped, and antidepressants are essential to alleviate suffering.

Although the DSM claims to be atheoretical, it is actually based on a range of philosophical assumptions, including physicalism, realism, and reductionism. The delineation of psychiatric disorders in the DSM is often based not on objective evidence but on the consensus of the book's authors and their values and theoretical beliefs, which is not a scientifically rigorous approach to classification. It is not clear that these disorders are really distinct entities rather than problems of living shared by all people. Furthermore, the DSM is based on Western cultural perspectives about which feelings or behavior are considered to be normal. A diagnosis can be helpful when it allows the sufferer to recognize that he or she has a well-recognized problem that others have also suffered. However, this approach tends to medicalize problems of living without considering cultural factors such as poverty and discrimination. The medical approach may over-pathologize the individual since many "disorders" are not discrete entities but are part of a spectrum of psychological states that shade into normality. This approach does not sufficiently consider the individual's strengths and capacity for self-help. It may stigmatize the patient, damage self-esteem, and make him feel helpless.

Biological psychiatry raises the question of the extent to which practitioners are unwittingly reinforcing or colluding with social forces and prejudices within our culture. By dealing with emotional problems as if they were only located within the individual rather than the cultural milieu, both psychiatrists and psychotherapists sometimes help people remain in situations in which the person's emotional distress is caused by exploitation by oppressive socio-political conditions such as poverty, colonialism, racism, or misogyny. Mental health practitioners have been guilty of trying to impose cultural norms and beliefs on their patients.

Mainstream psychotherapy has become somewhat medicalized in the sense that it uses diagnosis, symptom-based treatments, and techniques thought to be specific to particular diagnoses. All this in spite of the fact that the therapeutic relationship and factors such as the development of trust and the therapist's authenticity, empathy, and understanding are far more important than any technique. Values such as the discovery of the meaning of suffering are often lost when therapy becomes "scientized." The medical model approach to psychotherapy implies that there are or will be specific treatments for specific disorders, grounded in evidence-based approaches that are universally replicable. However, many sources of emotional distress, problems of living such as loneliness, grief, loss of hope, the fear of death, and lack of meaning in life, torment people seeking psychotherapeutic help, but only individual responses to these issues are relevant to the one who suffers. These situations are not illnesses or disorders. The psychotherapist's responses to such problems of living are conditioned by his or her personal philosophical commitments. Faced with an individual who is thinking of committing suicide, or one who is contemplating divorce or deciding whether to have an abortion, the psychotherapist's personal beliefs, feelings, and values are immediately engaged. There can be no such thing as objectivity in such a situation. The psychotherapist's precommitments about these questions color his or her approach to psychotherapy, but these issues cannot be solved by empirical methods because they occur in individual contexts, and human needs and personalities are very different. There are no clear answers to such problems of living, and the way the psychotherapist approaches the human condition profoundly affects the way in which he deals with them. These forms of suffering, and problems such as chronic hatred and envy, are not specific to any particular diagnosis and they do not have specific "evidence based" remedies. Many forms of emotional distress are suffered silently and cannot even be articulated.

Philosophical assumptions of schools of psychotherapy

All theories of psychotherapy have ontological and epistemological assumptions, an explicit or implicit view of human nature, and a view of the best way to understand people. These assumptions may be hidden, but they affect the ways in which the psychotherapist works. Schools of psychotherapy are often colored by the originator's image of humanity or his or her worldview. Thus, in his *Civilization and its discontents*, Freud sees society and human biology as inherently in opposition to each other. He writes that our sexual and aggressive drives must be tamed for civilization to function, but human nature resists attempts to civilize it, and conflict is inevitable, so that civilization is but a thin veneer. Even though this is a pessimistic view of humanity, this attitude became incorporated into the early years of psychoanalytic theory as if it were a fundamental truth. Competing views to those of Freud were largely marginalized at the time, partly because of Freud's strict demand for conformity to his theories. Adler's view of the human condition has been largely ignored by mainstream practitioners, but he stressed the fundamentally social nature of human beings who struggle to overcome personal and social difficulties. His view of human nature was essentially optimistic. Jung's model of the psyche was also ignored and accused of being too metaphysical. Jung's view that there is a transpersonal or universal level of the psyche, and an a priori God-image in the psyche, is only acceptable to a minority of practitioners, but to them it is important because it offers a spiritual dimension to their practice. However, it is anathema to mainstream psychologists who want to free the field from anything so unmeasurable.

It took some time before object relations theorists and psychoanalytic self psychologists developed the idea that human beings are inherently relationship seeking creatures and not simply driven by biological drives. Kohut questioned the inevitability of intergenerational conflict and pointed out the growth-enhancing and supportive behavior of healthy parents. He stressed the primacy of the development of the self rather than the primacy of instinctual drives. Other, hermeneutically oriented practitioners focused particularly on the social, cultural, and historical factors that affect human life, and studied the person's action in the outer world as opposed to the private inner world.

Psychotherapists tend to gravitate towards theories that embody their own vision of humanity, although they often find in practice that their theory is not always adequate to the human situations they face. There is a tendency for psychologists to ignore experiences, states of mind, and problems of living that are not amenable to their particular methodology. One of the risks of psychotherapy occurs when the therapist is overly attached to his or her theoretical orientation. There is then a risk he or she will impose or project a truth derived from theory onto his patient and not see the patient's reality. Therapists may justify their interventions on the basis of their preferred theory of therapy, but these justifications may be based on faith and personal commitments and often cannot be rigorously proven. Many schools of psychotherapy are based on rationales that have not been empirically verified. Psychotherapists often adhere to approaches based on nothing more than conviction, training, and personal preferences. Thus, when people improve with a particular approach, because of the importance of the non-specific factors common to all schools of psychotherapy (described below), one cannot assume that improvement occurred for the technical reasons that the theory postulates.

In today's climate it is impossible to believe that any single theory of psychotherapy could be universally applicable. Much of what goes on in psychotherapy is unconscious and not necessarily defined or understood by current theory. Rigid adherence to a particular theory of psychotherapy restricts other ways of looking at the psyche that might be equally valid. Perhaps the majority of modern therapists integrate more than one approach. A complicating factor when comparing schools of therapy is that what therapists do in practice may not correspond to their declared therapeutic preference. Especially when therapists are faced with a patient struggling with a serious life crisis, the therapist will often behave in a way that goes beyond the bounds of his stated theory of therapy. The therapist usually falls back on his or her human responses rather than theory. These responses are not scientifically based, but they may be very helpful.

Ontological and epistemological claims in psychoanalysis

Psychoanalysis has often been characterized as unscientific and unverifiable. Adolph Grünbaum (1986) believed it is impossible to be sure that the data obtained in psychoanalysis are not the result of suggestion, and it is difficult to prove that this practice has therapeutic value. Donald Spence (1987) complained that unlike the objectivity and openness of science, psychoanalysis is a self-referential, closed discourse, and its theories of the mind are based on empirically unprovable metaphors. He insists that scientific conclusions must be based on evidence, not authority. Bornstein (2001) predicted the demise of psychoanalysis unless it adopts empirical, research-based methodology. In response, Mills (2002) pointed out that this kind of critique ignores the wide range of psychoanalytic theories and recent advances such as relational theory. Psychoanalysis is not a mainstream discipline within academic psychology because it does not appeal to psychologists who prefer unambiguous answers to questions and research topics that are easier to manage and quantify. However, psychological truth cannot be exclusively defined by the consensus of empirically trained researchers and their quantitative methods. Their claim to absolute authority is not legitimate, and neither is the view that only empirical science is a valid means of inquiry, "at the expense of other equally viable and philosophically defensible methods such as discursive, dialectical, qualitative, phenomenological, hermeneutic, linguistic, historical, post-structuralist, social constructivist, narrative, de-constructivist, feminist, and logical approaches—each with their respective criteria" (ibid., p. 552). Mills goes on to point out that because the mind and human nature are very complex, psychoanalysis cannot jettison complexity. It must resist simplistic, reductionist strategies, which often characterize mainstream approaches to the psyche. Mills believes that what fuels Bornstein's argument is the conviction that only empirical science can deliver objective truth about psychological phenomena, ignoring the fact that psychotherapy is inherently subjective. Countertransference is inevitable, and so is the presence of the therapist's values and preconceptions. Outward observation of an individual is important, but so is inward or first-person observation. The unconscious cannot be directly observed or measured. The attempts to find precision and clear rules of psychotherapeutic practice may be defenses against affect and against acknowledging the transpersonal dimension of the psyche. However, there are legitimate criticisms of classical psychoanalysis, for example the fact that the analyst's theory was sometimes superimposed on the therapeutic situation to the extent that theory took precedence over the patient's subjective experience. Freud believed he could objectively study his patients' subjectivity on the basis of his theory. The modern emphasis on relational and experience-near interpretations has largely corrected this problem. The later development of object relations theory proposed an inner world consisting of the internal representations of outer relationships. This makes the question of what is inside and what is outside, and how much we can rely on our perception of the outer world, very complicated. It is not clear that our internal representations of others are objective truth because they are so colored by subjective factors. In Kohut's psychology, another person becomes a selfobject, or an intrapsychic combination of one's own self and the other, so subjectivism rules. The risk of extreme subjectivism is that it shades into relativism. An extreme intersubjectivist position such as that of Stolorow and Atwood (1979), which focuses only on the interactional field, is an epistemological stance that gets rid of objectivism altogether.

Ogden (2019) believes that Freud and Klein developed an epistemological form of psychoanalysis, based on knowing and understanding the patient's unconscious and inner world, while Winnicott and Bion contributed to the development of ontological psychoanalysis, which has to do with being, becoming, and the discovery of meaning. Ogden points out that these two forms of the discipline do not exist in pure forms; they "coexist in mutually enriching relationships with one another" (ibid., p. 663). Jung's psychology also has ontological commitments, such as the existence of the Self and the objective psyche. Kohut's attempt to strengthen the self is an ontological approach, while his emphasis on empathy is his epistemological method. From an epistemological point of view, dreams and the interpretation of the transference are particularly important approaches to the unconscious. Kohut (1977, pp. 31–32) noticed a parallel between self-psychology and the finding within quantum physics that the means of observation and the target of observation "constitute a unit that, in certain respects, is in principle indivisible." For him, only what can be observed empathically defines the range of the therapeutic field, making the consciousness of the participants critically important. Sucharov (1992) has suggested that complementary is an essential feature of self psychology since we need complementary modes of description to describe the interaction of observer and observed when they are both integral to a psychological phenomenon.

Jung makes several empirical observations in his study of the psyche, such as the existence of numinous imagery. He postulates that this emanates from or is produced by the Self or the objective psyche, which for him is ontologically fundamental. Since Jung wrote, many observers have attested to the existence of these phenomena. Jung's postulate is a parsimonious theory in the sense that it explains many recurrent experiences, even if it is difficult to know if and how it can be falsified.[25]

Brain, psyche, and quantum effects

Although the psyche cannot be entirely reduced to brain mechanisms, quantum effects in the brain may be relevant to psychological functioning. Even though the brain operates using classically understandable chemistry and physics at the macroscopic level, and quantum effects within such a large system as the brain may not be detectable, it is reasonable to assume that quantum effects *within* neurons affect their processes at a very small scale. This means that brain mechanisms are more complex than accounts based on interactions between macroscopic neurons.

Simon (2019) has suggested that quantum mechanisms may solve the hard problem of consciousness and the "binding" or "combination"[26] problem of conscious experience, perhaps as a result of quantum entanglement in the brain. Hameroff and Penrose (2014) have suggested that consciousness may emerge as a macroscopic state resulting from quantum-level computation in cytoskeletal microtubules[27] within neurons. The microtubular theory of consciousness has been applied to the problem of schizophrenia, which is said to be associated with micro-tubular abnormalities (Venkatasubramanian, 2015).

Stapp (2017) believes that the mind–brain or brain-consciousness connection is a quantum effect. Discussing ion channels in the brain, he notes:

Large amounts of quantum uncertainty are introduced by the passages of ions through ion channels. The small spatial diameters of these channels entail large uncertainties in the velocities of the ions emerging from them. A living person's brain is therefore a generator of huge amounts of quantum uncertainty. This uncertainty can percolate up to the macroscopic level without being perceived either by the person himself or by anyone else. Brains must therefore be treated quantum mechanically. That is what permits the behavior of a person's brain to be significantly influenced by the free choices made by that person's own conscious mind.

(Stapp, 2014, p. 13)

In other words, the mind chooses among different states of the brain, and the mind allows us to actualize the body's intentions—a form of mind-matter dualism. If there are quantum level processes within the brain that have random outcomes, our actions may not be fully determinable. However, it is also possible that the macroscopic environment of the brain destroys any coherent quantum state that might arise at the microscopic level.

Quantum level physical principles are being applied to various areas of neuroscience and psychology (Schwartz et al., 2005) and to cognition (Broekart et al., 2017; Bruza et al., 2015).

Metaphysics and psychology

What is metaphysics?

There are many definitions of metaphysics. The term has a long history, and it is used in different ways by different writers. The word itself literally means "after" or "beyond" the physical dimension, or whatever lies beyond our current capacity to study scientifically and verify empirically, such as notions of God or the soul. Metaphysics can also refer to belief in supernatural entities such as ghosts, which cannot be explained by the usual scientific means. Arguments about whether only material entities exist, and whether everything has a natural explanation, the doctrines of materialism and naturalism, or whether only mind exists, the doctrine of idealism, are metaphysical. Metaphysics also refers to the fundamental conditions that allow things to exist or to occur, so the word "metaphysics" is sometimes used to mean explanations about the whole of reality, for example by asking whether there is a First Cause of the universe or a cosmic plan for humanity. In his introduction to *Appearance and reality*, the philosopher F.H. Bradley speaks of metaphysics as "an attempt to know reality as against mere appearance, or the study of first principles or ultimate truths, or again the effort to comprehend the universe, not simply piecemeal or by fragments, but somehow as a whole." Whitehead (1979) describes metaphysics as the effort "to frame a coherent, logical, necessary system of general ideas in terms of which every element of our experience can be interpreted" (p. 39). Kastrup (2021, pp. 10–11) uses the term "metaphysics" to mean "the *essence of being* of things, creatures and phenomena ... a certain view of what nature is in and of itself, as opposed to how it *behaves* (which is the subject of science) or how it *appears* to observation (which is the subject of cognitive psychology and phenomenology)." This is a view of metaphysics viewed as the study of Being-as-such rather than any individual being or entity. Metaphysics tries to describe fundamental characteristics of reality such as the nature of existence, time, and change. Metaphysics raises questions such as whether causation really exists or whether there are simply regular conjunctions between events, an issue raised by the philosopher David Hume.

In Hume's *Enquiry concerning human understanding* (1748), he contended that the only meaningful ideas are either mathematical concepts or those that can be tested by experience. For him, notions such as "reality" or "mind" are actually meaningless or insignificant since we cannot define or test them. We cannot know what a correct answer to metaphysical questions would look like, so there is no point in asking them. He believed it would be more interesting to ask about the psychology of people who get involved in searching for answers to unanswerable questions.

Kant (2004 [1772]) questioned "whether such a thing as metaphysics is even possible" (p. 5). He believed that metaphysical thinking, such as ideas about God or the immortality of the soul, is "transcendent," in the sense that such ideas try to pass beyond the limits of what can be experienced. For him, such beliefs can only be maintained dogmatically but cannot be demonstrably proven. Metaphysics is a system of conceptual knowledge not based on empirical observation. However, he believed that it is impossible to eradicate metaphysical beliefs from the human mind because we are driven to ask such questions even though they cannot be answered empirically (Kant, 1950 [1787], B 21). Nevertheless, Kant believed that these beliefs are of moral value since we can base our conduct on them.

Kant believed that the mind makes an essential contribution to our experience of the world. While it is true that we must study the world empirically, we must also acknowledge that the mind tacitly employs innate categories such as cause and effect, space, and time, which help to constitute or structure our experience of the world. We only know the world after the mind has applied its own categories to an object.[28] For Kant, we cannot expand our knowledge beyond what the mind allows us to perceive—that is, we do not know things-in-themselves, the non-empirical world or the noumenal reality that may lie beyond phenomenal appearances, Kant therefore believed that we cannot know absolute reality as it is in itself, because any phenomenon we experience has already been structured by the mind, leading to an unbridgeable gap between reality itself and our experience of it. Arguments about the nature of the noumenal realm result in what Kant called antinomies, conclusions that can be both disproved and proved, so we have no way to know which of two opposing views on metaphysical questions are true. Thus, according to Kant, attempted proofs for questions such as the existence of God are doomed to failure. For Kant, the transcendent dimension is not knowable because it is beyond experience.

Jung was very influenced by his reading of Kant, although his appropriation of Kant has been criticized by several authors (e.g., de Voogd, 1984, Brooks 2011). Based on what he considered to be his Kantian epistemology, Jung denied that we could draw metaphysical conclusions from psychological experience. However, Jung deviates from Kant in his belief that although we cannot know the nature of the noumenal level of the archetype-as-such, we can gain some knowledge of it because of the symbols, images, and ideas it produces (CW 8, para. 417). It would go beyond Kant to say that the unknowable archetype-as-such is metaphysically real because it produces effects such as synchronistic events. Kant would have said that we cannot say anything about the status of noumenal things in themselves, but Jung believed that numinous symbols point to the presence of the psychoid archetype-as-such (CW 8, para. 417). Here he implies that what Kant saw as transcendental could be made accessible symbolically.

It was assumed by early-twentieth-century psychologists that their work was free of metaphysical assumptions. Psychology during the early years of Jung's professional life was characterized by "physics envy," which Leahey (2001) describes as a "Newtonian fantasy" that one day "a Newton will arise among psychologists and propound a rigorous theory of behavior delivering psychology unto the promised land of science" (p. 24). To avoid any appearance of practicing metaphysics, psychologists turned to a rigorously empirical approach, preferring quantitative measurements of human behavior. Psychotherapists who adopted this metaphysics of physicalism also unconsciously allied themselves with a medical model of the psyche.

The entire project of metaphysics has been called into question by adherents to scientism, the (over-valued) idea that the scientific worldview is the only valid one, and by physicalism, as if metaphysical speculation tries to describe a realm that does not exist. Many philosophers have seen speculative metaphysics as pretentious and misguided, only a form of mythmaking or fantasy that masquerades as a genuine source of knowledge. In this view, attempts to explain the nature of reality as a whole or to understand the meaning of life only lead to arbitrary, untestable speculations removed from experience. Therefore, for positivism and for logical empiricism, metaphysics has little cognitive value because metaphysical claims cannot be experimentally justified and there are no timeless answers of a metaphysical type. For skeptics, at best metaphysical speculation can be compared to poetry that expresses emotion; only science provides genuine knowledge. Metaphysical questions are sometimes seen as either meaningless or just scientific problems that have not been properly formulated. However, there are profound metaphysical questions, such as Heidegger's "Why is there something rather than nothing?" that cannot be answered by the methods of empirical science. Although early science developed in opposition to metaphysics, today there is interest in metaphysics among scientists who recognize that ontological questions and assumptions are inescapable. Although some scientists remain scornful of metaphysics, which they see as involving speculation that cannot be established scientifically, Trigg (2015) points out that quantum physicists are able to contemplate the existence of universes that are beyond human reach, for example in the Many Worlds theory of quantum mechanics. Physicists can reasonably posit the existence of entities that we cannot measure at the moment, for example by explaining fundamental particles in terms of string theory. By analogy, it is unreasonable to criticize Jung's ideas as too metaphysical because they are unprovable at the moment.

The metaphysics of science is a discipline that inquiries into the existence and nature of the phenomena that science studies, not simply the behavior of these phenomena. The distinction is important; for example, physicists understand the behavior of subatomic particles but do not necessarily know their essential nature. Analogously, psychologists may study the manifestations of the psyche without knowing its essential nature, which is a philosophical problem.

Some of the disagreements between schools of psychotherapy can be understood not only because of different methods but also because of differences about fundamental metaphysical questions. For example, the metaphysical belief that human beings are essentially material makes it reasonable to analyze behavior quantitatively. Cognitive behavioral psychology is based on a metaphysical theory of mind–body dualism that tends to be materialistic, brain-based, and computational. It also assumes that there is a mind-independent, objective reality that the patient's thought processes are distorting. This approach assumes that cognition is more important or more primary than affect. It leads to a rational, problem-solving approach to psychotherapy that sees the self as separate from the world, largely ignores the spiritual dimension, and does not grapple with questions of meaning and purpose in life. It tries to abolish mystery. Klein (2015) has pointed out that precommitments such as physicalism and determinism render mental events only epiphenomenal and so difficult to demarcate from purely biological explanations. Instead, he concludes that it is preferable for psychologists to accept mental events as primary and causal.

Skeptical writers have seen metaphysical ideas as nothing more than reflections of the psychological disposition of their authors; metaphysical distinctions such as those between the appearance of the world and its underlying reality are then seen as symptoms of psychological maladjustment. More generous philosophers see metaphysical inquiry as an important human function, even if we grant that there are connections between the individual's metaphysical beliefs and his or her psychological makeup.

Metaphysical speculation contrasts with the scientific approach to reality that focuses on limited explanations of small but measurable aspects of the world. However, the view that physical reality is all there is, and reality can only be known through the methods of science, is itself a form of metaphysics. Today, the relationship between science and metaphysics is more mutually tolerant than it was when Jung was writing. After Jung's death, during the later twentieth century, and especially in the last twenty years, it became clear that the distinctions that helped to justify the neat separation between science and metaphysics were not justifiable. It became less possible to insist on a distinction between statements based on empirical observation and statements based on theory (Kistler, 2020). It is now widely acknowledged that pre-existing metaphysical assumptions and commitments play a role in science. Indeed, there is now an active Society for the Metaphysics of Science, although there are several ways to understand this term. If Jung were writing today, he would be less reticent about his metaphysical claims. It may be that the fundamental questions of metaphysics will forever elude our ability to answer, but our curiosity about these mysteries will persist and is inescapable.

What are the helpful factors in psychotherapy?

In an important but sometimes forgotten work, Jerome Frank (1972, 1993) demonstrated various similarities between healing practices across many cultures and time periods. These practices have many non-specific features in common. They all improve the morale of the patient and combat demoralization. They include an emotionally charged and confidential relationship with a socially sanctioned practitioner, a healing setting, a rationale that gives plausible explanations or interpretations of the patient's symptoms and a logical reason for the treatment program. The allegiance of the therapist to his or her approach is an important component of the treatment. So is the healer's capacity to "persuade" the patient to face what he fears, either consciously or unconsciously, and the healer's ability to awaken hope, new meaning, and new ways for the patient to understand himself. It also helps if both participants believe in the treatment process. Frank found it implausible that the wide range of theories and approaches to psychotherapy could all be valid, but he believed that because they can all be helpful at times, factors they have in common must be important.

Later research confirms that successful psychotherapy requires a helpful therapeutic relationship, warmth, empathy, and the capacity to facilitate trust and the sense that the patient is understood. Such common factors are shared by practitioners of different schools of therapy (Wampold, 2015). Perhaps this is why some research suggests that psychotherapy is effective whether the interventions are interpersonal, psychodynamic, or cognitive-behavioral (Norcross, 2011). Wampold and Imel (2015) have pointed out that the assessment of the outcome of therapy is colored by psychologists' pre-conceived ideology. Advocates of cognitive behavioral therapy have claimed that this approach is superior to all others, although as noted earlier Shedler (2010) disputes these statistics and suggests that the data are in favor of psychodynamic approaches, whose effects last longer than other methods. These conflicting narratives point out the difficulty comparing schools of psychotherapy, partly because each of them has its own therapeutic goal and different views of success. Thus, psychodynamically oriented psychotherapists and Jungian practitioners often do not set out to reduce symptoms, but rather aim to improve self-understanding, strengthen the sense of self, foster the individuation process, develop the ego–Self axis, and so on. These prac-titioners do not believe that quantitative measures can determine the success or failure of their work, whose processes are unique to the individual.

To add to the problem of evaluating schools of psychotherapy, when patients improve their improvement is not always attributable to the therapist's declared theory. Therapists do not always do what they say they do, they do not always practice according to the ideas of their professed theory, and sometimes changes in the person's life unrelated to the therapy account for improvement. The mechanism of therapeutic change is still unclear. Some research suggests that the therapist's orientation and profes-sional allegiance are largely unimportant in determining the success of psy-chotherapy. Some therapists seem to have more success than others (Norcross, 2011), but the reasons for this are not clear. There is little evidence that the therapist's experience is a major factor. The practitioner's academic credentials are unrelated to the outcome of psychotherapy, in spite of guild and licensing requirements (Strupp & Hadley, 1979). Techniques such as EMDR may be helpful for specific problems, but overall, techniques have less impact than the non-specific factors in psychotherapy, including shared expectations, the therapist's capacity for empathy, and his or her personality and therapeutic presence. Research consistently shows that the therapeutic relationship seems to be more important than any particular modality. These factors do not lend themselves to scientific measurement. An unsolved problem is knowing how to match different types of psychological problem with the correct therapist. Overall, the validity of Jung's point that the main healing factor in psychotherapy is the therapist herself has become clear (CW 16).

Notes

1 Klein (2016) discusses the problems associated with the attempt to reduce psy-chology to brain science.
2 One foundation might be sensory experience of events in the world. The opposing view, coherentism, thinks of knowledge as a coherent, interlocking whole free of any absolute foundation.
3 Truth claims about what does or does not exist are sometimes supported by power structures and value judgments asserted by what those in power consider

to be true and valid knowledge (Haber, 1994). An example is the exertion of political power by the American Psychological Association, which attempts to impose its standards on licensing requirements in several states, as if its approach to psychotherapy is the only valid one. Power can be exerted in subtle ways in the psychotherapeutic relationship, for example by insisting on a specific theoretical approach. Masson (1993) and Guggenbühl-Craig (2015) have laid out the power shadow of this field, although I believe these critiques are less relevant today than they used to be because of advances in relational approaches to psychotherapy.

4 Determinism is the doctrine that a knowledge of the initial conditions of all the particles in a system would allow one to predict exactly how it will unfold at any given time. Classical Newtonian physics is deterministic, involving local cause–effect processes.

5 Einstein imagined himself chasing a beam of light; Kekulé discovered the structure of the benzene ring because of a dream in which he saw a snake biting its own tail.

6 Measurement is important to many research psychologists, but their task is difficult because unlike a physical object psychological characteristics and states of mind, such as love, are private, complex, difficult to define, and do not lend themselves to direct observation, leading to great difficulty in research replicability. The unpredictability of human nature further complicates the issue. There is a world of difference between the result of a psychometric test and the individual's subjective experience.

7 Gadamer was a foremost exponent of philosophical hermeneutics. He proposed that understanding requires conversation and the attempt of the interlocutors to grasp each other's point of view through dialog, rather than trying to understand people empathically, which Kohut taught. Gadamer did not believe we could arrive at truth using a specific method but only in dialectic and interaction, awaiting the emergence of what was previously unknown. Jung's approach is also based on dialectic, but he realized that the therapist is radically affected by the therapeutic interaction, in a way that he called "psychic infection" but today is called projective identification. Empathy plays a large part in this process.

8 The term "empirically supported" refers to techniques for treating specific disorders. This term is often used as if it were synonymous with evidence-based practice, usually implying randomized, controlled trials and quantitative methods of research.

9 Inductive approaches to science make many observations of a phenomena and then derive a general principle or theory to account for them.

10 In nonlinear systems, the output is not proportional to the input; a small change in input can result in a large change in output. Many natural systems, such as the brain, are nonlinear.

11 In the strong version of causal closure of the physical, there is nothing that can intervene in the closed systems of physical laws. However, theorists who believe that the mind emerges from lower levels of brain functioning believe that there can be downward causation of higher, mental levels onto the lower brain levels from which they emerged.

12 Folk psychology is our everyday way of making sense of people's actions and predicting behavior in terms of beliefs, intentions, desires, fears, hopes, and so on. When we use these terms, we have a theory about how these different states of mind operate to cause behavior. Folk psychology is the basis of much of our legal, educational, and psychotherapeutic practice. Folk psychology has been important in human evolution and is essential in everyday life, although it is not necessarily consistent with scientific psychology. The relationship between folk psychology

and scientific psychology is much debated. Eliminative materialists such as Paul Churchland (1979) would like to discard folk psychology entirely, because they believe that beliefs and desires do not really exist except as brain states, but this is an impractical stance for many psychotherapists for whom folk psychology has to be considered when working with people.

13 Postmodernism is in many ways the polar opposite attitude to positivism. Postmodernism stresses the subjective understanding of evidence, and insists that human behavior and meaning are contextual, always occurring in social and relational settings. Postmodern philosophers rejected the idea that truth is objective and waiting to be discovered, and they rejected the idea that positivism, empiricism, and rationalism are universally applicable, preferring to see knowledge in terms of socially constructed interpretations of the world (Slife & Williams, 1995). In this tradition, truth is often seen as relative to the observer. However, the idea that truth claims are always flawed is self-contradictory. Postmodern philosophers are appropriately criticized because they reject objective epistemological standards, but postmodern concerns cannot be entirely ignored by psychotherapists.

14 Moral psychology is the study of the ways in which morality and moral decision making are integrated into personality structure.

15 Today, most physicists do not believe in hidden variables, and the many worlds theory remains unprovable.

16 Classical physics is not completely deterministic because chaotic motion may occur, including noise in the firing of brain cells.

17 Entanglement refers to the fact that quantum connected particles behave as if they were a unit; when one changes, the other changes instantaneously, no matter how far apart they are.

18 Here I am speaking of the Copenhagen interpretation of quantum theory, which rejected determinism and strict causality in favor of a statistical or probabilistic approach. This interpretation rejected objectivity in favor of the view that our understanding of microphysical phenomena depends on how we choose to observe them. A quantum phenomenon does not have specific properties until it is observed, so there is no objective reality underlying the everyday world. This led to the controversial idea of observer-created reality, although the Copenhagen interpretation does not necessarily apply to the world of ordinary objects, and, in the opinion of some authors, consciousness does not necessarily play a role in the standard Copenhagen interpretation of quantum measurements.

Niels Bohr used the concept of complementarity to describe reality at the atomic level. The observer decides whether to design the experiment to detect light as a wave or as a particle. A particle is a localized entity with a clear trajectory, while a wave is spread out and capable of interference; they seem to be mutually exclusive entities. It is not clear whether either exists independently of the particular type of measurement employed. Complementarity means that these are alternative descriptions of the same phenomenon, but both are essential to understand the nature of light. Bohr thought that complementarity was the deepest insight into reality that quantum mechanics allows, but that is now widely disputed.

It may be that a photon has only one underlying reality but can exist in different states when observed differently.

Descriptors such as wave and particle may only be metaphors or symbolic devices that are used to make predictions under particular conditions. These terms do not necessarily describe the intrinsic nature of the phenomena themselves. Subatomic particles can be described in terms of conceptual or mathematical constructs, without knowing exactly what they are. Some physicists take the position that although they talk about microscopic entities as if they were literal things, they may only be concepts that describe what the measuring instrument does and what the calculations predict. The physicist only knows how an electron appears with respect to the way it is measured. This may be an essential limitation of the physicist's knowledge. Some versions of the Copenhagen interpretation say that an object that cannot be measured is not ontologically real, which is a positivist approach. Physicists committed to a positivist approach do not believe that interpretation of quantum mechanics is necessary. The only important fact for the pragmatist is that the theory corresponds to the observations and the predictions are correct.

Holton (1988) believes that Bohr was very influenced by William James, from whom Bohr borrowed the term complementarity. Heisenberg, Pauli, and Schrödinger were the other main drivers of the Copenhagen interpretation, although they had differences of opinion among themselves, so there was no unified Copenhagen interpretation.

19 Incidentally, the year in which Freud's *New introductory lectures on psychoanalysis* was published.

20 Storm (2020) has suggested that the "hard problem" of consciousness is related to intrinsic limitations in the human brain. Our early hominin ancestors did not experience the necessary evolutionary pressures that would have required them to deal with this problem, just as we do not have brain systems that allow us to directly perceive many aspects of reality such as magnetic fields.

21 Anthropologists describe a form of sudden death caused by being cursed or cast out after having broken a tribal taboo.

22 As an analogy, the mind-brain identity theorist would see the mind as made of neuronal activity the way what we call table salt is a combination of sodium and chlorine, while a functionalist would use a different analogy; an artificial kidney functions as a kidney even though it is not made of human tissue, so it does not matter what is carrying out the function. Functionalism and identity theory are not incompatible and may be combined.

23 Bertrand Russell (1992 [1927]) also pointed out that physics tells us about particles and forces only in extrinsic or descriptive terms, but nothing about their intrinsic nature. That is, we know what an electron does but not what it is. So, we cannot rule out the possibility that matter is intrinsically mental in some way.

24 See Pilecki et al. (2011). Some of the panel members who designed the DSM are reported to have had ties to pharmaceutical companies.

25 Karl Popper (1972) believed that science starts when a scientist invents a hypothesis or a conjecture that is subsequently tested by observation. Theories are the primary unit of science. He wrote that a scientific theory can never be regarded as absolutely certain because it is always open to the possibility of falsification. Theories must remain tentative, and only theories that can be falsified are true scientific theories. Observations can only confirm but not prove a theory. For some time, this idea became a touchstone belief among many researchers, but in the last few decades its influence has faded, in part because no theory can be falsified in isolation but only in the context of many other assumptions and theories. Furthermore, scientists do not simply abandon a theory when it is falsified; they modify it in terms of an overarching paradigm, a set of assumptions at a higher level than the theory. Thomas Kuhn suggested that science may advance in two ways. Normal science sorts out known problems with existing theories. Rarely, a revolution occurs when the assumptions of a previous paradigm are overthrown, and new assumptions are adopted. This may require abandoning strongly held view of reality. The theory of relativity is such a case.

26 Conscious experience receives information from different sense organs at the same time, but it is unified. The binding or combination problem is to explain how that unification is achieved.
27 Microtubules are protein filaments that form the cytoskeleton of cells.
28 Many philosophers and physicists today reject Kant's notion that the source of order in the universe is in the human mind; they prefer to see order emanating from natural laws such as the laws of physics, which can be relied on.

Chapter 2

Jung's philosophical and scientific claims

Jung's rejection of the idea that his work is metaphysical

Jung began his research at the beginning of the twentieth century, a time when psychology had only recently begun to differentiate itself from philosophy. He wanted to maintain the scientific credibility of his psychology during an era when science rigorously defined itself in opposition to metaphysical claims, which were thought to be lacking in rigor and to be merely dogmatic statements. The influential early-twentieth-century empiricists wanted to abandon all metaphysical claims, believing that science rests on the much more solid foundations of observation and logic (Carnap, 1936). Jung therefore felt he had to adopt an empirical, scientific position in the face of the hegemony of the materialism and positivism of his day. The question at issue is whether his work is truly empirical and to what extent it shades into the philosophical, in spite of his many disclaimers that this was not his intention.

Although Jung was often criticized for sounding too metaphysical,[1] he protested that he was reporting empirical findings and frequently denied that his work was metaphysical. He insisted that he was "an empiricist not a philosopher" (CW 9i, para. 149),[2] sometimes denying that his psychology had any philosophical significance. In a letter, he pointed out that "I have no doctrine and no philosophical system, but I have presented new *facts*" (Jung, 1975, p. 245). By "fact" he meant his observations of the psyche, which he saw as empirical data. He realized that: "Psychological truth by no means excludes metaphysical truth," but he believed that "psychology, as a science, has to hold aloof from all metaphysical assertions" (CW 5, para. 344). Jung wrote that he is "content with what can be experienced psychically" and insisted that he rejected metaphysical claims, which he saw as "laughable" (CW 13, para. 82). In fact, "I quite deliberately bring everything that purports to be metaphysical into the daylight of psychological understanding." He wanted to "dismiss without mercy the metaphysical claims of all esoteric teachings" (CW 13, para. 73). In his late *Mysterium coniunctionis*, Jung emphasized that:

DOI: 10.4324/9781032618456-2

I do not go in for either metaphysics or theology, but am concerned with psychological facts on the borderline of the knowable. So if I make use of certain expressions that are reminiscent of the language of theology, this is due solely to the poverty of language, and not because I am of the opinion that the subject-matter of theology is the same as that of psychology. Psychology is very definitely not a theology: it is a natural science that seeks to describe experienceable psychic phenomena.

(CW 14, p. vii)

Furthermore, "If we are convinced that we know the ultimate truth concerning metaphysical things, this means nothing more than that archetypal images have taken possession of our powers of thought and feeling" (CW 14, para. 787). Jung occasionally becomes very critical of metaphysics: "Any honest thinker has to admit the insecurity of all metaphysical positions ... He has also to admit the unwarrantable nature of all metaphysical assertions" (CW 11, para. 764). Jung believed that

"our metaphysical concepts are simply anthropomorphic images and opinions which express transcendental facts either not all or only in a very hypothetical manner ... we have no encouragement whatever to think that our metaphysical picture of the world corresponds to the transcendental reality"

(CW 14, para. 781).

This is true because: "Metaphysical assertions are *statements of the psyche*, and are therefore psychological" (CW 11, para. 835; emphasis in original). He says that: "All religious and metaphysical concepts rest upon archetypal foundations ... Metaphysics is, as it were, a physics or physiology of the archetypes" (CW 18, para. 1229). "It is the psyche which, by the divine creative power inherent in it, makes the metaphysical assertion; it posits the distinction between metaphysical entities. Not only is it the condition of all metaphysical reality, it is that reality" (CW 11, para. 836). Jung could make that claim because of the psyche's innate religious function, its capacity to produce numinous experiences. However, he often noted that these experiences do not necessarily have metaphysical implications about a divinity that may exist beyond the psyche.

Jung saw metaphysics as too dogmatic and based on a priori principles, in contrast to the openness of science, and he believed that no metaphysical assertion "can be proved to be true or untrue" (1975, p. 368). He also argued that metaphysical speculation by theologians expresses a dominant but unconscious complex in the theologian's psyche, which helps to explain the lack of agreement within this discipline.

Typical of Jung's occasionally defensive statements about his approach is this:

> Although I have often been called a philosopher, I am an empiricist and adhere as such to the phenomenological standpoint ... As this statement indicates, I approach psychological matters from a scientific and not from a philosophical standpoint ... I restrict myself to the observation of phenomena and I eschew any metaphysical or philosophical considerations.
>
> (CW 11, para. 2)

Jung makes this kind of claim in several places, even though later in the same paper he makes overtly metaphysical statements, such as: "the only form of existence of which we have immediate knowledge is psychic" (CW 11, para. 16) and then "Not only does the psyche exist, it is existence itself" (ibid., para. 18). Here he reveals his leanings towards philosophical idealism and the ontological primacy and irreducibility of the psyche.

Jung's denial that he was practicing metaphysics surfaces especially when he was criticized by theologians. We see this for example in his response to accusations that he reduces divinity to nothing but a psychological phenomenon. In this vein, Martin Buber (1952) insisted that Jung had overstepped the boundaries of scientific psychology and was intruding into matters of faith. In Jung's reply, he insisted that he was concerned with psychological phenomena "which can be proved empirically to be the bases of metaphysical concepts" (CW 18, para. 1506). He saw himself as describing demonstrable psychological facts (CW 11, para. 4).[3] He insisted that he adheres to a phenomenological approach that simply observes psychological phenomena, and "I eschew any metaphysical or philosophical considerations" (ibid., para. 2). He claimed to engage in a "comparative phenomenology of the mind" (McGuire and Hull, 1977). However, Jung's work is not purely phenomenological when he makes claims about the archetype-as-such, prior to its manifestation as a symbol. He believed that this level cannot be experienced in itself because it is transcendent, not capable of becoming conscious (CW 8, para. 417). Jung thinks that the "innermost nature" of the archetype is inaccessible to experience (CW 6, para. 659). His attempt to justify the idea of the archetype-as-such using Kantian epistemology has been criticized by several authors (e.g., de Voogd, 1984).[4] For example, Kant's noumenal realm is unknowable by definition, whereas Jung believed that the noumenal level of the archetype appears to consciousness in symbolic form. (Jung's claim to be a phenomenologist has been discussed by several authors such as Roger Brooke, who sees Jung's phenomenology as "undisciplined" and "unsophisticated"; Brooke, 1991, p. xvi.)

Because of his interest in subjects like Gnosticism, alchemy, and hermetic philosophy,[5] Jung was labelled as a mystic or an occultist, especially by the early psychoanalytic establishment. At the time, this characterization meant that the individual was not carrying out rigorous scientific research, and his claims were therefore of dubious validity and reliability. Not surprisingly, therefore, Jung resented this appellation by the Freudian tradition. In a 1957 interview with the psychologist Richard Evans, Jung declared that "Everyone who says I am a mystic is just an idiot."

Jung writes that he considers all metaphysical perspectives to be psychological projections rather than objective perspectives on reality itself. Furthermore:

> As a psychologist, therefore, I have neither the inclination nor the competence to mix myself up with metaphysics. Only, I have to get polemical when metaphysics encroaches on experience and interprets it in a way that is not justified empirically.
>
> (CW 9, ii, para. 98)

A good example of Jung's rejection of what he considered to be metaphysical claims is his skepticism about the notion of a Universal Mind of the kind found in Eastern philosophy:

> Psychology accordingly treats all metaphysical claims and assertions as mental phenomena, and regards them as statements about the mind and its structure that derive ultimately from certain unconscious dispositions. It does not consider them to be absolutely valid or even capable of establishing a metaphysical truth. We have no intellectual means of ascertaining whether this attitude is right or wrong. We only know that there is no evidence for, and no possibility of proving, the validity of a metaphysical postulate such as "Universal Mind." If the mind asserts the existence of a Universal Mind, we hold that it is merely making an assertion. We do not assume that by such an assertion the existence of a Universal Mind has been established. There is no argument against this reasoning, but no evidence, either, that our conclusion is ultimately right. In other words, it is just as possible that our mind is nothing but a perceptible manifestation of a Universal Mind. Yet we do not know, and we cannot even see, how it would be possible to recognize whether this is so or not. Psychology therefore holds that the mind cannot establish or assert anything beyond itself.
>
> (CW 11, para. 760)

This essay was written in 1939. In the same year, in *The integration of the personality*, Jung writes that the universal mind in Hindu philosophy "corresponds to what the West calls the unconscious" (p. 15). This implies that he did in fact believe that the collective unconscious can be seen as a universal mind. In spite of this link to the East, Jung rejected many Eastern metaphysical claims; he saw Eastern philosophers as "symbolic psychologists" whose claims should not be taken literally (CW 13, para. 74).

> It is perhaps not superfluous to mention that the East has produced nothing equivalent to what we call psychology, but rather philosophy or

metaphysics. Critical philosophy, the mother of modern psychology, is as foreign to the East as to medieval Europe. Thus the word "mind," as used in the East, has the connotation of something metaphysical. Our Western conception of mind has lost this connotation since the Middle Ages, and the word has now come to signify a "psychic function." Despite the fact that we neither know nor pretend to know what "psyche" is, we can deal with the phenomenon of "mind." We do not assume that the mind is a metaphysical entity or that there is any connection between an individual mind and a hypothetical Universal Mind. Our psychology is, therefore, a science of mere phenomena without any metaphysical implications.

(CW 11, para. 759)

Jung believes that the meaning of metaphysical concepts that have "lost their root connection with natural experience" can be recovered by relating them to psychological processes. For example, the metaphysical God of theism can be understood as the projection of the archetypal Self, the "God within," (CW7, para. 399). Once the connection of such metaphysical ideas to the psyche is restored, these psychological processes no longer need to be projected. This is important because: "Once metaphysical ideas have lost their capacity to recall and evoke the original experience, they have not only become useless but prove to be actual impediments on the road to wider development" (CW 9, ii, para. 65). Jung here expresses his concern that Christian metaphysical assertions of faith are often not connected to direct religious experience. This was a painful reality for Jung's father, a Christian pastor, who suffered greatly because he had no personal numinous experiences with which to ground his theological beliefs. It seems that Jung's experience with his father's strained relationship to Christian metaphysical doctrine and dogma turned Jung against this kind of speculation. Furthermore, he saw during two world wars that Christian metaphysical teaching had little or no effect on the barbaric behavior of its putative adherents. A significant element of Jung's work was a kind of re-mythologizing of the Christian tradition, a psychologically based understanding of the Christian story (Stein, 2018).

In his work on the God-image Jung takes the spiritual dimension seriously, which today is a minority view among many scientists and academics. Consequently, Jung's thought does not have much influence on the academic mainstream and is not taught in many universities. His approach is not compatible with the prevailing mechanistic, deterministic, positivist, and physicalist worldview that still underpins much of the academic world. The academy also tends to ignore or marginalize Jung because various of his observations, such as the idea of synchronicity, are difficult to pin down empirically. Synchronistic events occur unpredictably, they are not repeatable, they have no known mechanism of action, and they are not compatible with a purely physicalist worldview, so mainstream scientists are reluctant to engage with this idea. However, synchronicity seems to be an important complement to the law of cause and effect and offers a more complete worldview than one based only on causality. The experience of synchronicity has important spiritual implications; it shows that apparently separate psychological and physical events are in fact meaningfully connected parts of a larger whole.

Jung did not wish to reduce the experience of spirit to something that could be explained away by the scientific method. In part, that is why he studied esoteric material such as alchemy and astrology, which are usually considered to be peripheral to Western views of reality. In 1943, he wrote that his ideas "occupy an isolated outpost" (CW 7, p. 8) and he predicted that they would be slow to take root in the academic world. This process has barely begun. However, a change in perspective is demanded by the advent of quantum mechanics. Jung's work is more compatible with some of the implications of quantum mechanics than it is with Newtonian physics.

What did Jung mean by "metaphysical"?

What was Jung rejecting when he denied that his work was metaphysical? He uses the word in different senses, but generally he tends to associate metaphysics with doctrinal and dogmatic speculation and traditional theological ideas that have no basis in experience. If his own understanding of the term is considered, his repudiation of metaphysics makes sense.

One clue about Jung's meaning of the word "metaphysical" is given in his discussion of Christ as a projection of the image of the Self, the God within. He is at pains to point out that this parallel "is not to be taken as anything more than a psychological one … There is no question of any intrusion into the sphere of metaphysics, i.e., of faith" (CW 9 ii, para. 122). In this essay he equates metaphysics with religious belief, doctrine, and dogma for which there is no real evidence, ideas to which people adhere based only on blind faith. He seems to have been influenced by the fact that his father and his minister uncles had little or no personal spiritual experiences that would underpin the dogma and doctrine they preached and discussed (Jung, 1965, p. 73). His skepticism about this material is seen in his remark that religious dogma consists of "sacrosanct unintelligibility" (CW 11, para. 170). He attributes faith divested of personal experience to people "who for one reason or another think they know about unknowable things in the Beyond" (CW 18, para. 1503), which is an implicit critique of theological speculation. Based on his reading of Kant, Jung does not believe such transcendent knowledge of a metaphysical realm is accessible. Instead, he tends to see philosophical and metaphysical claims as the result of the philosopher's personal complexes, or as an expression of the archetypal level of the unconscious. In fact, "It is the psyche which, by the divine creative power inherent in it, makes the metaphysical assertion" (CW 11, para. 836). This is typical of his attempt to dismiss without mercy the metaphysical claims of all esoteric teachings ... I quite deliberately bring everything that purports to be metaphysical into the daylight of psychological understanding and do my best to prevent people from believing in nebulous power words ... I strip things of their metaphysical wrappings in order to make them objects of psychology.

(CW 13, para. 73)

Jung recognizes the importance of ancient metaphysical notions by people such as Plato, but mainly when he could use such ideas to make a psychological point. By converting metaphysical statements into psychological material, he believes that if there is something "ineffably metaphysical ... it would then have the best opportunity of showing itself" (ibid.). Jung believes that "our metaphysical concepts are simply anthropomorphic images and opinions which express transcendental facts only in a very hypothetical manner." He goes on to say that we do not know if our metaphysical ideas correspond to transcendental reality. When he says it is certain that "the world inside and outside ourselves rests on a transcendental background" (CW 14, para. 787), much depends on his meaning of the term "transcendental." Whereas Mills (2013) interprets this to refer to suprapersonal or cosmic processes, Saban (2014) believes this is a misreading of Jung's use of the world "transcendent," if this means going beyond the ego's epistemological limits, because the ego cannot have knowledge of the transcendent ontological level. However, it is possible to see Jung's use of the word transcendental as a reference to transpersonal levels of the psyche or to other realms of reality that exist even though the ego has no access to them.

Mills (2019, p. 2) complains that Jung sets up a "false binary" between science and philosophy and introduces "an obfuscating cleavage" between psychology and philosophy. Perhaps this is a little harsh; one can empathize with Jung's struggle with the science of his day, which was inadequate to deal with his observations of the psyche, and especially early in his career we can understand his psychological need to protect his work from accusations of being metaphysical. However, Jung's attempt to radically separate his scientific work from any hint of metaphysics is no longer necessary. Today, philosophy is seen as a complement to science. Since Jung's time, a new field of inquiry known as the metaphysics of science has arisen, which aims to either pursue metaphysical questions in the light of contemporary science or to interpret contemporary science in metaphysical terms. We can now discuss the metaphysical implications of Jung's psychology without being shy about them.

Jung and philosophy

There are several critiques and discussions of Jung as a philosopher (Saban, 2014; Segal 2014; Mills, 2014), in spite of the fact that Jung did not intend to be seen primarily as a philosopher. He often claims that his work is intended to be purely psychological and psychotherapeutic and not philosophical. For example, he writes that "I approach psychological matters from a scientific and not from a philosophical standpoint ... I eschew any metaphysical or philosophical considerations" (CW 11, para. 2). Nevertheless, he refers to many philosophers throughout his work. His personal philosophical stance is apparent throughout his writing and clearly influences his psychological theories, which have philosophical implications in areas other than psychology. Jung eventually acknowledged that although he was trying to be scientific, he discovered that "I had involved myself in a net of reflections which extend far beyond natural science and ramify into the fields of philosophy, theology, comparative religion, and the human sciences in general" (CW 8, para. 421). In a letter, Jung (1973, p. 194) referred to himself as a "philosopher manqué," evidently recognizing that his work had philosophical implications. Sometimes, the philosophical underpinning of Jung's work is implicit, while at other times it is on the surface. He often claimed to separate psychology and philosophy, although he realized that these disciplines are both "systems of opinion about objects which cannot be fully experienced and therefore cannot be adequately comprehended by a purely empirical approach" (CW 8 para. 659).

Especially in his early career, Jung was concerned that his observations of the psyche should be accorded scientific credence and not dismissed as mere speculation by materialists. He insisted that his work is empirical, but he extended the term empirical to include data gleaned from dreams and from the comparative observation of imagery and ideas from world religions and mythologies. He believed this material to be empirical in the sense that it can be observed, described, and compared. (The problem with this extension is that such data is less reliable and more prone to subjective distortion than the data of physical science.) Jung further stretched the notion of "empirical" in his belief that motifs from psychotic productions, fantasies, and dreams contain imagery that is demonstrably similar to that which occurs within mythology and folklore, even when such a parallel is not known to the dreamer (CW 5, para. 151). He hypothesized that all this material arises from the same archetypal level of the collective unconscious. However, the existence of this level is difficult to prove empirically, and Mills (2014) insists that it is a metaphysical idea. Because the collective unconscious can be seen as analogous to the idea of a Cosmic Mind, Mills (2014) believes that this idea shades into religious thinking, and thus only appeals to theologians and mystics. I would add that it also appeals to many Jungians who appreciate the spiritual dimension of Jung's work. But Mills is concerned that ontological claims of this kind without scientific evidence can be judged to be too subjective and motivated by purely psychological factors. He believes we should not deify the collective unconscious, because it is an unverifiable fiction that would "satisfy the wishful fantasies of imagination at the expense of reason, logic, and science" (Mills, 2019, p. 17). He sees the collective uncon-scious as a "signifier for the common psychological dynamics and char-acteristics of shared humanity ... a metaphor for a higher abstraction or ideal principle ordained with numinous value" (ibid., p. 6).

In his 1935 Tavistock lectures, Jung insisted that "There is nothing mys-tical about the collective unconscious" (CW 18, para. 84), because he felt he could reasonably postulate its existence on the basis of his observations of dream material, religions, and intrapsychic symbols, which he saw as psy-chological facts. However, Mills (2019) protests that Jung does not demon-strate that these universal structures derive from a collective source and believes that Jung conflates these contents with the collective unconscious itself, without explaining why the postulate of a collective mind is even necessary. Mills sees this idea as only "an intellectual intuition" parading as a scientific hypothesis and complains that Jung hypostasizes or reifies an abstraction. He believes that Jung succumbs to "a mystical metaphysical theory of consciousness that lacks argumentation, theoretical justification, or empirical support" (ibid., p. 35). However, there is empirical support for this view of consciousness in the Eastern spiritual traditions. Jung's intuition is consistent with meditative traditions that describe a field of Pure Con-sciousness that is beyond name and form. For people who meditate, this level of the psyche is a direct experience. It is not unreasonable to suggest that archetypal imagery has a source in a level of the psyche that is beyond image, such as the Buddhist storehouse consciousness (Ālaya-vijñāna), which con-sists of unconscious mental processes and is said to store the individual's past karma.

Jung's philosophical claims

In contrast to Jung's frequent denial that he practiced philosophy, he also wrote that "we psychotherapists ought really to be philosophers or philoso-phical doctors—or rather that we already are so" (CW 16, para. 181), and "philosophical problems belong in the highest degree to any empirical study of the psyche" (CW 10, para. 1042). In his own words: "Whether we will or no, philosophy keeps breaking through" (CW 7, para. 201). In his 1933 *Modern man in search of a soul*, Jung acknowledged that "philosophy and psychology are linked by indissoluble bonds ... Neither discipline can do without the other" (p. 179). He believed that psychological factors "furnish the implicit—and frequently even unconscious—primary assumptions" of philosophy (ibid.). Jung therefore included philosophical speculation within the overall compass of psychology. Because psychological processes underly philosophy: "I always think of psychology as encompassing the whole of the psyche, and that includes philosophy and theology" (CW 8, para. 525). In this way, Jung saw the psyche as superordinate to other disciplines, including science, because:

The psyche is the starting point for all human experience, and all the knowledge we have gained eventually leads back to it. The psyche is the beginning and end of all cognition. It is not only the object of science, but the subject also.

(CW 8, para. 261)

Further, "every science is a function of the psyche and all knowledge is rooted in it" (ibid., para. 357). Shamdasani (2003, p. 15) suggests that Jung believed that psychology constitutes the fundamental scientific discipline, upon which other disciplines should be based, because psychology is the only discipline that can "grasp the subjective factor that underlay other sciences." Shamdasani even suggests that Jung "conceived the cultural role of complex psychology to be to counter the fragmentation of the sciences and to provide a basis for a synthesis of all knowledge" (ibid., p. 22).

Jung's claims about a spiritual dimension of the psyche

Jung believes he can empirically demonstrate the existence of the Self, which he sees as an image of the divine within the psyche (CW 5, para. 612) or the "God within us" (CW 7, para. 399). He insists that this is a psychological rather than a metaphysical claim because he can demonstrate the numinous dream imagery the Self produces. He realizes that he cannot equate the intrapsychic Self with the divine as it is understood in the transcendent, metaphysical sense of the theisms, but he asserts that the Self is the "most immediate experience of the divine which is psychologically possible to imagine" (CW 11, para. 396). If there is a divinity beyond the psyche, it could only be experienced by means of the psyche (CW 18, para. 1589). He says that the intrapsychic experience of the Self is qualitatively indistinguishable from traditional accounts of the experience of the divine. The Self produces "symbolism which has always characterized and expressed the Deity" (CW 11, para. 757). Jung admits that we do not know the relationship between intrapsychic images of the Self and the metaphysical God of the theisms, but he also believes there is "an original behind the [intrapsychic] image" (CW 18, para. 1589). He says that the question of a transcendent deity beyond the psyche lies beyond the province of psychology, so he can safely leave that question to the theologians.

Each symbolic manifestation of the Self can only represent a fragment of it. Because the Self is the totality of the psyche, it has to include within it all possible opposites, such as matter and spirit or good and evil. Jung therefore thinks of the Self as the union of opposites, sometimes using the term *complexio oppositorum* (CW 11, para. 716) and sometimes *coincidentia oppositorum* (CW 12, para. 259).[6] The conflict produced by the tension of opposites within the psyche and their eventual union is a central issue within Jung's metapsychology.[7] He saw this tension as the "ineradicable and indispensable" precondition of all psychic life (CW 14, para. 206), and he believed that the most important problems of life "are fundamentally insoluble," expressing a necessary polarity. The opposites within the psyche tend to compensate for each other, but when the tension between them becomes intolerable, the two conflicting poles must be reconciled at a higher level, or perhaps the problem is simply outgrown (CW 13, para. 17). The resolution of such oppositions is brought about by the transcendent function, which creates an often irrational, symbolic resolution to the conflict, perhaps through creative fantasy or the imagination, leading to a more encompassing attitude to what initially seemed to be an insoluble dilemma. Drob (2017, p. 24) articulates the ways in which this union of opposites is "an 'echo' of an original unity that has been sundered by thought and language." The idea of an absolute, non-dual, unitary level of reality in which there is no differentiation and separation, which Jung refers to as the unus mundus,[8] is common to several spiritual traditions.

A clearly metaphysical speculation is Jung's idea that the Self needs human consciousness to become conscious of its own internal dualities, especially its own darkness, as he claimed in *Answer to Job*. This idea has important metaphysical implications. Although he tries to maintain his position as an empirical scientist, this is an example of what Mills (2014, p. 234) refers to as Jung's "cryptic supernaturalism." For Mills, Jung's metaphysics are grounded in psychologism, the reduction of all phenomena to psychological entities. This critique was also one of Martin Buber's objections to Jung's approach to religion. However, Jung would deny that his observations are reductive; what his critics call psychologism is based on Jung's insistence on the reality and primacy of the psyche, our inability to get beyond the psyche, and the fact that the psyche is ultimately the medium and possibly the genesis of all religious experience. He points out:

> it is only through the psyche that we can establish that God acts upon us, but we are unable to distinguish whether these actions emanate from God or from the unconscious. We cannot tell whether God and the unconscious are two different entities.
>
> (CW 11, para. 757)

Jung saw all the gods and goddesses of the various religious pantheons (including the biblical God) as manifestations of archetypal imagery emerging from the archetypal level of the psyche (CW 11, para. 8; CW 12, para. 9). When this level is experienced directly it produces a numinous experience, of the kind experienced by Moses at the burning bush or Paul on the road to Damascus. These kinds of experiences are reported by all religious traditions, but rather than seeing them as emerging from a heavenly realm, Jung sees them as manifestations of a spiritual dimension of the psyche This is one of the most important ways in which Jung's approach to spirituality differs from traditional theistic claims, which see the divine as beyond the psyche. Jung's assertion that the psyche has an intrinsic "authentic religious function" (CW 11, para. 3) is itself a metaphysical claim. It means that *Homo sapiens* is intrinsically *Homo religiosus*, as many scholars of religion have long claimed. The psyche's capacity to produce numinous experiences, and the presence of the Self as the God within, account for the fact that human beings have a thirst for the sacred and an intrinsic drive towards transcendence and meaning making. However, Jung denied that he was offering a metaphysical explanation of numinous experience, insisting only that in order to understand it "use must be made of certain parallel religious or metaphysical ideas which have not only been associated with it from ancient times but are constantly used to formulate and elucidate it" (CW 14, para. 781).

The psyche produces numinous imagery that has nothing to do with traditional accounts of divinity, but which has the quality of Otto's *mysterium tremendum et fascinans*. In other words, a numinous experience may have the quality of an experience of the sacred or the holy but be entirely novel and unorthodox (Corbett, 2019). Jung's claims that the psyche has an innate religious function, and that numinous material that arises from the unconscious is consonant with imagery from the world's theistic traditions, have important metaphysical implications. These claims mean that the individual may develop a personal relationship with the archetypal level of the psyche, which does not require membership in a historical tradition, a sacred text, or a religious hierarchy. Not surprisingly, Jung was attacked by religionists who realized the implications of his stress on individual numinous experiences, which may and often does contradict theological doctrine and dogma. These experiences are forms of personal revelation, another potential challenge to established religious traditions that insist that the revelations described within their religious text are the only valid ones.

Jung's stress on numinous experience and its relationship to traditional descriptions of the experience of divinity makes him more than a pure phenomenologist or a scientist. Although he insists on the psychological origin of his ideas about God, he also makes statements about God that are clearly metaphysical. He presumes the existence of God with comments such as: "God is a psychic fact of immediate experience ... .it can be the most immediate and hence the most real of experiences, which can neither be ridiculed or disproved" (CW 8, para. 625). He writes that "man's vital energy or libido is the divine pneuma" (Jung, 1973, p. 384), and he refers to God as "the supreme and ultimately decisive factor" (Jung, 1976, p. 366). These comments make it clear that Jung believed there is a God that produces the experience of God. I don't think Jung uses this term metaphorically; I believe he felt—and many Jungians feel—that the Self is really the divine manifesting itself within the psyche.

Jung makes other explicitly metaphysical assertions, especially in his letters to pastors written late in his life. These letters often informally expand upon ideas that are not fully developed in the *Collected works*, and they sometimes reveal his personal beliefs. For example, he writes that "God is certainly Being itself" (Jung, 1975, p. 73). Or God is a "superior deciding power to which you may give various names like instinct, fate, unconscious, faith, etc." (1975, p. 301). These are clearly metaphysical claims. There are many similar metaphysical assertions throughout the *Collected works*, such as the comment that God is "reality itself" (CW 11, para. 631).

The resistance Jung encountered about his theory that the psyche produces spiritual experiences was in part the result of the taboo against spirituality in the scientific community of his time, especially among psychologists who wanted their discipline to be an entirely secular pursuit. Jung's interest in the spiritual dimension is partly why he is ostracized by the academy but embraced by many people in the wider culture. Harald Walach (2017) believes that the taboo against spirituality in science still operates. He also describes how the creative leaps of scientists such as Einstein, who developed intuitive insights that see the larger story behind the data, are akin to a spiritual insight into the inner structure of reality. They may arise in a state of reverie, meditation, or in a dream, and they cannot be completely explained. Creative ideas that are arrived at intuitively can be subsequently tested inductively by empirical research. The point is that reason and objectivity alone are insufficient to explore reality; we also need the imaginative capacity.

Jung's psyche-based ontology and epistemology

For Jung, the psyche is ontologically fundamental and irreducible. There are no grounds for regarding it as an epiphenomenon of the working of the brain: "on the contrary, there is every reason to regard it, at least hypothetically, as a factor sui generis" (CW 9i, para. 117), "*essentially different* from physicochemical processes" (CW 9i, para. 118; emphasis in original). Jung sees the psyche as a domain in its own right. He notes that when we ask what the psyche actually is, "all science ends" (CW 11, para. 533). In particular, the extent of the unconscious is unknowable. He insists that we have no idea of the nature of the unconscious, whose existence is only a posit. The unconscious cannot be hypostasized; it is not a discrete entity whose metaphysical essence we understand. Its extent is not known. The unconscious "designates only my *unknowing*" (Jung, 1973, p. 411; emphasis in original). "The concept of the unconscious is an assumption for the sake of convenience" (CW 11, para. 64). Jung views the unconscious as a kind of consciousness in its own right; he notes that perception, thinking, feeling, volition, and intention go on in the unconscious as though a subject were present Jung (CW 8, para. 362). Rather than being comparable to traditional monotheism, the unconscious contains many archetypal centers of consciousness that he refers to as scintillae, or sparks of light in the darkness (ibid., paras. 388 and 396). He believes that "the collective unconscious is anything but an incapsulated personal system; it is sheer objectivity, as wide as the world ... There I am utterly one with the world ... but this self is the world, if only a consciousness could see it" (CW 9i, para. 46). This latter passage, which approaches a non-dual view of reality, is metaphysically very significant; Jung equates the Self with the world, so that the psyche extends beyond the personal. This is an idealist point of view that sees consciousness and the world as inseparable. In one of Jung's most radical comments about the psyche he says that "at bottom the psyche is simply 'world'" (CW 9i, para. 291), clearly merging psyche and matter. Kastrup claims that Jung equates matter with the collective unconscious, quoting a letter of Jung in which he says:

> So far as we can see, the collective unconscious is identical with Nature ... I have nothing against the assumption that the psyche is a quality of matter or matter the concrete aspect of the psyche, provided that "psyche" is defined as the collective unconscious.
>
> (Jung, 1975, p. 540)

Kastrup (2021, p. 95) makes the case that for Jung, *"the external physical world and the collective unconscious are one and the same thing presenting itself to us in two different ways"* (emphasis in original). This idea would collapse psyche and world into a unity, as we see in synchronistic events. It describes Jung's monistic approach to reality.

Jung acknowledges that his epistemological approach is limited by the fact that there is no Archimedean point from which to judge the psyche: "only the psyche can observe the psyche" (CW 9i, para. 384). He emphasizes that we cannot get out of the psyche to study it; we study the psyche by means of the psyche and from within it, so it can never be fully objectified. Notably however, Jung avoids defining exactly what he means by "psyche," because "no one knows what 'psyche' is, and one knows just as little how far into nature 'psyche' extends" (CW 8, para. 806). Also: "The only thing that can be established with certainty, in the present state of our knowledge, is our ignorance of the nature of the psyche" (CW 9i, para. 117). The psyche "remains an insoluble puzzle and an incomprehensible wonder, an object of abiding complexity" (CW 10, para. 526). However, in spite of the psyche's inscrutability, it remains the central reality for Jung. For him: "The psyche is the greatest of all cosmic wonders and the *sine qua non* of the world as an object" (CW 8, para. 357). No wonder he calls the psyche the "God-given essence of man" (CW 10, para. 265). Not surprisingly, many contemporary Jungians informally use the term "psyche" as a God-term.

Jung's theoretical approach and his epistemology are integrally related. Papadopoulos (2006) believes that Jung did not write directly about his epistemology and methodology, but they are "interwoven into the very fabric of his theories and overall psychology" (p. 7) and they need to be extracted in order to be examined. Papadopoulos discerns two opposing epistemological stances in Jung's work. One is his insistence that he is an empiricist and a phenomenologist, the other a Gnostic stance based on the importance of direct experience, particularly of numinous material. The Gnostic Jung is essentialist and universalist (presumably referring to the idea of the Self and the collective unconscious), the other is "constructionist and relational" (ibid., p. 48). Papadopoulos believes that Jung was not aware that these attitudes are antithetical. I believe that Jung realized that his metapsychology,[9] his theory or philosophy of psychology, required both approaches in order to account for the full range of human experience. They are complementary in Bohr's sense of that word, meaning that both are required for a full description, even though they seem mutually contradictory. It seems unlikely that Jung was unaware of the tensions between them, but he had difficulty finding a suitable way to describe their relationship without reducing either of them. Main (2013) has also argued that Jung's psychology can be understood both empirically, without reference to transcendent reality, and also metaphysically, so that he has a "double perspective." One sees this tension in the contrast between Jung's call for a new myth because modern man has lost his soul, while at the same time he is skeptical about metaphysics and insists on being thought of as an empiricist.

Deciphering Jung's ontology and epistemology is made more difficult because at times Jung deliberately embraced ambiguity: "The language I speak must be ambiguous ... I strive consciously and deliberately for ambiguity of expression, because it is superior to unequivocalness and reflects the nature of life" (Jung, 1975, p. 70). This, because he saw that psychological truths are often paradoxical and impossible to pin down.

Jung's claim of the existence of the Self is an ontological claim, and his approach to it by means of the dream is an epistemological claim. To claim that the intrapsychic Self is a God-image is a metaphysical claim; to suggest that we can study it by examining numinous imagery is an epistemological claim, even though, as Jung realized, such images "point to something ineffable" and we do not know how clearly religious images reflect their transcendental objects (CW 11, para. 555). It is typical of Jung to acknowledge such epistemological limitations; he was always interested in the psychological meaning of religious experience, acknowledging that we cannot know its underlying nature.

One question raised by Jung's idea of the Self is whether it is only a function of his epistemological approach to the psyche, or whether he has discovered something ontologically real in its own right. This question raises the larger issue of the relationship between Jung's ontology and his epistemology. If he had used another approach to the psyche, for example that used by the meditative traditions, he might have arrived at a different conclusion about the Self, more akin to descriptions of the Ātman-Brahman of the Upaniṣadic tradition. That tradition does not focus on the symbolic manifestations of the Self but sees it as Pure Consciousness. An important critique of Jung's notion of the Self is that of Robin Brooks (2019). She points out that Jung focuses too much on the psyche and ignores the biological body, embodied experience, and the material environment in the formation of selfhood. However, in a paper on schizophrenia, Jung (CW 3, para. 582) notes:

> The reason that led me to conjecture a localization of a physiological basis for this archetype [the Self] in the brain-stem was the psychological fact that besides being specifically characterized by the ordering and orienting role its uniting properties are predominantly affective. I would conjecture that such a subcortical system might somehow reflect characteristics of the archetypal forms in the unconscious.

Jung notes that the Self "has its roots in the body" (CW 13, para. 242). His use of the light spectrum as a metaphor for the archetype (CW 8, para. 414) clearly indicates that the archetype has a somatic and a psychological pole. He sees body and mind as inseparable and based in an unknown common substrate at the psychoid level. This connection is sometimes seen when dreams reflect somatic states. His notion of individuation includes the embodiment of the individual's archetypal potentials into the empirical personality, and these potentials are endowed by the Self.

Like Brooks, Warren Colman (2017, p. 36) believes that Jung divides mind and world too much, and his psychology is not sufficiently embodied. Colman believes that Jung does not pay sufficient attention to everyday reality. His view of the archetypal forces in the psyche is too contained within its own sphere and does not take into account "geography, climate, competition for resources, and social and political conflict" (ibid.), and the interaction of states of mind and the state of the social world. Colman wants to see the soul as a function of our way of being in the world, and he relocates the mind in general in the form of embodied action in the world. It is surely true that the environment and the body shape mental activity, as the field of embodied cognition points out. However, it seems implausible to me that the psyche, at least the autonomous level of the unconscious, can be reduced to "situated cognition" that corresponds to the physical environment, or that all our cognitive operations are based on bodily experience. The mind can disconnect from the environment and imagine what is not physically present, and abstract thought may not be embodied. The relationship between the archetypal unconscious and the body remains to be clarified.

Jung's implicit metaphysical claims

Jung's concepts of the collective unconscious and the Self have metaphysical implications, which Jung chose not to make part of his scientific writing.

Although he repudiated links to metaphysics in his technical work, in his quasi-autobiographical *Memories, dreams, reflections*, he writes that; "In the end the only events in my life worth telling are those when the imperishable world erupted into this transitory one" (Jung, 1965, p. 4). This kind of statement clearly reveals his personal belief system, which we can also see as early as his Zofingia lectures of 1896–7, in which as a student Jung spoke of the limits of materialistic science, the need to "allow the immaterial to retain its immaterial properties," the soul as a life-force, the importance of empiricism, the centrality of teleology, the evidence for spiritualist phenomena, and the importance of mystery in religion. Some of these attitudes did not change much during his life. Jung remained interested in spiritualism, and he had various anomalous or paranormal experiences throughout his life, which he did not deal with reductively (Main, 1998). Mills (2014) points out the tension between Jung's spiritual predilections and his scientific aspirations. Giegerich describes the tension between Jung's modern thinking, which realizes that metaphysics is dead, and his rejection of modernity and his metaphysical approach to the soul. Anderson (2021, p. 50) sees this as a conflict within Jung that he never acknowledged. Anderson believes that Jung's metaphysical speculation "serves as a sort of dog whistle to those of a metaphysical frame of mind," and this has contributed to tragic splits within training institutes. However, Shamdasani (2003, p. 2) believes that Jung was "[i]intent on reconciling science and religion through psychology." Jung would not give up either the scientific status of his ideas or their metaphysical and spiritual implications. Although these might seem to be contradictory, one can see them as epistemologically complementary in the wave-particle sense; both are necessary to describe the psyche.

Jung always saw his own metaphysically colored suggestions as only hypotheses. Thus, he insisted that his statements about the intrapsychic God-image do not prove the existence of God; they demonstrate "only the existence of an archetypal God-image" (CW 11, para. 102). However, he makes several implicit assertions that suggest his belief in a metaphysical dimension, for example when he says that the word "archetype," which has its etymological roots in the Greek word *typos*, meaning an imprint (in the psyche), "presupposes an imprinter" (CW 12, para. 15). In other words, his metaphysical ideas subtly insert themselves into his scientific (empirical, observational) work. Giegerich (2008) believes that Jung's claim that the archetype is an imprint in the psyche smuggles in the metaphysical idea of God. The notion that the archetypal level of the psyche is the source of the gods and goddesses of the world's religions is nothing if not a metaphysical statement. It contrasts vividly with the theistic notion of a divinity in a heavenly realm beyond the psyche. Jung believed that all religious imagery emerges from the archetypal level of the psyche (CW 8, para. 405). Indeed, in the following statement from his *Memories, dreams, reflections*, Jung seems to imply that "God" is virtually a synonym for the unconscious:

I prefer the term "the unconscious," knowing that I might equally well speak of "God" or "daimon" if I wished to express myself in mythic language. When I do use such mythic language, I am aware that "mana," "daimon," and "God" are synonyms for the unconscious—that is to say, we know just as much or just as little about them as about the latter.

(Jung, 1965, pp. 336–337)

This comment recalls the early complaint from the Freudian community that Jung is really some kind of mystic rather than a psychologist. He describes the collective unconscious as "suprapersonal" (CW 9i, para. 3), but the exact meaning of this word is not clear—one can take it to mean simply collective, although it is often taken to refer to a spiritual dimension.

Jung became less unwilling to make metaphysical claims as he aged. An example of his changed attitude is seen in the change in his attitude to spirits. In his 1928 *Contributions to analytical psychology*, he saw spirits as "unconscious, autonomous complexes that appear as projections because they are not associated with the ego" (p. 258). In a footnote he added to his paper on the psychological foundations of belief in spirits, originally given to the Society for Psychical Research in 1919, Jung wrote that "I see no proof whatever of the existence of real spirits ... I must regard this whole territory as an appendix of psychology," (CW 8, para. 600). However, in a later (1948) footnote to this essay he added that "I no longer feel as certain as I did in 1919, when I wrote this sentence ... I doubt whether an exclusively psychological approach can do justice to the phenomena in question" (ibid., note 15). In a letter he notes that spirits may be only the personification of the unconscious, and "archetypes can behave exactly like real spirits" (Jung, 1973, p. 432), but also that "in the long run I have to admit that the spirit hypothesis yields better results in practice than any other" (ibid., p. 431). In a late letter, Jung admits that although the psychological aspects of synchronicity are important, "I am equally interested, at times even more so, in the metaphysical aspects of the phenomena" (Jung, 1975, p. 344).

Main (1998) pointed out that Jung drew several metaphysical inferences from the empirical observation of synchronicity, such as the notion of the unus mundus and the idea that the psyche exists "in a continuum outside time and space," (Jung, 1975, p. 561). Jung's 1951 *Aion* discusses the astrological notion of the precession of the equinoxes and the Platonic Year, the apparent backward motion of the sun's movement against the signs of the zodiac, due to the slant and slight wobble of the earth's axis. This book, and his 1952 account of synchronicity, also suggest that Jung had become less reticent about revealing his more esoteric interests. This change may have in part resulted from the fact that in 1944, a heart attack led to an altered state of consciousness in which Jung had an extraordinarily numinous experience (Jung, 1965). He felt he was floating high above the earth. A dark block of stone, as big as a house, appeared, at the entrance of which a Hindu sat in the lotus position, expecting Jung. It then seemed that everything earthly "was being sloughed away ... the whole phantasmagoria of earthly existence fell away or was stripped from me" (ibid., p. 291). What remained was his essence, or his "objective form." An archetypal image of his physician then appeared, who told Jung he had to return, much to his disappointment, since he had to return from the spiritual realm to the "box system" in which individuals seem to be separate from the totality. During his illness, Jung also had a series of ecstatic states, filled with the highest happiness and "eternal bliss" that was impossible to describe. This was clearly a glimpse of the ānanda or bliss described by the Upaniṣadic description of the divine as sat, chit, ānanda. He also had a series of kabbalistic visions, and a vision of the *hierosgamos* or sacred marriage. Jung describes these visions as "the most tremendous things I have ever experienced" (ibid., p. 295), as a result of which he said that "I have never since entirely freed myself of the impression that this life is a segment of existence which is enacted in a three-dimensional boxlike universe especially set up for it." These visions were "utterly real; there was nothing subjective about them; they all had the quality of absolute objectivity." It is important that Jung insists on the objective reality of these mystical experiences. They confirmed his belief in the ontological reality of the spiritual dimension of reality, they gave him new courage, and allowed the "acceptance of my own nature" (ibid., p. 297). It is impossible to imagine that such events had no effect on his subsequent writing, if only as an unspoken background. After this experience, he became less concerned with being seen as an empirical scientist. He reveals his real beliefs in his later works, for example, saying: "That the world inside and outside ourselves rests on a transcendental background is certain as our own existence" (CW 14, para. 787).

As well as his affirmation of a spiritual dimension, Jung takes other controversial positions, such as his acknowledgment of the reality of parapsychological phenomena such as mediumship, clairvoyance, psychokinetic events, prophetic visions, and telepathy. He had many such experiences during the course of his life. Main (1998, 2022) lists Jung's childhood apparition of floating heads, the experience of a splitting table and an exploding breadknife, the detonation in a bookcase while visiting Freud, various prophetic visions before the first world war, and the haunting of his house, all described in his autobiography. Jung was also influenced by the parapsychological work of J.B. Rhine, with whom he corresponded.

Jung noted telepathic influence in dreams (CW 8, para. 503), and he pointed out that telepathy is easier to ignore than explain. He asserts that "telepathic phenomena are undeniable facts ... The hypothetical possibility that the psyche touches on a form of existence outside space and time presents a scientific question mark that merits serious consideration" (CW 8, para. 814). Telepathy suggests that the psyche has a "relatively trans-spatial and trans-temporal nature," and thus seems to be able to annul space and time, but we lack "the scientific and intellectual equipment for adequately evaluating the facts of telepathy" (CW 8, para. 813).[10] Jung typically describes psi phenomena in the context of synchronicity, although this could not explain some of them such as apparitions. It is however tempting to invoke synchronicity when parapsychological events occur, for example when a clock stops or a mirror breaks at the same time as a death occurs, or if we dream of a death at the same time as it occurs. Jung's main interest was in the meaning of such events to the subject. As Main (1998, 2004) points out, Jung's model of the psyche was shaped to accommodate anomalous phenomena of this kind, which tend to be ignored or dismissed by mainstream science. He believed that because of them the assumptions of mainstream science had to be expanded. Main also notes that Jung's interest in anomalous phenomena was influenced by his concern for the disenchanted condition of modern society, meaning its pervasive lack of meaning and mystery. Main points out that Jung saw his work as a compensation for society's extreme rationalism and overvaluation of material science. Jung referred to the modern world as "desacralized," and he was concerned with its massmindedness, its loss of connection to the psyche, its loss of conscious individuality, and its worship of collective ideals (CW 10, para. 722). He believed the solution was the discovery of "a deeper source" of our spiritual life (McGuire et al., 1977, p. 230), although not necessarily in its traditional form. For Jung, attention to numinous material, anomalous events, and synchronicity were an important part of this discovery.

Jung was subject to a good deal of criticism because of his interest in esoteric matters, but he was interested in them because he realized that they express an important dimension of human experience. The value of a psychological approach to traditions such as alchemy, religion, the I Ching, and astrology is to reveal elusive levels of psychological reality that otherwise would remain inaccessible. Jung approached this material phenomenologically and symbolically rather than literally. He was careful to avoid discussing the truth claims of these systems. Thus, in his work on Christianity, he was interested in the role such belief played in the life of the individual, remaining agnostic about whether its dogmatic assertions were true or false. Although Jung respected the importance of reason, he was also sensitive to the mysteries at the heart of human existence, and he had a sense of the transcendent dimension that underlies it. Many of the esoteric texts Jung studied contain profound intuitive wisdom. Anticipating rejection because of the intellectual atmosphere of the times in which he wrote, Jung often had to alternate between direct statements of the importance of religious experience and ideas such as synchronicity, followed by an immediate disclaimer that seems to soften their importance. This hedging was an acknowledgement of the conventional rationality of his audience. However, he was well aware of the importance of intuitive, subjective, nonrational psychological processes whose nature eludes materialistic science.

Jung's teleological view

Teleology was an important part of Jung's epistemology, in part because the meaning of some events only becomes evident in terms of their end points or final effects. As early as 1916 (CW 4, para. 687) Jung wrote that "the nature of the human mind compels us to take the finalistic view" as well as a causal view of events. He believed that the life of the individual, and the individuation process, have a purpose towards which the major events in a person's life seem to be pointing. It is as if such events, which often involve important synchronicities, move the subject in a particular direction and are thus part of the destiny of the individual. "Life is teleology *par excellence*; it is the intrinsic striving toward a goal" (CW 8, para. 798). This view is seen in particular in relation to his synthetic or finalistic approach to symptoms.[11] This is a controversial philosophical point of view, since (as Darwin pointed out) the detection of order in a system does not necessarily mean that the order is purposive, for which there may be no empirical evidence. It is even difficult to prove there are order and purpose in nature since their appearance may simply result from the human imposition of pattern onto chaos. Many modern scientists, especially those who view the mind as neurologically based, view teleology as incompatible with physical causality. In classical physics, what happens is not affected by any future goal. However, the psyche does seem to be goal directed, and seems to have "foreknowledge of some kind" (CW 8, para. 931). Jung's teleological approach looks for aims rather than only causes. It is very different than a deterministic, mechanical, and linear approach to the psyche based on past events.

Jung's idealism: the reality and primacy of the psyche

Jung believes that the psyche is "the most tremendous fact of human life" and "indisputably real" (CW 9i, para. 206). As evidence for this claim, he points out that the psyche is real because it has real effects. Jung grants ontological and epistemological primacy to the psyche; "we are hopelessly cooped up in an exclusively psychic world" (1965, p. 385). He makes an even stronger claim when he says that "Not only does the psyche exist, it is existence itself" (CW 8, para. 18). In a letter, (1973, p. 540) he says that "the psyche is an οὐσία," a Greek term, variously translated as an essence or substance, but "knowledge of the psychic substance is impossible for us" because the psyche always observes itself, with no Archimedean point outside it (CW 9i, para. 384), meaning that we cannot get beyond it to observe it. Since the psyche is irreducible it cannot be contrasted with anything non-psychic; any conception would itself be psychological. "In reality the psyche is the mother and the maker, the subject and even the possibility of consciousness itself" (CW 11, para. 141). For Jung, "The psyche is the world's pivot: ... the one great condition for the existence of a world at all" (CW 8, para. 423). "Psychic existence is the only category of existence of which we have *immediate* knowledge, since nothing can be known unless it first appears as a psychic image" (CW 11, para. 769).[12] In fact, "physical existence is merely an inference, since we know of matter only in so far as we perceive psychic images mediated by the senses" (CW11, para. 16). In these ways, he makes an ontological or metaphysical claim about the primacy and reality of the psyche, and its extension beyond the human level. His overall attitude to the psyche is very much like that of an idealist philosopher.[13]

Jung refutes materialist approaches to the psyche in several places, insisting that: "the psyche is a phenomenal world in itself, which can be reduced neither to the brain nor to metaphysics" (CW 14, para. 667). For example: "the psyche's attachment to the brain can be affirmed with far less certitude today than it could fifty years ago" (CW 8, para. 812). In several places, he insists that "the psyche deserves to be taken as a phenomenon in its own right; there are no grounds at all for regarding it as a mere epiphenomenon" (CW 8, para. 10). Or: "The psyche as such cannot be explained in terms of physiological chemistry" (CW 8, para. 375). As well: "Despite the materialistic tendency to understand the psyche as a mere reflection or imprint of physical and chemical processes, there is not a single proof of this hypothesis ... the materialistic hypothesis is much too bold" (CW 9i, para. 117). In a letter, Jung subscribes to William James's transmission theory of brain functioning, which postulates that "the brain might be a transformer station" that allows the psyche to be perceived (Jung, 1975, p. 45). Jung therefore suggests that when a part of the brain is destroyed and a function is lost, only the "transmitter" of that function has been lost (ibid., p. 160).

Jung often sounds as if he is committed to metaphysical idealism, in which consciousness or the psyche is the ground of being, or consciousness is the ultimate reality. In the idealist view, the natural world is purely phenomenal, the extrinsic appearance of mental processes. Subjective idealists believe that there is no ontologically distinct, objective physical world; the perception of the world is the world; our perception of it is not simply a representation of the world in the mind. In this view, the idea that there is an external world independent of our perception of it is only an explanatory model, constructed in thought; it is not a fact that can be demonstrated empirically.

Typical of Jung's idealist attitude is this comment:

> All that I experience is psychic. Even physical pain is a psychic image which I experience; my sense impressions—for all that they force upon me a world of impenetrable objects occupying space—are psychic images, and these alone constitute my immediate experience, for they alone are the immediate objects of my consciousness.
>
> (CW 8, para. 680)

Or: "It is my mind, with its store of images, that gives the world color and sound ... Thus there is, in a certain sense, nothing that is directly experienced except the mind itself" (CW 8, para. 623). Jung sounds like an idealist philosopher when he says that "the only form of existence of which have immediate knowledge is psychic ... physical existence is a mere inference, since we know of matter only in so far as we perceive psychic images" (CW 11, para. 16). Here, the psyche is primary, and matter is indistinguishable from psyche. "Far from being a material world, this is a psychic world, which allows us to make only indirect and hypothetical inferences about the real nature of matter" (CW8, para. 747). Furthermore, "nothing can be known unless it first appears as a psychic image ... to the extent that the world does not assume the form of a psychic image, it is virtually non-existent" (CW 11, para. 769). When Jung points out that there is no Archimedean point beyond the psyche from which we may observe it, he infers that we are entirely contained within it. He equates psyche with consciousness, in the formula "*psyche = consciousness*" (CW 8, para. 380; emphasis in original). Clearly, he sees psyche or consciousness as an irreducible, primary feature of existence, in line with various contemporary philosophers of consciousness.

Kastrup (2021) makes a strong case for idealism as the very ground of Jung's thinking, arguing that "Jung was a metaphysical idealist in the tradition of German idealism" (pp. 7–8). Kastrup also notes a place in which Jung appears to contradict absolute idealism by saying that "psyche and matter are two different aspects of one and the same thing" (CW 8, para. 418). Kastrup points out that this sounds like dual-aspect monism, implying a concealed metaphysical substrate that is neither psyche nor matter. This seems to contradict Jung's position in the letter quoted above that the psyche is an oὐσία, or ousia, an ancient Greek word for an essence that exists in and of itself, independent of anything else. Kastrup resolves this apparent inconsistency on the basis of his own idealist ontology, which he also finds in Jung. In this approach, matter is entirely explained in terms of mind (Kastrup, 2019)—the opposite of the physicalist approach, which explains mind in terms of matter (brain functioning). Kastrup suggests that both the objective psyche and the world of matter are "conceptual inferences of ego-consciousness" (p. 94). The objective world and the objective psyche are "essentially the same entity" (ibid.) Both impinge on ego consciousness, the objective world through the sense organs and the objective psyche across an internal barrier, through which dreams arise. Kastrup believes that reality consists of patterns of excitation of a universal mind, which corresponds to Jung's objective psyche. Kastrup thinks that metaphysical idealism is the only way to make sense of the experimental results in quantum mechanics that are affected by the consciousness of the physicist.

Controversies around Jung as a philosopher

Although Jung does not set out to be a philosopher, his ideas have "profound philosophical implications," as Kastrup (2021, p. 74) and Mills (2013) have pointed out. Mills sees the heart of Jung's metaphysics in his claim of innate, impersonal, archetypal processes that organize the psyche, as parts of its deep structure. They seem to be a dimension of the psyche that is super-imposed on human experience but is outside our usual conscious perception. The archetypes constitute a kind of universal mind that operates within all human beings. For Jung, this archetypal level of the psyche is ontologically real, not simply a metaphor or a social construction. Mills therefore believes that Jung was an ontologist who wanted to defend a universal theory of mind. However, Jung's status as a philosopher and his philosophical claims are controversial and have been critiqued by several authors. Saban (2014) believes that it is not clear that Jung's comments about the collective uncon-scious were intended to be read ontologically rather than purely psychologi-cally. Saban acknowledges the implicit metaphysical or ontological claims underlying the idea of the collective unconscious and the archetypes, but he does not believe that Jung is trying to establish the ontological existence of anything supernatural, or that the archetypes are supernatural agents of some kind. He sees archetypes as merely concepts, and he focuses on Jung's frequent characterization of them as hypotheses. This opinion is typical of an approach to Jung that tries to avoid his implicit and explicit spiritual claims about the nature of the archetypes.

Mills (2014, p. 231) believes that the "archetypal and collective uncon-scious by definition are not empirical because they cannot be seen, measured, observed, tested, verified, falsified, or refuted." Accordingly, by definition, they are metaphysical postulates. He suggests that "Jung's thought has the potential to be extended into a more formalized, systematic philosophy" (ibid., p. 228). In fact:

> If all the experiences we have are conditioned by and come from a col-lective psyche as the primordial base dispersed as ontic forms super-imposed on all the various layers that comprise human psychic reality, and that we ultimately only know and experience them as our inner world, then if this is not a grand philosophy, I don't know what else it would be.
>
> (Mills, 2014, p. 231)

Here, Mills suggests that for Jung the collective psyche is an ontic reality. This view has been challenged, for example by Whitney (2018), who believes that Jung's view of the unconscious is purely psychological, and not ontic, in part because Jung himself wrote that: "The concept of the unconscious is for me an exclusively psychological concept, and not a philosophical concept of a metaphysical nature" (CW 6, para. 837). Whitney (2018, p. 119) believes that depth psychology is "rooted in epistemology" rather than ontology, and that Jung has conflated purely psychological theorizing into an ontology. However, the quote that Whitney uses to support her contention was written in 1921, and Jung's thinking evolved greatly in the following 40 years. In most cases Jung does treat the objective psyche as a metaphysical category in its own right, for example when he refers to the unconscious as a "supra-consciousness" (CW 13, para. 229), implying that it has a transpersonal or spiritual level. If this level of the psyche can be equated with the Pure Consciousness of the Upaniṣadic traditions, this would allow an important bridge between them and Jung (Corbett, 2023).

The reality of the psyche is Jung's ontological ground. For him, nothing can be more fundamental or more irreducible. This approach has metaphysical implications. Rather than taking a position in which the mind or matter are primary, Jung insists on a purely intrapsychic position (he refers to it as *esse in anima*), which is a metaphysical position that takes the psyche as the only way we can know the world. Psychic reality is the primary datum of our experience. "The psyche creates reality every day" (CW 6, para. 78), and since the psyche is real, its contents are real. He writes that "everything in my immediate experience is psychic in the first place" (Jung, 1975. p. 70.) However, Nagy (1991, p. 31) believes that Jung's subjectivism is excessive, and "makes nonsense of scientific endeavors." For her, such an extreme subjectivist approach "has often had the devastating effect of squelching critical thinking and creating a kind of confessional atmosphere" (p. 32) in Jungian groups. It is true that this problem sometimes happens, but it seems to be due to an excessive idealization of Jung and an inability to see beyond his theories, rather than his philosophical idealism.

In a further contribution to the question of Jung's status as a philosopher, Mills (2014, p. 227) points out that "regardless of whether Jung identified himself as a philosopher or not, his thought is deeply philosophical and assumes a stance toward ultimate reality, hence constitutes a position on being and becoming, which makes Jung's project a metaphysics of presence and concealment." Mills goes on to say that it is important for Jungians to embrace the philosophical implications of Jung's thought, and: "To say that Jung did not intend for his so-called psychological theories to be interpreted as philosophical does not negate his ontological commitments." Mills believes that Jung's work constitutes a "treatise on human nature" (p. 229). Mills (2019, p. 4) urges that: "It is time for Jungians to welcome the philosophical positions inherent in Jung's writings in order to engage or revise them."

Segal (2014) takes issue with Mills on several points and is very critical of Jung's philosophical stance, especially on his professed Kantianism, saying that although Jung was a fabulous psychologist, as a thinker he was an embarrassment. While Mills asserts that the collective unconscious is ontologically real for Jung, Segal counters that the claim that the collective unconscious exists is not itself an ontological claim; it is a claim about something *within* reality rather than a claim about reality itself. This seems to be a distinction without an important difference, and it ignores many of

Jung's comments about the irreducible primacy of the psyche and his belief that the psyche is "existence itself" (CW 8, para. 18).

Some of Jung's critics make arguments that are debatable. Brooks (2011) believes that Jung's epistemology adopts a dualistic foundationalism in his distinctions such as mind/matter, conscious/unconscious, and various others. This critique ignores Jung's obvious monism, found in his oft-repeated notion that mind and matter are two aspects of the same reality, and his emphasis on the unus mundus. Brooks' other major complaint is that Jung's work is based on the idea of an isolated mind containing a priori cognitions and innate structures, but this critique ignores the fact that the objective psyche is transpersonal, and all human beings participate in it; the collective unconscious and the Self are identical in all people (CW 8, p. 436). Because we are connected at the level of the objective psyche, the mind in Jung's model is not isolated. Furthermore, Jung is clear that the Self is the same in all of us, which is another source of linkage between people, but Brooks objects to the essentialism fundamental to Jung's notion of the Self. She approvingly quotes various authors who see the Self as socially constructed, ignoring Jung's idea that the Self is the "God within" (CW 7, para. 399) and so cannot be merely a social construction.

The archetypes

Jung's metaphysical ideas are particularly noticeable in his discussion of the nature of the archetypes.[14] It is important to note that his opinions about the archetypes and the objective psyche changed over time and remained unsystematized. The meaning of the word is sometimes ambiguous. Jung first used the term "archetype" in 1919, where he referred to them as "*a priori* determinants of all psychic processes" that force our manner of perception and apprehension into specifically human patterns (CW 8, para. 270). Early on, Jung referred to the archetypes as "primordial images," a term borrowed from the historian Jacob Burckhardt (CW 5, para. 45, note 45). Because of the presence of the archetypal level of the psyche, common motifs arise in disparate cultures, religions, myths, and other symbol systems. The fundamental structures of these patterns are constant, but they are given local contents, folkloric and cultural coloring, and different names in different places. All human beings participate in this collective level of the psyche, so that imagery from any mythological or religious tradition may arise in the dream material of any individual, regardless of her or his personal background. Jung takes it for granted that the objective psyche exists independently of any individual mind. He believes that myth is the primordial language of the archetypal level of the psyche, "and no intellectual formulation comes anywhere near the richness and expressiveness of mythical imagery" (CW 12, para. 28). There are archetypal levels of the psyche, containing profound truths, that can best be expressed using mythic imagery because no other medium is adequate. Jung's notion of the archetype was an attempt to create a theory about the processes behind his empirical observation of numinous phenomena.

Jung subsequently developed a range of descriptions of the archetypes, and his ideas about them evolved, although some aspects of the idea persisted through time. At times he referred to the archetypes as such[15] as unknowable or "irrepresentable" basic forms that can only be grasped approximately; they appear within consciousness as symbols, ideas, and images (CW 8, para. 417). The archetype is a fundamental psycho-physical template within the mind–body, a form or potential for experience that is given a specific content by the circumstances of the individual's life (CW 11, para. 845). The archetypes are "unconscious organizers of our ideas" (CW 9ii, para. 278), known only through their effects on consciousness (CW 8, para. 412) and not subject to human will (CW 11, para. 557). The archetypes therefore exist outside human intentionality, but they affect much human experience. In a letter to Wolfgang Pauli, Jung says that Pauli's idea that probability is related to the archetype is "most illuminating. In fact, the archetype represents nothing but the probability of psychic events" (Meier, 2001, p. 69).

In themselves, prior to their symbolic manifestations, the archetypes have an "innermost essence" that "can never become wholly conscious" (Jung, 1973, p. 313). The problem here is that if the archetype-as-such is not the same as its images, how do we know it exists? This is partly why some authors merge the archetype and its images (Brooke, 1991). But this merger is not compatible with Jung's concept, which is that we only experience the archetype in the form of a symbol or as an unconscious influence on our behavior, while the underlying archetype itself is an inference. For Jung the psyche rests on an "unknowable metaphysical background" (CW 11, para. 558). When Jung uses this kind of language, he implicitly invokes the spiritual dimension of the archetypes and takes the idea beyond a purely empirical or phenomenological approach. This gives them a depth that prevents the archetype becoming merely an ego-level phenomenon.

Jung makes several allusions to the similarity between the archetype and Plato's Ideas.[16] For example, discussing the mother archetype, he says:

> Were I a philosopher, I should continue in this Platonic strain and say: Somewhere, in "a place beyond the skies," there is a prototype or primordial image of the mother that is pre-existent and supraordinate to all phenomena in which the "maternal," in the broadest sense of the term, is manifest. But I am an empiricist, not a philosopher.
>
> (CW 9i, para. 149)

In spite of Jung's denial at the end of this paragraph, this seems like a subtle hint about his real metaphysical belief. He sees the archetypes as "active-living dispositions, ideas in the Platonic sense, that preform and continually inform our thoughts and feelings and actions" (ibid., para. 154). The arche-type is "an explanatory paraphrase" of the Platonic ideas (CW 9i, para. 5). In this Platonic sense the archetype is a spiritual principle that conditions the human mind. Like Plato's Ideas, Jung says that the archetypes are "universal and impersonal" (CW 9i, para. 90), but there are differences in that Plato's Forms are cognitive, transcendent, or cosmic rather than psychological prin-ciples. They do not have the affective quality of the archetypes, nor do they appear as mythological motifs or as immanent symbols within the psyche. Furthermore, archetypal images are dynamic rather than fixed, often compensating for something within the individual psyche.

Jung sees the archetypes as dynamic agencies, "living subjects" (CW 11, para. 757) that seem to have intentionality, autonomy, and independence (ibid., 758). The archetypes can be seen as carriers of information about the patterned ways in which the psyche works. In this way, they can be seen to be analogous to the laws of physics, which describe the orderly behavior of matter. Importantly, if the archetypes organize the psyche, they cannot themselves be psychological, any more than the laws of physics can them-selves be physical. The archetypes can therefore be seen as spiritual princi-ples, and indeed at times Jung sees the archetypes as attributes of the divine (Jung, 1975, p. 130). He sometimes speaks of them as if they were metaphy-sical ultimates. This causes confusion and debate, given that Jung often denies that his ideas are metaphysical. There is a great deal of resistance to attributing metaphysical status to the archetypes among contemporary wri-ters such as Wolfgang Giegerich (2012a), Jon Mills (2019), and Jean Knox (2003), but Jung's notion of the Self as a God-image is clearly metaphysical.

A major philosophical issue raised here is whether archetypes, (which includes mathematical forms), exist independently of the human mind, which seems to have been Jung's belief. The archetypes are not only psychological; Jung also talks about the archetypes as "attributes of instincts" (Jung, 1965, p. 347), and he says he cannot refute the possibility that these "form patterns" are identical with the instincts (CW 8, para. 404). To relate the instinctual and the psychological, in his 1954 essay On the Nature of the Psyche, Jung uses the light spectrum as an analogy (CW 8, para. 414); the blue or ultraviolet end of the archetype is its spiritual dimension, and the red or infrared end is the somatic pole. His model therefore suggests that the archetype is bipolar. One pole is in the body in the form of an instinct and the other is in the mind or spirit. The spiritual dimension at the ultraviolet end is on the same spectrum as the infrared biological or instinctual level of the psyche. The middle of the spectrum contains the psyche as we experience it. Since the light spectrum is unitary, I see this metaphor as an allusion to Jung's monism of matter and spirit, which cannot be separated. Both are manifestations of the same underlying reality. Jung is clear about this in a letter to Pauli, in which he says that "the physical and the psychic matrix is identical" (Meier, 2001, p. 126), and in various places he makes comments such as: "Spirit and matter may well be forms of one and the same transcendental being" (CW 9i, para. 392). In other words, matter, spirit, and consciousness are not sharply distinguished in his model—they are continuous, a manifestation of the same substrate. Marie-Louise von Franz (1988) points out that matter may appear at the "ultraviolet" or spiritual pole in the form of parapsychological phenomena. Therefore, she suggests that our division of matter and psyche is only valid subjectively, imposed on us by the structures of our consciousness, and does not correspond to the wholeness of reality. Jung writes that "matter has a psychic aspect, and the psyche a physical aspect ... all reality would be grounded on an as yet unknown substrate possessing material and at the same time psychic qualities" (CW 10, para. 780). Both psyche and matter are complementary aspects of one reality, which Jung described using the medieval term "unus mundus." This view has been developed by Atmanspacher in several publications (e.g., Atmanspacher, 2012a, 2012b). This approach is known as dual-aspect monism, which suggests that there is a fundamental metaphysical substrate to both psyche and matter, a common ontological ground that is neither psychological nor material. However, this view is not necessarily consistent with Jung's comment (discussed below) that the psyche is an οὐσία (a being or substance) in its own right, since dual-aspect monism would make the psyche reducible to a deeper substrate and not fundamental or primary.

In his early work, Jung assumes a biological approach to the archetype, which he says is genetically encoded and engraved on the mind as a result of the repeated experiences of our early archaic ancestors. These experiences left a deposit in the psyche (CW 7, para. 109) that become predispositions that were subsequently passed on in the form of inherited potentials. In an early paper, Jung writes that archetypes are "inherited with the brain structure—indeed they are its psychic aspect" (CW 10, para. 53).[17] Or, the collective unconscious "contains the whole spiritual heritage of mankind's evolution, born anew in the brain structure of every individual" (CW 8, para. 342). Jung linked the idea of the archetypes to the theory of evolution in order to give it some biological basis. When he talks about the archetype as inherited, it has a discredited Lamarckian flavor, although Anthony Stevens (1982) shows that this is not the case. It seems that Jung stressed the biological aspects of the archetype in his early writing because this seemed to give the idea scientific credence. In this attempt he was probably influenced by Freud's biological approach to the psyche and by the materialistic temper of the times. Stevens (1982, p. 29) believed that to emphasize the spiritual nature of the archetypes is to adopt an "esoteric path," which neglects the behavioral, phylogenetic, and biological implications of the idea, which divorces analytical psychology from the mainstream of biological science. However, to acknowledge the spiritual dimension of the archetype is not to ignore its biological aspects. In any case, as Steele (1982) pointed out, it is not necessary link the archetypes with biological inheritance, because the strength of the idea is its hermeneutic approach, resting on meaning, and the attempt to introduce biological causality would be a category mistake. I prefer the proposal that the concept of the archetype tries to integrate biology, spirit, and psyche. As Jung puts it, the separation of psychology from biology is artificial "because the human psyche lives in indissoluble union with the body" (CW 8, para. 232). At its irrepresentable level, the archetype structures both psyche and matter (CW 8, para. 964).

In its spiritual dimension, the archetypal level of the psyche can be compared to the idea of a World Soul (CW 8, para. 390). This aspect of Jung's theory inevitably leads to complaints of supernaturalism and mysticism, which is understandable since the Self is a God-term for Jung. Nevertheless, the concepts of the collective unconscious and the archetype have metaphysical implications if one believes they are spiritual entities, which Jung appears to have done, based on comments such as: "If one assumes that God affects the psychic background and activates it or actually is it, then the archetypes are, so to speak, organs (tools) of God" (Jung, 1975, p. 130)—clearly an ontological claim about the spiritual nature of the archetypes. He wrote to Herbert Read (one of the humanist editors of the *Collected works*) that archetypes "are and always have been numinous and therefore 'divine.' In a very generalizing way we can therefore define them as attributes of the creator" (ibid., p. 606). Mills (2019) summarily dismisses any such spiritual connotation as the result of Jung's Christian upbringing.

If the archetypes have a spiritual or transpersonal dimension, they cannot be inherited as if they were purely material. Unfortunately, however, the idea that the archetypes are inherited biologically has been repeated so often in the secondary literature that it has been transmitted as if it were Jung's final view on the subject. However, showing how his thinking had changed, in a 1947 letter to Medard Boss, Jung writes that: "You are utterly mistaken in saying that I have described the archetypes as given with the brain structure" (Jung, 1975, p. xl.). In his final work, Jung says that their nature makes them "incapable of precise definition" (Jung, 1964, p. 96). He was very cautious about the question of the nature and origin of the archetypes: "Not for a moment dare we succumb to the illusion that an archetype can be finally explained and disposed of. Even the best attempts at explanation are only more or less successful translations into another metaphorical language" (CW 9i, para. 271). In his later writing, Jung says that the origin of the archetype is unknown, just as the origin of the psyche is unknown and is an unanswerable metaphysical problem (CW 9i, para. 187). He suggests that the archetype "did not ever come into existence as a phenomenon of organic life but entered into the picture with life itself" (CW 11, note 2, p. 149).

The archetypes are clearly ontologically primary for Jung. In fact, Mills (2014, p. 231) points out that if the notion of the archetypes does not entail an ontological premise, the idea of the collective unconscious and the archetypes are "bankrupt ideas." Not only are the archetypes important to Jung's ontology, his idea that archetypal processes organize human knowledge is important to his epistemology. The fact that in a dream we can experience imagery from a mythological or religious tradition of which we have no conscious knowledge suggests that we participate in a non-material, archetypal source of psychological life that underpins our experience. This is clearly a metaphysical position. Jung's notion of the archetype is reminiscent of Schopenhauer's notion of the will, except that for him the will is blind, whereas for Jung the archetype has a definite direction and meaning. The information carried by the archetypes is one source of their meaning when we experience them symbolically.

Jung was clearly not a physicalist, but there are several explanations for the archetypes that describe them as a result of brain activity (Hogenson, 2019). Mills (2019) thinks that archetypal imagery can be explained in terms of innate cognitive processes that have evolved for the purposes of adaptation. Mills restricts his understanding of the archetypes to Jung's early belief that they are inherited, ignoring Jung's later insistence that they are *not* given with brain structure. Several authors similarly see the archetypes as emergent structures or biologically based image schemas, not innate but resulting from the interaction of brain functioning, genes, and the environment (Knox, 2004). Tresan (1996) used a physicalist combination of emergentism, supervenience, and complexity theory to describe the archetypes. Rather than seeing the archetypes as biologically based, Pietikainen (1998) suggested that they are symbolic forms that are products of culture rather than biology. Roesler (2012) also sees archetypes as emergent cultural phenomena. They can be seen as purely psychological processes or even as redundant (Colman, 2018). The genetic explanation seems rather weak, since it is doubtful that the enormous range of psychological manifestations of the archetypes could all be accounted for genetically. At the moment, it is impossible to prove any of these explanations, so one simply has to take a position based on the way one interprets Jung's words. An underlying predisposition to atheism is obvious in those authors who dismiss the spiritual dimension of the archetype.

Before leaving this subject, I should note that there is a prosaic way to understand the similarities between the motifs of disparate mythologies and religious systems without invoking the idea of the archetypes or a collective level of the psyche. It may be that stories and rituals are simply transmitted culturally over long periods of historical time, and some of these ideas may have diffused or migrated to other cultures. Or these similarities might arise because all human beings face similar problems and solve them with the same brain structures. Jung might counter that similar imagery arises in cultures that have no known contact with each other, and diffusion or neurological explanations do not account for the numinosity of archetypal experiences. Stolorow and Atwood (1979) account for this intensity by attributing the archetype to intrapsychic, "*primitive, highly aggrandized, omnipotent objects*" (p. 75; emphasis in original) that are experienced as autonomous entities operating independently of the subject's volition. That is, the archetypes are the residues of object imagoes in the psyche. (In this context, it is worth remembering Freud's notion of "archaic remnants" or "phylogenetic memories" in the psyche, found in his 1939 *Moses and mono-theism.*) This theory is a typical psychoanalytic reduction that does not account for the range of archetypal, mythic imagery that emerges in dreams, much of which the subject has never consciously experienced. Many psy-choanalysts now assume the existence of innate psychological structures that affect behavior, and they acknowledge that the unconscious may have a creative dimension.

Part of the resistance to the idea of the archetype is based on the fact that since the seventeenth century much Western thought has preferred to think that the mind only contains material that has entered it through sensory experience, that there are no innate principles in the mind. Jung's notion of the archetypal level of the psyche refutes this epistemological assertion since archetypal processes are innate and independent of sensory experience. The idea that the mind contains information at birth sounds too mystical to people who believe that distinctive human behavior can only be obtained by learning. However, modern cognitive science suggests that all human beings have innate cognitive, physical, and behavioral capacities (Brown, 1991), the doctrine of nativism. These are often thought to be based on modular structures in the mind with specific functions, some of which account for the beliefs of folk psychology. According to Fodor (1983) these modules or brain sub-systems are associated with specific neuronal structures. Much cognitive processing goes on at an unconscious level. Noam Chomsky postulated innate cognitive structures that are required for the acquisition of one's native language. However, cognitive scientists believe that our innate mental abilities evolved during human evolution and are only relevant to dealing with the environment. Jung's notion of innate archetypal processes is much more complex, and they cannot be the product of evolution if they are viewed as spiritual principles. They are metaphysically primary for Jung and their origin is not knowable.

The psychoid

Jung's postulate of a psychoid realm is a metaphysical claim, first made public by Jung in 1947 (CW 8, para. 368), where he insists the term is an adjective and not a noun. He does not define the term clearly. It seems to represent an unknowable level of reality from which the archetypes and syn-chronistic events emerge. At that level, body and psyche or matter and spirit are not differentiated. Or the term denotes a bridging function between body and mind (Addison, 2009, 2017 provides a valuable survey of the idea). The psychoid "points to the sphere of the unus mundus" or the unitary level of reality (CW 10, para. 852) in which reality is psychophysically neutral. This is an ontological postulate that is not amenable to empirical verification, and Jung acknowledges that it is a "metaphysical speculation" (CW 14, para. 660). In his last work, *Mysterium coniunctionis*, Jung claims that numinous experiences arise from the psychoid level.

Jung uses the term psychoid in part to refer to the essential nature of the archetype, or the archetype-as-such, which cannot be made conscious because it is transcendent (CW 8, para. 417). The archetype manifests itself in images, but the archetypes "have a nature that cannot with certainty be designated as psychic" (CW 8, para. 439). In a letter, Jung (1975, p. 22) talks about the psychoid level of the archetype as a "mere model[18] or postulate," but also that it is "an 'arranger' of psychic forms inside and outside the psyche." As an example, he uses this idea to account for the synchronistic events this level produced around the figure of Christ. In another letter he says that the psychoid level of the archetype is transcendental and "thus relatively beyond the categories of number, time, and space" (ibid., p. 318). In these places, he clearly refers to the archetype as a metaphysical agent, a far cry from his early biological understanding.

Brooks (2011) thinks that the idea of the psychoid is not a coherent theoretical idea. Mills (2014) sees the concept of the psychoid as without logical or rational justification and believes it to be an unintelligible aspect of Jung's philosophy. However, the idea is heuristically useful even if it is only speculative and yet to be proven to be real. Speculatively, the psychoid dimension may correspond to the level of the quantum wave function, and so may be part of a long-sought after bridge between depth psychology and quantum mechanics. The idea is no more incoherent than David Bohm's concept of an implicate quantum realm of wholeness out of which the explicate order of separate objects arises.

Jung as a scientist

Segal (2018, p. 86) believes that "Jungian analyses of persons and things are unscientific." He complains that Jung never tests his hypothesis of the archetype, does not try to falsify it, and the theory cannot be shown to have predictive value (Segal, 2014). Overall, for Segal, Jungian psychology is a pseudoscience. However, Segal's argument is overstated in various ways. While it is true that Popper (1968) argued that falsifiability demarcates (empirical) science from nonscience, he did not claim that falsifiability is the only criterion that can guide science. Neither did he claim that all scientific theories are falsifiable. Popper believed that scientific theories start with generalizations and conjectures in the mind of the researcher, whose validity is tested until they are falsified. According to Popper, a theory can be falsified by *conclusive* empirical evidence, but contemporary philosophers of science consider this criterion to be too strong a requirement (Hansson 2006).

At best, Popper is offering a methodological recommendation, not a description of what scientists do in practice. There might be useful scientific theories that are unlikely to ever be falsified.[19] Jung's notion of the archetypal dimension of the psyche could in principle be falsified if what he sees as archetypal processes could be shown to be illusory, or if a better explanation for them is found. However, it is not clear what evidence would definitively falsify the notion of the Self as an explanation for numinous experiences. Empiricists can be tolerant of novel hypotheses without ruling them out in principle, especially if they seem to explain the observed evidence. New theories, such as early atomic theory or the postulate of the neutrino, sometimes go beyond empirical evidence but are proven over time.

Popper's approach is now regarded as inadequate. Various philosophers of science have pointed out that there are many instances in the history of science that are inconsistent with Popper's criterion. Some scientific ideas are not verifiable or falsifiable in principle; for example, many theories in astrophysics cannot be falsified because our data about the early universe is incomplete. Kuhn (1962) pointed out that in practice, theories that are partially refuted by data, or theories that cannot be falsified, are not always discarded by scientists, especially when they are useful. Science often proceeds by comparing competing theories and not by falsifying them, and in scientific practice the discarding of a theory on the basis of falsification is the exception rather than the rule. Hansson (2006) has convincingly shown that the criterion of falsification relies on an incorrect view of the nature of scientific inquiry. It is of limited value and can itself be falsified. He quotes Ernest Nagel (1979a, p. 76), who pointed out that Popper's "conception of the role of falsification in the use and development of theories is an oversimplification that is close to being a caricature of scientific procedure." Furthermore, it is simply not reasonable to insist that all knowledge requires experimental evidence that is repeatable and publicly demonstrable. Some events are unique, very private, or very rare. Empirically reliable observations are sufficient to establish that they occurred, and their cause does not need to be explained to ensure that they are significant.

Kuhn (1962) suggested that science is carried out by a community of workers who agree on specific principles but also struggle over the interpretation of data. Those who succeed in this struggle introduce a new paradigm or worldview, which becomes the way in which existing data are interpreted. Until that time, facts that contradict the existing framework are usually seen to be irrelevant or anomalous, or they are reinterpreted. The need for a new paradigm emerges when a sufficient number of anomalies have accumulated that cannot be accommodated by existing theories, whereupon a new theory emerges that accounts for the anomalies. When a new paradigm emerges it "cannot be justified by proof" (p. 151). There may be no logical connection between the old and new paradigms, and it may not be possible to derive the new approach from the old approach. Changes in scientific theories are not simply additive, as if new data adds to previous knowledge. No theory encompasses all observations. New paradigms influence both the type of research that is done, the interpretation of the results, and new hypotheses. Some scientists are never convinced of the new way of thinking and resist it indefinitely. Others accept the new paradigm on faith before it can be proven. Jung's approach to the Self and the archetypal psyche is an approach to psychology that takes into account various types of experience that cannot be discussed within the framework of mainstream psychology, such as synchronicity. His work might be the beginning of the development of a new paradigm for the study of the psyche. His approach to the psyche considers the subjective element to be essential and inevitable, rather than trying to be objective, and it emphasizes the discovery of meaning. Jung wanted to avoid the reductive approach of experimental psychology. He pointed out that his work tackles "the darkest and most desperate problems of the soul," dealing with the "hopes and fears, the pains and joys" of real life, with no laboratory equipment (CW 17, paras. 169–171).

Analytical psychology differs from experimental psychology in that it does not attempt to isolate individual functions (sense functions, emotional phenomena, thought-processes, etc.) and then subject them to experimental conditions for purposes of investigation. It is far more concerned with the total manifestations of the psyche as a natural phenomenon.

Jung believed that existing scientific theories "are not adequate to the nature of the unconscious" (CW 16, para. 478), because their terminology has no affinity with its symbolism. There seems to be no way around the inevitably subjective perspective involved in the interpretation of this material. Neuroscience is of no help in understanding a complex symbol that has arisen from the unconscious. Knowing that the individual is in a state of REM sleep tells us nothing about the dream content or its meaning. Each discipline has its own parameters and requires its own approaches.

Looking back on his life, Jung (1965, p. 222) wrote that "My life is what I have done, my scientific work; the one is inseparable from the other", pointing out that his life and his science, or his subjectivity and his objective observations, are inextricably linked. Although science is an "affair of the intellect," for the purpose of studying the psyche, "the leading role is given to *life* itself," (CW 6, para. 84), and: "Inasmuch as the intellect rigidly adheres to the absolute aim of science it cuts itself off from the springs of life" (ibid., para. 86). Subjectivity cannot be eradicated from the study of the psyche. Therefore, feeling and fantasy are important to practical psychology; even though they are only approached abstractly and intellectually by science, in life and in psychotherapeutic practice they can unite the opposites of thinking and feeling, leading to a comprehensive psychology.

One of the difficulties Jung noted when studying the psyche was "the personal equation," or the effects of the psychologist's own subjectivity on the material he studies. "Nowhere does the observer interfere more drastically with the experiment than in psychology" (CW 17, para. 160). Based on his understanding of quantum mechanics, Jung writes that we need a concept of reality "that takes account of the uncontrollable effects the observer has upon the system observed, the result being that reality forfeits something of its objective character" (CW 8, para. 438).

Saban (2022) believes that the dynamic tension between the scientific and the imaginative aspects of Jung's work are related to his number 1 and number 2 personalities,[20] and the tension between them is central to his notion of individuation. Saban points out that it is impossible to try to ground Jung's work on the basis of natural science; doing so would have "neutered, tamed, and domesticated Jung's psychology," since Jung is trying to subvert traditional science by pointing out the essential role of subjectivity (ibid., p. 10) and by relentlessly criticizing materialistic and reductive approaches to the psyche. Saban (ibid., p. 14) sees Jung's psychology as transdisciplinary, a "trickster science that does its work in the realm of the liminal," in the boundaries between disciplines such as psychology and neuroscience where new ideas emerge. It is Jung's fascination with material that lies on the boundaries of knowledge that makes him open to subjects that cannot be encompassed by traditional science, such as mythology, parapsychology, astrology, the *I Ching*, and alchemy. Interest in this kind of material also marginalizes Jung in academic psychology, which prefers to dismiss this kind of material and limit itself to reductionist and positivist explanations of reality. However, Jung felt that rather than ignoring or discounting these phenomena, the psychology underpinning them should be explored. They are a part of his syncretic approach to the psyche. In his 1957 essay "The undiscovered self," Jung (CW 10, para. 498) expressed the concern that science based solely on statistics and abstract knowledge "imparts an unrealistic, rational picture of the world" that ignores the individual, but the individual is the "irrational datum, [and] is the true and authentic carrier of reality" as opposed to scientific concepts of people.

Jung was often accused of being unscientific, but the material he studied is often not amenable to the methods of the natural sciences, which was the standard being applied by his critics. It is not unusual for scientists to introduce ideas and concepts that cannot be measured or explained at the time. Jung proposes a radically new approach to the unconscious, and significant new methods of investigation often face stubborn objections; one thinks of Semmelweis's discovery of the way to prevent sepsis in childbirth and Wegener's theory of continental drift, both of which were initially derided. The scientific study of the unconscious is obviously made difficult because of the nature of the subject matter and because the human personality is irreducibly unique, whereas science is predicated on generalities and reproducibility. Nevertheless, although it is difficult to make generalized statements about unique individuals, he notes that individuality is not absolute, "and therefore it is possible to make statements of general validity, i.e., scientific statements" about parts of the psyche that are amenable to comparison (CW 16, para. 1).

Jung realized the limitation of the natural science approach to psychology because it forces nature "to give an answer oriented to the human question" (CW 8, para. 821) so that nature cannot answer "out of the fullness of its possibilities" (ibid., para. 864). The unconscious cannot be studied experimentally and quantitatively; it produces unique, non-reproducible phenomena such as numinous experiences, which can only be described but not explained. Although their source is unknown, the existence of these phenomena is undeniable. Jung's theory of the objective psyche is at least consistent with the observable facts. The explanatory power of unobserved (and possibly unobservable) entities is well known to science. Many useful theories can achieve no more than this.

It does not seem reasonable to hold Jung to a higher standard than applies in other areas of science. At the moment, string theory in physics is not testable experimentally, and it postulates ten or eleven hidden dimensions of reality. Proponents hope to be able to demonstrate its validity in the future, but at the moment there is no falsifiable test of the idea. The notion of a "multiverse" or many worlds in quantum mechanics is unprovable. Most physicists see a role for such speculation. It is not unusual for some aspects of a scientific theory to conflict with other parts of the same theory or with other well-established theories. The difficulty in reconciling some aspects of quantum theory with general relativity is well known.[21] There is no reason that Jungian theory cannot be reconciled with the wider range of depth psychological theories such as object relations theory and psychoanalytic self-psychology.

With regard to Segal's critique about replicability, I would note that replicability is a problem not only in psychological and medical research but also in the humanities in general, where exact replication cannot meet the standards required of the physical sciences because of the nature of the objects studied and the methods available. Jung offers a range of evidence for his theories, which is standard practice. One line of evidence that his therapeutic approach is effective is found in Roesler's review of the findings of several studies:

> Jungian therapy leads not only to a significant reduction of symptoms and of interpersonal and other problems but also to a restructuring of the personality with the effect that the patients can deal with upcoming problems much better after the end of therapy.
>
> (Roesler, 2018, p. 308)

Not only have these therapeutic observations been replicated, but observations of synchronistic events have also been replicated countless times by clinicians, leading to a general sense of confidence in the validity of this idea. The concept of synchronicity, and the idea of the archetypal psyche, are empirically useful ideas that fit the observable phenomena, although the observer is susceptible to the criticism of confirmation bias—seeing what one wants to see. There are calls to subject Jung's ideas to the scientific method (Jones, 2014), but the empirical, quantitative methods of mainstream psychology are too crude for this purpose (Kime, 2018). Segal's critique ignores the fact that Jung did not believe that science is the only way to know the world or that its methods are privileged, although he did write that we can gain access to the psyche "by the methods of natural science" (CW 8, para. 441). If so, his work is at the stage of scientific investigation characterized by empirical observation, the compiling of data and the relationship between data, classification, and the development of general rules and concepts. At the moment his theory does not lend itself to the kind of prediction beloved of the physical sciences, which scientists believe help to either verify or falsify a theory. The unpredictable uniqueness of the individual combined with acausal ordering principles such as synchronicity do not lend themselves to being studied using statistical methods. The study of the complexity of human subjectivity requires its own methods that cannot simply be copied from the physical sciences. It is very difficult to operationalize concepts such as individuation, which cannot be studied quantitatively. Since this process is unique to the individual it is by definition not repeatable. Meanwhile, the idea that the archetypes are ordering principles of an unknown kind is a useful hypothesis that fits much of the observed material, and there is broad consensus about its value among psychotherapists with a Jungian orientation. The notion of the archetype may only be a metaphorical way of describing our sense that the psyche is ordered, but metaphors are also widely deployed in physics (an example is the "Big Bang"), because they are essential ways of talking about our relationship to reality.

Saban (2022) locates Jung's science in the context of the contrasting, interactive and oppositional practices of science described by the philosophers Deleuze and Guattari. Saban describes Jung's empiricism or pragmatism in terms of what these authors refer to as nomad science, which is malleable, inventive, and fluid, in contrast to royal or state science which privileges the stable, deterministic, rational, and standardized approach to science. Another approach to Jung's psychology would be to see it in terms of the work of Bruno Latour (1988), for whom Jung's theories are at a stage of "science-in-the-making," consisting of hypotheses that are still unsettled and controversial. This kind of science progresses through publication, discussion, and repeated observation, which gradually removes or confirms doubt about the hypotheses. Latour says that hypotheses gradually accumulate allies and dissenters; this is a social process, in which different communities may evolve different interpretations of the same evidence. These controversies are essential. Science typically proceeds using a series of proposals and counterproposals.

The unity of psyche and matter in Jung's work

Synchronicity

Jung's concept of synchronicity describes a situation in which a subjective, psychological process corresponds in a meaningful way to a physical event that occurs at about the same time,[22] even though the inner and the outer events do not cause each other. For example, one dreams of a plane crash at the same time as a physical plane crash occurs. Synchronicity therefore meaningfully links our subjectivity with the outer world. Skeptics resist this idea, because the theory contravenes ordinary notions of cause and effect and undermines the idea that the material world is independent of our psychology. The notion of an acausal connecting principle between physical and mental events drastically expands the perspectives of psychology and psychotherapy and radically opposes traditional positivism and determinism.

Synchronicity links the apparently separate domains of matter and psyche by virtue of a common meaning. An important question is whence that meaning arises. For Jung: "Synchronicity postulates a meaning which is a priori in relation to human consciousness and apparently exists outside man" (CW 8, para. 942). Here, Jung discusses the possibility of meaning that is not simply derived by the individual who experiences the event; the meaning may be given by the objective psyche rather than being projected into the situation by the subject. Although this cannot be proved scientifically, when Jung refers to objective or "self-subsistent meaning" (ibid., para. 945), he is suggesting that meaning seems to have an archetypal basis and may represent an unknown factor within nature that "appears to us as meaning" (ibid., para. 916). Hypothetically "one and the same (transcendental) meaning might manifest itself simultaneously in the human psyche and in the arrangement of an external and independent event" (ibid., para. 915). However, "we have absolutely no scientific means of proving the existence of an *objective* meaning which is not just a psychic product" (ibid.) even though we do not know what meaning is in itself. In a letter, Jung (1975, p. 495) writes that the coincidence of a physical and an endopsychic event "presupposes … an all-pervading, latent meaning which can be recognized by consciousness" but which is independent of ego consciousness. He refers to meaning that is transcendental (CW 8 para. 915) and a priori in relation to human consciousness (ibid., para. 942). Colman (2011) prefers the opposing view, that the meaning attributed to a synchronistic event is a purely human construction, generated out of the interaction of the mind and nature. He is not happy with the implication of a universal mind or any other religious connotation. But Jung clearly emphasizes an "archetype of meaning" (CW 9i, paras. 66, 79), appearing as an archetypal figure in the form of imagery such as the Wise Old Man (ibid., para. 682), who represents "the archetype of the spirit, who symbolizes the pre-existent meaning hidden in the chaos of life"

(CW 9i, para. 74). Meaning that arises from this kind of archetypal source rather than the personal psyche carries more numinosity than personal levels of meaning. Objective meaning becomes an ordering principle in its own right, and an intrinsic constituent of nature. It is not an accident that synchronistic events tend to occur during periods of heightened emotional significance such as births, deaths, creative work, or psychotherapy, all situations in which the issue of meaning becomes paramount.[23]

There has been some controversy about Jung's use of the term *sinngemäß Koinzidenz*, usually translated as "meaningful coincidence." Giegerich (2012a) saw a mistranslation of the German word "meaningful," *sinngemäß*, in this phrase. He thought that Jung was not referring to transcendent meaning, or Meaning, but simply that the mental and physical events mean roughly the same thing; they are comparable or equivalent to each other. (*Sinngemäß* can also mean analogous.) Giegerich dismisses Jung's idea of the unus mundus and synchronicity as an opening to the sacred as "mystifying and sentimental waffle." On the contrary, for those of us with a spiritual orientation to Jung's work, these ideas are important components of his approach to the psyche. In his reply to Giegerich, while also critical of the idea of the unus mundus, Colman noted that German speakers such as Marie-Louise von Franz do not share Giegerich's interpretation of the word "meaningful."

Robert Aziz (1990) finds four levels of meaning in Jung's use of the idea of synchronicity. One is that the two events simply parallel each other because they have the same content, while another level is the numinous quality of the experience or its emotional power. The third level is of meaning refers to the significance of the event from the point of view of the subject's individuation process, and the fourth level is the event's objective or archetypal meaning, which underpins all these levels. This was clearly the most important level for Jung, who believed that the numinous charge of a synchronistic event correlates with an underlying constellated archetype (CW 8, paras. 841, 845). However, these levels are not mutually exclusive. If the archetypal level of meaning can be integrated, it contributes to and merges with the personal level. The spiritual quality of a synchronistic event often occurs because these experiences have a numinous, "meant to be" quality, which makes the subject realize she is part of a larger whole, not separate from the totality, which Jung (CW 8, para. 960) refers to as a "unity of being". To ignore this dimension of synchronicity is to diminish its importance.

Both Pauli and Jung saw the phenomenon of synchronicity as an example of acausal orderedness that is a function of the deep structure of nature. They hoped that understanding synchronicity might help to unify depth psychology and physics. They tried to construct a unified vision of reality by showing how the apparently separate domains of quantum physics and the archetypal psyche might be related to each other at a deep level. In Jung's words:

The common background of microphysics and depth-psychology is as much physical as psychic and therefore neither, but rather a third thing, a neutral nature which can at most be grasped in hints since in essence it is transcendental.

(CW 14, para. 768)

By focusing on synchronicity, these authors were trying find "an acausal connecting principle" alongside space, time, and causality (CW 8, para. 968), to which Jung added synchronicity as a fourth category of universal principles. He wrote that he had a "fervent interest" in the metaphysical aspects of synchronicity, and when a synchronistic event happens, how it seems "that even inanimate objects are capable of behaving as if they were acquainted with my thoughts" (Jung, 1975, p. 344). This comment belongs to Jung's project of restoring meaning to matter, rather than seeing the material world as entirely despiritualized as a result of scientific rationalism, which was a major concern of Jung (CW 8, paras. 140–141). Synchronistic events restore our sense of an underlying spiritual order, in which something deeper than ordinary causality is at work. Synchronicity is "only a particular instance of general acausal orderedness" that the observer is able to recognize (CW 8, para. 965). Both Jung and Pauli were interested in developing a broader, wholistic scientific sensibility that takes the psyche as well as matter into account. Pauli is an exemplar of this possibility, since he was so interested in his dreams, which seemed to comment on concepts in physics "in a qualitative and figurative—i.e., symbolic—sense" (Meier, 2001, p. 179).

Jung and Pauli wanted to develop an acausal principle within nature that includes both quantum level phenomena and synchronistic events. It was clear to them that psychology needs more than simply causal explanations for events. Jung's theory of synchronicity implies an unknown metaphysical ordering principle, not dependent on causality, that meaningfully links the inner and outer worlds and links matter and psyche. It would be a mistake to say that there is an archetype *causing* synchronistic events, but Jung points out that they "can easily be shown to have a direct connection with an archetype" (CW 8, para. 912) or they occur in situations in which an archetypal pattern is constellated. It is as if the archetype acts as a mediating principle or vehicle of linkage between matter and psyche or even between the individual and the cosmos. The archetype is an expression of an underlying pattern in which physical and mental processes are equivalent. Marie-Louise von Franz (1984, p. 271) wrote that synchronistic events allow such latent archetypal meaning to become visible. For her, following Jung, human beings do not create this meaning, we only realize it, "but it is already latently existent in nature itself, independent of our conscious realization." This kind of meaning "points to a connection with what we call the Self" (ibid., p. 273). She points out that while the archetype does not cause synchronistic events, it becomes manifest in them.

Based on synchronicity and his observation of psi phenomena such as telepathy, and prospective dreams, Jung believes that

> the space-time barrier can be annulled. The annulling factor would then be the psyche ... it could even break through the barriers of space and time precisely because of a quality essential to it, that is, its relatively trans-spatial and trans-temporal nature.
>
> (CW 8, para. 813)

"It follows either that the psyche cannot be localized in space, or that space is relative to the psyche" (CW 8, para. 996). It is an everyday experience that in dreams ordinary time and space are abolished. Time and space behave differently in the unconscious from the way we experience them consciously. Following Kant, Jung thought that space and time "are hypostasized concepts born of the discriminating activity of the conscious mind ... They are, therefore, essentially psychic in origin" (CW 8, para. 840).

Jung's monism: the unus mundus

Synchronicity led Jung to the idea that matter and psyche are both rooted in a unitary level of reality, which he referred to as the unus mundus, whose existence is part of Jung's picture of the world. "Everything that happens, however, happens in the same 'one world,' and ... events must possess an *a priori* aspect of unity" (CW 14, para. 662). Elsewhere: "we have every reason to suppose that there is only *one* world, where matter and psyche and are the same thing, which we discriminate for the purposes of cognition" (Jung, 1975, p. 342). The unus mundus is a kind of potential world in which empirical phenomena are inherent. Furthermore: "in the Unus Mundus ... there is no incommensurability between so-called matter and so-called psyche" (ibid., p. 400). The unus mundus is the unitary background of the empirical world.

In Jung's words:

> Undoubtedly the idea of the Unus Mundus is founded on the assumption that the multiplicity of the empirical world rests on an underlying unity, and that not two or more fundamentally different worlds exist side by side or are mingled with one another. Rather, everything divided and different belongs to one and the same world, which is not the world of sense.
>
> (CW 14, para. 767)

Jung's stress on the unus mundus is consistent with the idea in quantum mechanics that there are levels of reality that are outside of space and time, but which generate events that emerge into spacetime. In line with the notion that consciousness is a crucial factor in quantum measurement, Mansfield and Spiegelman (1991) suggest that just as an irreversible measurement transforms the potentiality of the quantum wave function into an actuality, reflective consciousness brings the transcendent realm into the empirical world of multiplicity: "The primordial unity of the unus mundus is shattered by reflective consciousness" (p. 285). Mansfield and Spiegelman (1989) have suggested various ways in which non-local, quantum correlations may be connected to the interconnected world view demanded by the idea of synchronicity. However, their view depends on controversial interpretations of quantum mechanics that make consciousness essential, which many physicists deny.

Jung generally talks about matter and psyche as "two different aspects of one and the same thing" (CW 8, para. 418). His sense that matter and psyche are ultimately not separable is seen in comments such as this: "somewhere our unconscious becomes material ... Somewhere there is a place where the two ends meet ... And that is the place where one cannot say whether it is matter, or what one calls psyche" (Jung, 1988, p. 441). Jung writes "we do not know whether what we on the empirical plane regard as physical may not, in the Unknown beyond our experience, be identical with what on this side of the border we distinguish from the physical as psychic" (CW 14, para. 765). As well: "Spirit and matter may well be forms of one and the same transcendental being" (CW 9i, para. 392). As he put it, "the spirit is the life of the body seen from within and the body the outward manifestation of the life of the spirit—the two being really one" (CW 10, para. 195). When Jung (CW 9i, para. 41) says that the unconscious psyche "reaches down" into the sympathetic nervous system, he seems to be merging the psyche with the material level of the nervous system as if they are not separate. He sees mind and body as "the expression of a single entity whose essential nature is not knowable ... two sides of the same coin," divided only as necessary for conscious discrimination, so that we separate "one and the same fact into two aspects, to which we illegitimately attribute an independent existence" (CW 8, para. 619). The psyche and the body have the same "underlying unitary nature" (CW 14, para. 768). We observe the same unitary reality from the outside as the material world and from the inside as the psyche. However, Jung thought that the unitary level of Being is beyond our powers of comprehension, since "in essence it is transcendental" (CW 14, para. 768). Atmanspacher sees Jung's approach as a form of dual-aspect monism (Atmanspacher, 2012a, Atmanspacher & Fuchs, 2014; Atmanspacher & Rickle, 2022), while Goodwyn (2019) believes that neutral monism is the best approach to Jungian theory (these are described on p. 34).

Some implications of Jung's work for spirituality and religion

Jung's work has important applications in the areas of spirituality and religion. Indeed, for some Jungians, his approach to spirituality is more useful and nearer to experience than the approach of the theistic traditions

(Corbett, 2011, 2019, 2021). Jung's religious attitude permeates his writing, and this is one source of mainstream resistance to his psychological theories. Although some contemporary Jungians resist the spiritual implications of Jung's work, preferring to focus on its psychotherapeutic applications, the spiritual dimension has been important to many of his followers for whom it has soteriological as well as purely psychological value.

Jung challenges traditional theism in several ways. He sees the unconscious as the source of religious experience, a notion that was anathema to both traditional religionists such as Martin Buber and to many psychoanalysts such as Eric Fromm. Although Jung does not completely equate the metaphysical God of the theistic traditions with the Self, he believes that the imagery that the Self produces cannot be distinguished from symbolism that has always "characterized and expressed the Deity" (CW 11, para. 757). Jung sees all the gods and goddesses of world religions and mythologies as manifestations of the objective psyche. These are archetypal processes that have been given local folkloric and historical names. He sees any form of numinous experience as an encounter with the objective psyche, regardless of the content of the experience. For him, only the emotional quality of the experience is important. Jung's notion of the Self as the "God within" the psyche (CW 7, para. 399) is radically different than notions of divinity inhabiting a transcendent heavenly realm. Furthermore, unlike traditional Christian accounts of divinity as only good and loving, in his *Answer to Job* Jung insists that our God-image must include a dark side that is responsible for evil and suffering (CW 11, para. 662). A further incompatibility with Christian theology is found in Jung's idea that the Self may be projected onto any local divinity and cannot be confined to Christ. Jung sees Christ as too limited an image of the Self, in part because this image is depicted as entirely benevolent, and also because it is exclusively masculine and does not include the feminine aspects of the divine. Jung also saw the imagery that arises from the unconscious as forms of revelation that may contravene traditional theological notions, an idea that makes his approach unacceptable to traditions that insist on one particular form of revelation, which is a claim based on authority. But Jung believes that "The claim to authority is naturally not in itself sufficient to establish a metaphysical truth" (CW 14, para. 785). It is true that the testimony of an inspired person is the experience of a "will transcending his consciousness," and naturally this is felt to be divine (ibid.) However, Jung "cannot see that it proves the existence of a transcendent God." Jung asserts that it is wiser "not to drag the supreme metaphysical factor into our calculations … but, more modestly, to make an unknown psychic or perhaps psychoid factor" responsible for such inspirations (CW 14, para. 786). As evidence, Jung points to the divergence of inspiration among different religious traditions, each insisting on its own unique rightness. For Jung, although the religious individual is free to "accept whatever metaphysical explanations he pleases about the origin of these images," Jung sees himself as a scientist who "cannot take heaven by storm" but must abide within the bounds of scientific interpretation (CW 12, para. 16).

Jung felt obliged to speak the language of empirical science in order for his psychology to be taken seriously. By claiming the mantle of science, he was also attempting avoid major entanglements with the custodians of traditional religion, although in this he did not fully succeed, since notables such as Martin Buber accused him of straying out of the territory of psychology into theology. However, Jung was obviously a deeply religious individual who shrewdly disguised what is in practice a psychological approach to spirituality that allows each person to find his or her personal approach to it. There is no reason for those who value his approach to continue to disguise the fact that his is a religious approach to the psyche. He points out that the psyche has an "authentic religious function" (CW 11, para. 3), which produces numinous experiences, and the psyche is "shot through with religious feelings and ideas" (CW 4, para. 781).

Metaphysical claims in Jung's *Answer to Job*

Nowhere are Jung's metaphysics clearer than in his late *Answer to Job*, where he argues that the divine has created human consciousness to act as a reflecting mirror to itself. His basic idea is that the divine is the totality of consciousness, but it is undifferentiated and requires human consciousness to differentiate the opposites within it, "in order to exist in reality" (CW 11, para. 575).

In the biblical story of Job, Jung believes that Yahweh allows Job to suffer atrocious cruelty because Yahweh is unconscious of the antinomies or opposites within itself. His behavior is the behavior of "an unconscious being" (CW 11, paras. 567, 600). There is an "unconscious split" in the divine nature (ibid., para. 623). In particular, Yahweh is unconscious of his own dark side, which was ultimately responsible for Job's suffering. God incarnates the opposites within its own nature into the human level of the psyche, and humanity must "bend to this burden ... [humanity] becomes a vessel filled with divine conflict" (para. 659). It is then the human task to differentiate the divine opposites and make them conscious within human consciousness, which renders the divine a service, since it would otherwise remain unconscious of the opposites within it. The contradictions within the God-image—at once loving, terrifying, and compassionate, but also indifferent to evil and suffering—must be symbolically resolved within the ego, in dialog with the depths of the psyche. Thus, the human-divine interaction is mutually redemptive. This process is a part of Jung's approach to the problem of suffering, which has meaning in terms of the resolution of the contradictions within the divine. As Jung put it in his essay on the Trinity, the human achievement of consciousness is "to put it metaphysically ... part of the divine life-process. In other words, God becomes manifest in the human act of reflection" (CW 11, para. 238). The idea that God created humanity to act as a reflecting consciousness is part of Jung's personal myth. Note how different is this model compared to classical notions of a self-sufficient, entirely transcendent deity that inserts itself into history from a heavenly beyond. Jung's notion is an overtly metaphysical statement, unless the word "God" refers only to the Self, or the God-image in the psyche, as Jung often insisted. However, although he tries to maintain this distinction theoretically, in his writing it is sometimes difficult to know whether he is referring to the Self or to the divine as understood traditionally.

Jung's psychology and its possible connections to quantum mechanics

In collaboration with Wolfgang Pauli, Jung was one of the first thinkers to investigate what quantum mechanics and depth psychology may have in common. The ontological implications of quantum physics are often said to have some similarities to Jung's psychology (von Franz, 1988). He believed that:

> Sooner or later nuclear physics and the psychology of the unconscious will draw closer together as both of them, independently of one another and from opposite directions, push forward into transcendental territory, the one with the concept of the atom, the other with that of the archetype.
>
> (CW 9, ii, para. 412)

In his discussion of the importance of the observer to quantum experiments, Jung writes that "the relative or partial identity of psyche and physical continuum is of the greatest importance theoretically ... by bridging over the seeming incommensurability between the physical world and the psychic" (CW 8, para. 440). Jung asked Pauli to comment on this idea, and Pauli wrote:

> the epistemological situation with regard to the concepts "conscious" and "unconscious" seems to offer a pretty close analogy to the under-mentioned "complementarity" situation in physics ... It is undeniable that the development of "microphysics" has brought the way in which nature is described in this science very much closer to that of the newer psychology.
>
> (CW 8, fn. 130, p. 229)

However, a major proviso here is that Pauli adhered to an interpretation of quantum mechanics that stressed the importance of consciousness in the collapse of the wave function, which would provide a link to psychology, but this interpretation is now widely called into question and many physicists do not think consciousness is implicated in the outcome of their experiments.

In spite of this caveat, various authors try to link quantum mechanics and depth psychology. Ponte and Schäfer suggest that the non-material levels of the archetypes emerge from a cosmic, non-empirical realm of non-material wholeness described by quantum mechanics, which they see as synonymous with Jung's unus mundus (Schäfer, 2013; Ponte & Schäfer, 2013). These authors see quantum waves as pure forms or mind-like patterns of information; they see quantum wave functions as representing the archetypes that underly physical reality. This leads these authors to support the idea that consciousness is a cosmic property. This is an appealing story but there is no way to validate it. In her discussion of the overlap of quantum mechanics and depth psychology, von Franz (1988, p. 245) points out that for Jung the archetypes are systems of psychic energy, which is consistent with the physicist's attempt to understand reality in terms of fields of energy. However, the use of the same word may only be an analogy and not a likeness.

Quantum theory tells us that hidden behind the apparently separate objects of the physical world is an entangled world in which classical locality does not apply. Writers such as Mansfield (1995) and Peat (1987) suggest that from this nonlocal dimension arise synchronistic experiences, which demonstrates how inextricably the psyche is a part of the world, and how the psyche may have nonlocal effects. Writers who try to link quantum mechanics to psychology point out that quantum entanglement implies that at some preconceptual level, apparently disparate features of the universe are connected into a unified whole, in ways that are not causal, but which may be the result of acausal order. The fact that the early Copenhagen interpretation of quantum mechanics implies a "radical departure from the causal description of nature" (Bohr, 1934, p. 84) is consistent with Jung's stress on the importance of acausal synchronistic events, which he sees as an example of an acausal level of order in nature. The separateness that we perceive between apparently disparate events may be purely a function of the limitations of our brains and sense organs. This means that apparently isolated events may be connected to other events occurring somewhere else that we know nothing about—as the theory of synchronicity describes.

Mansfield and Spiegelman (1989) link nonlocality to Jung's idea of synchronicity, but Mansfield also warns:

> It would be poor scholarship and a disservice to both physics and depth psychology to make too many easy parallels and use them as a hunting license for affirming all kinds of parapsychological phenomena. This is slippery ground. Tread with caution.
>
> (Mansfield & Spiegelman, 1989)

Notes

1 Hearnshaw (2020, p. 166) referred to Jung's "strongly mystical strains" and his "flirtations ... with occultism." Hughes (2002, p. 160) wrote that Jung's mind was "profoundly confused" and he was a "mystagogue" parading as a man of science. Rieff (1973, pp. 97–98) dismissed Jung's work as "a language of faith ... revelatory ... a private religion and an antiscience." Wilson (1984, p. 9) claimed that Jung was an occultist in disguise and a "guru of the Western world." Fromm (quoted in Wehr, 1987, p. 475) dismissed Jung as a "blend of outmoded superstition, indeterminate heathen idol-worship, and vague talk about God." Other harsh Freudian critiques were rendered by Jones (1959), who says that Jung descended into "pseudo-philosophy," and Glover (1991, p. 134), who dismissed Jung's writing as a "mishmash of oriental philosophy with bowdlerized psychology." In this context, it is worth noting that several of Freud's ideas such as the libido theory and the death instinct are not empirically provable.

2 Perhaps not realizing that the focus on empiricism is itself a philosophical position.

3 Although Jung often insists that only reports empirical facts, philosophers of science point out that there are no facts independent of interpretation and the observer's pre-existing theories and philosophical stance. Jung would assert that he tried to minimize these factors in order not to dilute the psychological validity of his observations, but he would not deny the importance of the "personal equation" or the researcher's subjectivity.

4 Although Jung often refers to Kant, especially when he wants to criticize metaphysical ideas, it has also been said that Kant's ideas are themselves a form of metaphysics that are not empirically provable.

5 Hoeller (1982) believes it would be a mistake to reject Jung's connection to the hermetic chain of esoteric thinkers with whom Jung felt an affinity, and his work should not be confined to the field of psychotherapy.

6 Nicholas of Cusa (1401–1464) believed this term to be the least imperfect way of talking about God, who is beyond the coincidence of opposites. Henderson (2010) has shown how Jung misappropriated Cusa's usage.

7 Metapsychology refers to philosophical speculation about the psyche, or speculation about the fundamental principles underlying psychological theory.

8 The term unus mundus arose in Scholastic philosophy. It describes a kind of potential plan in the mind of God before he created the world.

9 Tresan (1996, p. 400) believes that: "There is essentially no Jungian metapsychology." However, I suggest that ideas such as Jung's combination of reductive and synthetic approaches to symptoms, his belief that the psyche is a self-regulating system, combined with the soteriological aspects of his work do constitute his metapsychology. Perhaps the clearest statement of Jung's metapsychology is found in his essay on synchronicity, first published in *The interpretation of nature and the psyche* in 1955. This was a joint work by Jung and Pauli.

10 It is interesting that Freud privately maintained membership in the British and American societies for psychical research and corresponded with some psychic researchers. Early psychoanalytic interest in telepathy is described by Ullman (2011).

11 The finalistic or synthetic approach to symptoms suggests that they have teleological purpose, moving the individual in a direction that otherwise he or she might not take.

12 Here, incidentally, he notes that "The East bases itself on psychic reality, that is, upon the psyche as the main and unique condition of existence" (CW 11, para. 770).

13 Philosophical idealism comes in various forms. One version says that we cannot prove the existence of the world independently of human consciousness. This is

the position Jung often takes. A stronger version, as found in Advaita Vedānta, says that the world is identical with consciousness, or at least that consciousness is the essence of the world. Idealism argues that since we only know the world in the mind, we only know objects as they appear in our mental representation of them. It may be that matter exists, but we cannot know it except through the mind.

14 The word "archetype" is derived from the Greek root *arkhē*, meaning an origin, or beginning, and *typos*, meaning an imprint. The etymology of the word thus "presupposes an imprinter" (CW 12, para. 15)—but we do not know what this was. It implies a spiritual source. A phrase such as "intrapsychic organizing principle" does not have the religious connotation of the word "archetype," but that is the word Jung chose.

15 Jung's distinction between the archetype *an sich*, as it is in itself or in its own nature, rather than its symbolic expression in the psyche, may correspond to the way in which quantum theory suggests that physical reality emerges from a non-empirical realm of potential. Speculatively, this quantum realm might correspond to the objective psyche or to the psychoid dimension.

16 Plato believed that the physical world is less real than the ideal realm of absolute Ideas or Forms that are the perfect, spiritual essence of all things. Objects and qualities in the world are imitations of the Ideas, which are eternal and unchangeable.

17 One critique of this idea is that it only allows for variations on archaic or original archetypal themes. It does not adequately allow for creative variations on these themes or historical shifts in their expression.

18 It is important that Jung uses the word "model," since models can only approximate reality, and are always selective and incomplete. Models are often simply heuristic aids to our imagination. The model works only to the extent that it corresponds to our observations of reality; it is a symbolic and inevitably over-simplified way to think about reality. As Jung puts it, "A model does not assert that something *is* so, it simply illustrates a particular mode of observation" (CW 8, para. 381). Jung is clear that his notion of the archetype is such a model or "an auxiliary idea which can be exchanged at any time for a better formula" (CW 11, para. 460.) He protested that he was not developing a "system" (Jung, 1975, p. 192). As early as 1927 he insisted that his work was "not a Weltanschauung but a science" that provides the building material with which a Weltanschauung might be built up or torn down (CW 8, para. 730).

19 Popper believed that hypotheses can be falsified but not finally verified inductively, since they can be falsified by a single observation. Thus, the theory that "all swans are white" cannot be fully verified by any number of observations of white swans, because it is falsified by seeing one black swan.

20 Number 1 was an ordinary schoolboy, a child of the times, while number 2 was timeless, wise, spiritual, attuned to the inner world and a kind of guiding light.

21 The problem is that spacetime is a smooth constant according to general relativity theory, only warped by large masses, but quantum mechanics says that quanta are constantly changing and in motion, which means that gravity would not work the way Einstein predicted. If general relativity is correct, matter would not fluctuate constantly and we would know where matter is and its momentum, which contradicts quantum mechanics. String theory might reconcile the two theories, but it cannot be proven at the moment.

22 One of the debates in this area is exactly how close in time the events must be to qualify as synchronistic. Pauli raised this issue in various letters to Jung (e.g., Meier, 2001, p. 46). At times the meaningful inner and outer events occur virtually simultaneously, in which case the connection is clear, but it is debatable how much

time may elapse between events for them to be considered truly synchronistic. The two events are easier to notice when they occur close in time, but they may be meaningfully connected even when separated in time.

23 The discovery of meaning was very important to Jung. We see this at the beginning of his career when he tried to understand the meaning of the utterances of psychotic patients at the Burghölzli. In *Memories, dreams, reflections*, he emphasized the importance of finding meaning in suffering (Jung, 1965, p. 340). He believed that "a creation without the reflecting consciousness of man has no discernable meaning," so that "the hypothesis of latent meaning endows man with a cosmogonic significance."

Chapter 3

Possible connections between quantum mechanics and depth psychology

The twenty-six-year relationship, largely based on letters, between Jung and the quantum physicist Wolfgang Pauli significantly affected the intellectual development of both men. They wanted to expand the boundaries of their respective disciplines to discover possible links or overlaps between them, in spite of the apparent gulf between physics and psychology. To discuss the feasibility of this project, this chapter provides an overview of some quantum mechanical concepts and controversies, addresses the question of whether the view of reality suggested by quantum mechanics is relevant to psychology and psychotherapy, discusses the controversial role of consciousness in quantum mechanics, and describes some of the philosophical issues it raises.

A caution to psychologists

I must acknowledge the difficulty the psychologist faces when trying to be open to a field as complex as quantum physics, in which the psychologist has no expertise. Because of the formidable mathematics[1] involved in quantum mechanics, the best the psychologist can hope to achieve is to try to approach the physics as it has been described by physicists using symbolic and analogic language (Herbert, 1987; Becker, 2018). In this way, we can at least focus on the conceptual problems involved and the possible role of the psyche. There is a risk in this process; in recent decades there has been a great deal of misappropriation of concepts from quantum mechanics applied to other disciplines, including spirituality, social sciences, and the humanities. The extent to which observations from quantum mechanics can be applied to psychotherapy and psychology is still not clear. In part this is because the role of consciousness or the psyche of the observer in quantum mechanics is controversial. A further problem is that in spite of the considerable empirical success of quantum mechanics, there is uncertainty about what quantum mechanics actually claims about the nature of matter and how macroscopic reality is brought into being. The field is fraught with enigmas and often contradictory concepts. Quantum theory is most valuable in predicting the

DOI: 10.4324/9781032618456-3

outcome of experiments, but if one asks what the theory says about the philosophical problems involved, such as the relationship of the result of the experiments to the consciousness of the experimenter, or the question of whether a quantum level object has determinate properties independent of our observation of it, one tends to receive a "shut up and calculate" type of response.[2] Physicists prefer to deal with objective phenomena, and when the presence of an observer seems to affect the outcome of an experiment they become uncomfortable.

Quantum[3] mechanics describes the workings of the subatomic dimension of reality, out of which matter as we know it is formed. Quantum mechanics makes many strange and paradoxical claims, which often seem counter-intuitive. However, quantum theory is currently the best available theory for understanding the behavior of matter, and it is now thought to have super-seded Newtonian mechanics, which today is seen as a special case encom-passed by the wider scope of quantum mechanics. Many physicists are content to use quantum theory for its practical value without investigating what it means about the nature of physical reality, which quantum theory tells us is not what it appears to be. Perhaps because of a resistance to the challenging philosophical implications of this theory, for some years the conceptual or foundational problems at the core of quantum physics were ignored by physicists. However, several philosophers and philosophically oriented physicists now take an interest in them (Lewis, 2016). It is clear that the paradoxes at the heart of quantum mechanics cannot be resolved using our usual forms of logic, where an object exists irrespective of how it is observed; at the quantum level, observation or measurement makes a crucial difference.

The technical issues surrounding different interpretations of quantum mechanics are very complex, and many fundamental conceptual issues remain unsolved and controversial. It is difficult to find an approach to any major contended area that would meet the agreement of all physicists and philosophers. This situation is a major limitation, but a connection between the psyche and quantum physics remains a possibility because of the possi-ble—but controversial–role of consciousness and the participation of the experimenter in the outcome of experiments. However, consciousness is a problem for physicists because it has non-physical characteristics: it cannot be well defined; it is private; it cannot be measured; and it has intangible properties, so there is considerable resistance to acknowledging its impor-tance. Modern materialistic science is naturalistic and averse to the idea that there may be a psychological influence on physical experiments, partly because it is impossible to imagine how this might happen. For many physi-cists therefore, consciousness is something they would like to ignore, as did classical Newtonian physics. Most physicists would prefer to get rid of the role of the observer entirely and rely on instruments and the mathematics of quantum mechanics as described by the quantum wave function.

The quantum wave function

A wave function is a mathematical formalism, a description in mathematical terms, that describes information about a quantum system such as its state and properties.[4] Quantum-level particles such as photons or electrons are represented mathematically by a spread-out probability wave, named after its discoverer, Erwin Schrödinger. Before the quantum object is measured it seems to exist as a potential in all possible states that can be measured, a phenomenon known as superposition. Superposition means the wave function has different possibilities of manifestation in space-time, or it is a combination of all possibilities. According to the classical Copenhagen[5] interpretation of quantum mechanics, the wave function only "collapses" or restructures itself into a particle with a specific location when it is measured.[6] Until it is measured, the system appears to exist in multiple potential states at the same time. The collapse is sudden, and its development is nondeterministic, meaning that the exact state after collapse cannot be predicted. In a way, before measurement, the quantum is spread out in space and time rather than being at a single point. There is considerable debate about exactly what constitutes a measurement, how the collapse occurs, how it is controlled, whether collapse is the correct way to describe what happens when a measurement is made, whether the consciousness of the experimenter is a factor in the process, and how to describe the nature of the transitional state during the process of measurement.[7] Unobserved quantum phenomena do not obey the spacetime constraints of classical particles.

Collapse of the wave function involves randomness, discontinuity, and probability. When a system is observed or measured, it seems to behave randomly rather than deterministically. The experimenter can predict the relative probability of particular outcomes with high precision but cannot be sure exactly which one will occur, or why one particular outcome occurs on a specific occasion. The system seems to "choose" between the available alternatives, leading some observers to suggest (in a modified form of panpsychism) that there is a primitive or protomental form of consciousness at the microphysical level (Klemm et al., 2008).

When a photon appears as a particle, it does so because the measurement being carried out is geared to observing the characteristics of particles.[8] When collapse occurs, the particle immediately (mysteriously) disappears from everywhere else it could have been before the event, so there is only one defined outcome. Information about previous possible states is lost. Perhaps there are unknown factors that would make the evolution of the collapse completely predictable. It is possible that the outcome of a measurement reflects what actually exists, or measurement may only fix one possibility of an indeterminate state that had multiple possibilities of expression. Without measurement, a quantum event only has the potential to exist in the observer's spacetime. If the event is not measured, it will continue to propagate through space-time until it is observed. Prior to the measurement there is no way to know exactly how or where the quantum will materialize.

Exactly what it means to exist in a state of superposition is not understood and might represent the limits of human understanding. An additional problem is that it is not clear exactly what it is that is waving; the wave equation does not necessarily describe anything material such as a wave moving through water; it describes the probability of finding a photon or electron at a particular place. We do not know the underlying ontological nature of quantum waves. It is not clear whether the wave is only a mathematical construct, a representation of the probability of a particular event happening, or whether it is a real physical entity. Or perhaps there is no physical reality underlying the wave, in which case all we can know is the result of measurements. For some approaches to quantum theory, the wave is a link between consciousness and the physical world because the observer decides how to measure it, but for many physicists the observer's consciousness has no influence on the outcome of a measurement, which can be made with an instrument.

The quantum wave function is not a physical object in the ordinary sense; it is a mathematical description of a probability, which consists of a range of possible positions, velocities, spin, and charge, all at the same time. There has been a debate between physicists who believe that the wave function is ontologically real, in which case it actually represents the quantum state, and those such as Niels Bohr and Werner Heisenberg, who see it only epistemologically, as a description of what we can know about the quantum state. For these theorists, quantum mechanics is a practical tool for making predictions, not a theory of the nature of reality, which may be a construct determined by our observations of it. According to Heisenberg, the wave function is not a wave in the sense of a physical substance; it represents a change in our knowledge of the system. Bohr wrote: "In our description of nature the purpose is not to disclose the real essence of phenomena but only to track down as far as possible relations between the multifold aspects of our experience" (Bohr, 1934, p. 18). That is, in the original Copenhagen interpretation, quantum theory cannot describe a world independent of human observers. This interpretation is incomplete because it does not describe what happens when a measurement is made. The theory requires a "cut" or boundary between the quantum system being observed and the observer or the instrument doing the measurement but does not say exactly where the cut occurs and does not give any reason for the sudden change to the wave function when it is measured. This attitude avoids the metaphysical issue involved, such as the ontological nature of the wave, and this problem cannot be firmly settled at the moment. (There is considerable debate about how to interpret Bohr's philosophy of quantum theory.)

Fields and particles

At the quantum level matter is much more subtle than it is at the macroscopic level. Quantum physicists are not sure about the fundamental nature of reality at the quantum level because they do not know the exact nature of particles and fields in the quantum realm. Particles such as electrons can behave like waves, and fields like light can behave like particles. Particles are objects that have a definite location. Fields (like gravity) are spread out through space, with a particular value at any point. Some theorists believe that only fields exist; a quantum particle is the local excitation of a field. Hobson (2013) demonstrates the case that fields are the fundamental constituents of reality. In this view, a field is a property of an area of space that manifests itself as a physical effect. When the field oscillates it is known as a wave, which is a disturbance in the shape of a medium. There are many different types of field, and some physicists believe they are all aspects of an as yet undiscovered single, unified field. When fields are observed or measured, they may appear as particles such as electrons. However, there is no such thing as a separate particle; electrons are ripples in an electron field, a photon is a disturbance in a photon field; the disturbance actually is the electron or photon. Thus, there is no radical distinction between particles and fields, although it seems likely that quantized fields are the fundamental ontological ground of the universe and particles are derivatives of fields. Matter is an emergent property of the interaction of fields.

We have mental images of fields and particles, but we do not know what they actually are in their essential nature. It is not even clear whether they are separate things or only relationships between things. In some accounts of quantum mechanics such as that of Carlo Rovelli (2021), relationships are the fundamental building blocks of the universe. Relationships are all that exist. Objects are not fundamental.[9] In Rovelli's interpretation of quantum mechanics, every property of the world is seen as relative to an observer. There are no absolute physical quantities, only relational properties in the context of an observation. Observation creates a world that is relative to the observer alone, not to others. We live in our own observational worlds. There is no privileged, realist view and no absolute physical properties, only contextual properties. However, it is reasonable to assume that we live in a consensually agreed upon reality in which different observational worlds are consistent with each other. Yet another view sees properties as the only fundamental category; what we call a thing is actually a bundle of properties such as color and shape. Writing about this approach, Kuhlmann (2013) describes an electron as a bundle of properties including mass, charge, spin, position, and velocity. A particle is the collection of its specific properties.

The Copenhagen interpretation of quantum mechanics

The approach to quantum physics derived by Bohr and Heisenberg is known as the Copenhagen interpretation, which has been the standard model of the quantum world since the late 1920s. It was not seriously challenged for several decades. Today this interpretation is less influential than it has been, and there are several ways to understand it. There is little agreement about what this approach to quantum theory postulates to exist at the fundamental level of reality. The theory is typically used only as a way of mathematically predicting the result of experiments, with no commitment to any underlying ontology. At the moment there are more than a dozen influential interpretations of quantum mechanics and a range of minority interpretations.

Typically, the Copenhagen interpretation is understood to say that an objective determination of the nature of a quantum object cannot be made until it is measured. The experimenter decides whether to measure the quantum state as either a wave or a particle.[10] It is not clear how quantum level objects exist independently of our observations of them; perhaps only the observed properties of a quantum level object exist. An observation or measurement occurs whenever a quantum-level object interacts with a macroscopic instrument, for example when a photon lands on a piece of sensitive photographic film. In the traditional view, the macroscopic realm is described by classical physics, and quantum level reality is governed by the Schrödinger equation, which gives probabilistic information about a quantum system. Bohr separated these two levels, but today quantum mechanics is increasingly applied to larger objects than was hitherto possible. We do not notice quantum effects at the macroscopic level because they are only detectable with special instruments.

For several of the founders of the Copenhagen approach, quantum physics is only an instrument for calculating the probability of the result of an experiment. The question is whether probability is inherent in quantum systems, or even a part of the deep nature of nature, or whether probability is only epistemological, a reflection of our lack of knowledge. Heisenberg (1958a) believed that rather than telling us the nature of an objective reality, quantum mechanics only gives us a description of it. Bohr[11] is also reported to have said that there is no quantum world as such, only "an abstract quantum description" (quoted in Herbert, 1987, p. 17). In that case, physics tells us what we can say about nature based on the way we study it, rather than giving us knowledge of what nature is. Because the property that is observed depends on the physicist's method of observation, one way the theory has been explained is to say that there is no deep reality; reality is created by our observation of it. The physicist John Wheeler restated this idea by saying that "no elementary phenomenon is a phenomenon until it is an observed phenomenon" (Wheeler & Zurek, 1983, p. 204). For him, the observed universe appears according to the way questions are asked of it. The form the universe takes is a matter of perspective. This idea dissolves or at least blurs the subject–object distinction. The alternative view is that this complementarity is a feature of the thing observed rather than in the observer.

The Copenhagen interpretation of quantum mechanics is often said to be incompatible with ordinary materialism because of the role it attributes to conscious observation. The Copenhagen interpretation renounces strict realism in favor of what can be calculated mathematically. Some physicists believe that the question of what exactly is going on at the quantum level prior to observation cannot be answered. Because this theory predicts only the probability that an object will be found in a specific region, at the quantum level nature seems to be intrinsically random. In the standard understanding of the Copenhagen interpretation, there are no deterministic explanations of reality at the microphysical level because it can only be described statistically, mathematically, and probabilistically. Max Born (who developed the statistical interpretation of the wave function) and the physicist von Neumann believed that it was impossible to develop a deterministic interpretation of quantum physics (Born, 1949; von Neumann, 1955 [1932]). In their view, the observer has become what Wheeler and Zurek (1983) referred to as a participator in the universe because the consciousness of the observer brings the universe into existence. Although Wheeler believed that we can no longer say that there is a world independent of our observation of it, he also wrote that consciousness "has nothing to do with the quantum process" itself, and although meaning is important it is a "separate part of the story, important but not to be confused with 'quantum phenomenon'" (ibid., p. 196). Another influential group of physicists such as Albert Einstein, Louis de Broglie, Erwin Schrödinger, and David Bohm have been scientific realists—they believe there is a real world that is independent of the way we observe it. In this view, we have not yet discovered the causal mechanisms that determine the behavior of matter at the quantum level, and the reason physicists invoke ideas such as randomness is simply due to lack of knowledge. We have an incomplete description of reality. In this view, randomness is an epistemic approach to reality, not necessarily an ontological feature of reality.

In the early years of quantum mechanics, many physicists, including Einstein, insisted that quantum mechanics must be incomplete because of unknown, currently unobservable hidden variables that in principle would allow the physicist to predict the outcome of an experiment and restore objectivity and determinism. One such alternative to randomness is David Bohm's theory, which suggests that particles have pilot waves that determine the particles' motion, so that particles behave in a predictable manner and have a definite position whether or not they are being observed. Bohm's theory is objective and deterministic and does not need non-material elements such as consciousness. However, pilot waves are undetectable. Today, opinion is shifting towards the view that randomness is a deep property of nature and there are no hidden variables. The quantum level of reality is characterized by indeterminacy because quantum fields do not have precise positions or velocities.

Because the Copenhagen interpretation of quantum mechanics stresses irreducible randomness in the laws of nature, it sees epistemological uncertainty as an inherent property of the microphysical world. Another example of this uncertainty is Heisenberg's uncertainty principle, which says we cannot accurately know both a particle's speed and position at the same time. The act of observation of an electron when it is hit by a photon alters the electron's momentum. That is, the properties of the particle are affected by the act of measurement. Initially, Heisenberg thought that uncertainty was an epistemic problem due to our inability to measure the electron, but he and Bohr eventually decided on a model in which uncertainty is inherent in the nature of the electron; precise momentum and position do not exist simultaneously. Measurement selects a single position from a range of possibilities. Many possibilities then become one physical reality; human observation changes the ontological reality of what might have been a wave into a particle. There seems to be no way to know what a particle is doing in between two consecutive measurements. Bohr believed that the main issue is indeterminacy rather than uncertainty.[12]

For some decades, the Copenhagen approach was standard, as if it were the only possible way to understand the quantum dimension. In part this was because it was endorsed by John von Neumann, a towering figure of the time. However, many people rejected this interpretation because it does not allow a predictable explanation for the existence of the real world, which presumably exists even when it is not being observed. Quantum physics works extremely well at the level of prediction, but it is difficult to say what it says about the deep nature of the world.

If a subatomic particle is only a potential before it is observed, how do we explain the existence of macroscopic, solid objects that are made of these particles? This is something of an enigma, which is why some theorists believe that quantum theory is not a complete description of what is really happening even though quantum mechanics works very well in practice. One response is to point to the phenomenon of decoherence, which means the loss of the quantum properties of a quantum object because of interaction with the macroscopic environment, which is a kind of observation. Decoherence does not fully explain how the macroscopic environment becomes definite, and so does not solve the measurement problem. It is debatable whether decoherence explains the role of observation in localizing our macroscopic experience of reality. Most physicists are unwilling to discard the idea that the objects they study exist and behave independently of the way they are observed.

Pauli and Jung

Although many hopes were built on the prospect that the consciousness of the observer plays a role in quantum mechanics, the nature of the relationship between consciousness and physical reality remains controversial. If consciousness is important, the psyche would be relevant to quantum mechanics. The possibility that physics and psychology, or matter and psyche, might find common ground gripped the attention of Jung and the physicist Wolfgang Pauli, as we see from the letters between them, which continued for 26 years between 1932 and 1958 (Meier, 2001). Pauli was involved in the development of the early Copenhagen interpretation of quantum mechanics, which recognizes the integral status of the observer in quantum experiments, in contrast to the classical attempt to isolate the physicist's subjectivity in the study of matter. Like Jung, Pauli believed that deep connections must exist between the psyche and matter, in his words "because otherwise the human mind would not be able to discover concepts which fit nature at all" (quoted in Gieser, 2004, p. viii). He was therefore committed to trying to understand the role of the observer's consciousness in quantum mechanics, and the relationship between subjective and objective reality.

Pauli greatly influenced Jung's thinking on the subject of physics and psychology (Zabriski, 1995; Card, 1991a, 1991b). Both men were concerned with the possibility of building bridges between these disciplines, or even finding a unified basis for them, especially in areas such as synchronicity, which seems to offer what Jung called a "contact point" between these fields (Meier, 2001, p. 128; Atmanspacher & Primas, 1996). Pauli (1955, p. 210) wrote that "It would be most satisfactory if physics and psyche could be seen as complementary aspects of the same reality." In a letter, Pauli writes that for him "the relationship between physics and psychology is that of a mirror image" (Meier, 2001, p. 165).[13] Jung believed that physics and psychology have "a genuine and authentic relationship of complementarity" (CW 8, para. 440). He suggested that the common ground shared by physics and psychology will be found in the fact that numbers are organizing principles of both the inner and outer world. Marie-Louise von Franz further developed this idea in her *Number and time* (von Franz, 1974).

In a 1953 letter to Pauli, Jung wrote that only in the psyche of the individual can the "essential identity of Idea and Matter be experienced and perceived" (Meier, 2001, p. 100). He believed that psyche and matter are "indistinguishable in conceptual terms, which makes them *virtually identical*; only on a secondary level are they different, as different aspects of Being" (ibid., p. 126; emphasis in original). In a letter to Jung, Pauli wrote that he too saw mind and matter as "two aspects of one and the same abstract fact" (ibid., p. 159). He believed that "now that matter has also become an abstract *invisible reality* for the modern physicist, the prospects for a psychophysical monism have become much more favorable" (ibid. p. 87). In a letter quoted by Atmanspacher, (2012b, p. 6), Pauli suggested that the relationship between psyche and physis "could be conceived as complementary aspects of the same reality." (This dual-aspect approach to the mind–body question sounds like Spinoza's monism, discussed on p. 34.) Complementarity means that both descriptions are necessary to describe the situation, even if they are incompatible in some respects. Perhaps the problem with the mirror analogy is that the image in a mirror does not influence the object reflected, but mind and body seem to influence each other.

Thanks to his relationship with Jung, Pauli realized the importance of the unconscious and its archetypal dimension in the pursuit of empirical knowledge. We see this especially in his essay on Kepler (Jung and Pauli, 1955), where he describes archetypes as irrational ordering principles in the unconscious that act as a bridge between sense perceptions and ideas because they transcend the matter-psyche distinction. They also link the outer world and consciousness. Pauli saw archetypes as a necessary presupposition for developing scientific theories. He believed that an entirely objective description of the world is impossible because inaccessible psychological processes in the unconscious affect observation and theory formation.

Pauli (1994a, p. 41) pointed out that although consciousness logically requires a "cut" between subject and object, the boundary, or the position of the cut is "to a certain extent arbitrary." He also noted that every observation that makes something conscious "constitutes an interference with the unconscious contents that is in principle uncontrollable; this limits the objective character of the reality of the unconscious and invests reality with a certain subjectivity" (ibid., p. 42). Because of the role of the experimenter in the outcome of quantum mechanical experiments, in the light of his understanding of the Copenhagen interpretation of quantum mechanics, Pauli wrote that "the state of an object is not assumed any longer to remain independent of the way in which the possible sources of information about the object are irrevocably altered by observation" (ibid., p. 33). That is, there cannot be a purely objective observer; the observer creates "a new state of the observed system" (Pauli, 1994b [1954], p. 33). This also applies to our study of the unconscious, because,

> every bringing into consciousness, i.e., observation, constitutes an interference with the unconscious contents that is in principle uncontrollable; this limits the objective character of the reality of the unconscious and invests reality with a certain subjectivity.
>
> (Pauli, 1994b [1954], p. 42)

Pauli had strongly held philosophical views (Laurikainen, 1987). He was concerned to identify principles of order in the universe, and he was fascinated by the possibility of a shared background that orders both the psyche and matter. He wondered if it would be possible to develop a "neutral" language to describe both the psyche and matter (Meier, 2001, p. 82), which, if they could be joined, would help to heal an important cultural split.

Pauli believed that the advent of quantum mechanics had undermined belief in the rational nature of reality and also in the determinism and strict causality of classical physics, because the laws of quantum physics are probabilistic. At the quantum level, it is only possible to find statistical values for physical events, but not individual values, which are not predictable. There is no rational description for an individual quantum event, such as the decay of a radioactive atom, only for the average behavior of a large number of comparable events. To Pauli therefore, the unpredictable scattering of events around a mean suggests that reality itself is irrational. (Perhaps nonrational would be a better term.) He associated irrationality in part with the existence of the unconscious, because of which science cannot be entirely separated from the subjectivity of the scientist, which is one reason he thought that physics and psychology cannot be fully separated. He believed that the irrational nature of reality has been repressed in modern times. The typical counterargument is that statistical calculations are themselves rational, so if nature obeys statistical laws, that does not mean reality is irrational. Pauli might counter that this rationality only applies to theory, and when theory is applied to experimental results, irrationality is found because individual events cannot be predicted unambiguously. The Heisenberg uncertainty principle[14] puts limits on our capacity to describe reality; our attempts at rational descriptions of reality are always incomplete. Furthermore, a rational description of a particle should not contain contradictory properties, such as being both a wave and a particle at the same time, so in Pauli's mind, complementarity presupposes the irrational nature of reality (Laurikainen, 1990).

In a previously unpublished essay (Meier, 2001, p. 192), Pauli suggests that concepts in physics might be symbolically represented in the unconscious. For example, he reports a dream in which: "Brass tones are engraved on a metal plate." He associated brass with timeless indestructibility, which is a common mythic association, and the tones with music and feeling, which physics cannot express. The tones are also related to physics because tones are an acoustic phenomenon that Pauli linked to the ancient idea of the music of the spheres (he was reading Kepler at the time).[15] The dream suggests an imprint of the archetype on matter. In the same paper (ibid., p. 194), he suggests that *"psychic contents, and hence archetypes too, only alter because they are being observed*, i.e., as the result of an intervention on the part of human consciousness" (emphasis in original). He then offers a further dream in which science and psychology are reconciled using mathematical symbols. His underlying point is that "physis and psyche are indivisibly linked 'archetypally.'" Like Jung, Pauli believes that reality includes both the inner and outer worlds, and the archetypes form a connecting link between them. This idea has important implications; if matter and psyche form a whole, complementary to each other as Pauli (1994a, 1994b) suggested, we cannot explain the psyche solely in terms of the body or brain.

In his essay on Kepler, Pauli (1955) notes the influence of archetypal ideas on science. He saw Jung's work as "serious evidence that what is developing is indicative of a close fusion of psychology with the scientific experience of the processes in the material physical world" (Meier, 2001, p. 32). Jung also believed that: "Sooner or later nuclear physics and the psychology of the unconscious will draw closer together as both of them, independently of one another and from opposite directions, push forward into transcendental territory" (CW 9ii, para. 412). I should acknowledge that the average physicist would resist the notion that he or she is working in anything other than ordinary material territory.

In his correspondence with Jung (Meier, 2001), Pauli stresses the importance of wholeness. He saw matter, spirit, physics, and psychology as complementary aspects of reality, and not separable. Unlike many physicists therefore, Pauli acknowledges the importance of spirit, and he realized that contemporary physics had ignored feelings, morality, and values. Like Jung, Pauli saw the mind–body question as centrally important, so that physics and psychology are complementary sciences. Both men were interested in the discovery of a natural principle that would include quantum phenomena, synchronicity, and meaning. They were both searching for a philosophy of nature that would abolish the boundary between physics and psychology. If this were possible it would greatly increase the importance of synchronicity.

An important caveat is that Pauli's attempt to integrate depth psychology and quantum mechanics may have been in part related to his unresolved transference to Jung, reflecting an unconscious desire to bring them closer. Or perhaps there was an unconscious competitive element between them. From a practical point of view, as Peat (1987) points out, Pauli and Jung never could achieve a final unification of psyche and matter, and that remains a goal. Their project largely hinges on the questions of whether consciousness is truly involved with phenomena at the quantum level and whether synchronistic events express a matter-psyche connection. Pauli clearly adhered to a relatively subjectivist interpretation of quantum mechanics, which has the potential to make the psyche relevant to this field. At the time of their correspondence, the role of consciousness in quantum mechanics was considered to be important by several physicists. Today, however, this idea is widely challenged.

Even though no less a physicist than Wolfgang Pauli saw the importance of quantum mechanics for philosophy and psychology, mainstream psychology and much psychotherapy training have largely avoided the important philosophical questions raised by quantum mechanics. For example, in most but not all its interpretations, quantum mechanics undermines determinism and raises important questions about the relationship between the observer and that which is observed. The quantum world is characterized by indeterminism, interconnectedness, and non-locality while the macroscopic world is characterized by determinism, locality, and apparent separateness. Which of these characteristics is true of the psyche, and in what situations and at what level? Perhaps the characteristics of the quantum realm are more applicable to the unconscious than to the realm of the ego.

Many psychologists avoid these issues, partly because of their conceptual difficulties and partly due to inertia and tradition. The psychologist who adheres to research methodology in line with classical (Newtonian, pre-quantum) physics can reasonably argue that quantum effects are not noticeable at the macroscopic level of our everyday experience and cannot necessarily be extrapolated to the macroscopic level. However, quantum effects within the brain may affect our psychology in unknown ways. There is an often-discussed possibility that quantum processes in the brain are responsible for consciousness (Penrose, 1987, Stapp, 2011, 2014). However, we must be cautious about applying quantum physical principles to the psyche or to the human condition in general, since we do not know to what extent these domains are incommensurable. The possible application of quantum principles to practical psychology and psychotherapy remains to be worked out. It is not yet clear how processes such as indeterminism, nonlocality, and randomness are relevant to psychology, but synchronicity suggests that acausality is an important factor.

The measurement question: is consciousness necessary?

In the twentieth century, the consciousness of an observer seemed to make an entry into physics in both quantum mechanics and relativity theory. The theory of relativity says that the measurement of space and time is different for observers in different frames of reference. However, the important factors are the frame of reference or the state of motion of the observer relative to other observers, not the observer's consciousness per se. An automated device would suffice to record space-time dilation[16] in a high-speed rocket. So here, the consciousness of the observer is clearly not involved.

The controversial view that consciousness is important in determining the outcome of quantum mechanical experiments arose in the early years of quantum mechanics, in part because unobserved quantum phenomena are radically different than observed phenomena. At the moment a quantum wave function is observed or measured, what were previously many possibilities becomes *either* a wave *or* a particle. Accordingly, some of the early theorists of the Copenhagen interpretation, such as Heisenberg and Pauli, had a subjectivist account of quantum mechanics that made the experimenter's consciousness essential in determining the outcome of an experiment. Physicists such as von Neumann (1955 [1932]) suggested that human consciousness is an integral part of the measurement process in quantum mechanics. Consciousness and human choices seemed to enter into the quantum level processes that appear to us as macroscopic empirical phenomena. At the very least, quantum phenomena and the observer seemed to be an inseparable whole. However, many people who hoped that the role of consciousness might join quantum mechanics and psychology have become disappointed. Most quantum physicists today do not subscribe to the idea that consciousness is a factor in the outcome of quantum mechanical experiments, and most believe that there is an objective physical world outside the human mind and independent of it. These physicists believe that they affect the quantum system by means of the macroscopic instrument with which they measure it, not because of their consciousness. An observation only requires the irreversible recording of observation by an instrument, whether or not the result is seen by a conscious observer.

Physicists who do see a role for consciousness rely on the fact that, unless it is observed, a quantum system seems to have no definitive properties. For example, whether a photon appears as a wave or particle depend on how the experimenter decides to measure it (Rosenblum & Kuttner, 2011). Because the wave function is said to collapse in the act of measurement, selecting one of various possible outcomes, the experimenter's conscious choice seems to be an integral aspect of the process of observation. However, although it seems that the observer's choice about whether to observe the electron as a wave or particle makes a difference, in practice the choice could be made randomly and arbitrarily by an automated mechanical device. People who insisted on the role of consciousness in determining the outcome of an experiment were unable to answer questions such as whether an animal's consciousness would be sufficient, or how quantum wave collapse occurred in the long span of time before human consciousness appeared. No one has any idea *how* consciousness could interact with the wave form, assuming this is more than simply a mathematical reality. The experimenter's role may be purely passive rather than creative. Physicists who object to the role of consciousness prefer a completely physical and objectivist interpretation of their experiments. For example, Bunge (2006) strongly objects to the idea that electrons may not exist until they are observed or that they lack intrinsic properties but only acquire the properties with which the experimenter endows them.

It is not clear exactly what constitutes a measurement or an observation. Measurement in quantum mechanics may be synonymous with any type of interaction, either with a measuring instrument *or* with the consciousness of the physicist. If the act of measurement "creates" a particle, it is debatable at what moment this occurs—whether this happens when the particle reaches a detector that records the result, or when the experimenter looks at the result. People who believe that human consciousness is necessary for collapse to happen believe that the consciousness of the observer who reads the output of the detector is the final stage that collapses the wave function and creates the particle. However, because observations are carried out by macroscopic instruments, many physicists believe that the collapse of the quantum wave occurs when the instrument registers it, and not when the experimenter later reads the instrument. In that case, consciousness was not involved in the collapse. Probably most contemporary physicists believe that consciousness or measurement is not the only way to trigger the collapse of the wave function; interaction with another particle or an instrument may also do so. It is not known how the collapse of the wave function occurs, but most physicists assume that some objective physical event is responsible.

The problem is that if consciousness is not physical, we cannot conceive how it could interact with the physical world. Yet physicists such as John Wheeler (1997) argued that the presence of conscious observers collapses the wave function, thus allowing the universe to exist—which might imply it did not exist before human consciousness appeared. As the astronomer Martin Rees is reported to have said: "The universe exists because we are aware of it" (quoted in Rosenblum & Kuttner, 2011, p. 257). If consciousness is involved, part of the problem would be to understand how the universe existed before it was being observed. Many contemporary quantum physicists insist that consciousness cannot be necessary to make the location of a quantum object an actuality, in part because quantum processes have been going on since the Big Bang without being observed. Physical reality existed for billions of years before conscious observers appeared.[17] To deal with this objection Manousakis (2006) postulates a universal stream of consciousness that contains all individual streams of consciousness. This sounds akin to the Upaniṣadic notion of the ontological primacy of Pure Consciousness, which is the eternal ground of reality.

If consciousness is involved in the appearance of a wave or particle, the boundary between mind and matter is then blurred or, for some idealist thinkers, it is non-existent; the mind is an inseparable part of nature, not independent of it. If it is true that the consciousness of the observer affects the outcome of quantum level experiments, the quantum level is a bridge or place of contact between consciousness and matter. In this view, one cannot separate subjectivity and what used to be thought of as an objective material world. The important caveat here is that about half the mainstream interpretations of quantum mechanics do not require the role of a conscious observer. We have no idea what consciousness is, and no idea how the quantum wave collapses, so we are explaining a mystery with another mystery. Furthermore, according to a strict interpretation of this theory, a human observer would only exist when he or she is being observed, leading to an infinite regress unless the observer observes himself. The central claim that understanding quantum mechanics *requires* a conscious observer has therefore been roundly discounted by many physicists who believe it is based on misunderstandings and distortions of quantum mechanics. These theorists believe that interaction with a detector leads to decoherence before conscious observation occurs (Nauenberg, 2007, p. 1612; Becker, 2018). Yu and Nicolić (2011) describe an experimental arrangement in which the collapse of the wave function is dissociated from any conscious representation of the outcome of the measurement, and the human observer has no special role in this process. Sepetyi (2018) reviews and refutes the claim that the consciousness of a human observer is necessary for the collapse of the quantum wave into a classical particle. He insists that "quantum mechanical collapses are [a] matter of some objective physical conditions rather than of conscious observation" (p. 104). The convincing work of physicists such as Zurek (1991) and Carpenter and Anderson (2006) strongly suggests that "measurement" has nothing to do with human beings; it has to do with the interaction of quantum events and the macroscopic environment, for example when an electron hits a viewing screen and is detected. Its precise position is not affected by whether a human being observes it. Some physicists postulate that collapse can occur spontaneously without measurement or conscious observation. Gravity is another proposed candidate for quantum state reduction. If the role of consciousness in the outcome of a quantum experiment is finally discounted, the promise of finding a unifying principle between psyche and matter is diminished. This means that quantum mechanics may not offer the kind of overlap of psychology and physics, or psyche and matter, that Jung and Pauli hoped for.

If the macroscopic measuring apparatus is the significant factor in the collapse of the wave function, no human involvement is necessary. It is true that a conscious observer had to choose the experimental setup, but once the observer has chosen the design, no further consciousness may be necessary. It is important to note that although the experimenter choses either to find a particle or a wave, it is not certain that the system possessed that property before the experiment was performed. Somehow, the mind of the experimenter and the physical experiment are a combined psychophysical system. Importantly however, although the experimenter is an integral component of the situation, he cannot control the outcome, so he does not actually determine reality.

In spite of the controversy around the role of consciousness, various important physicists still embrace the idea that consciousness collapses the wave function (Rosenblum & Kuttner, 2011). For them, the world does not exist until it is observed (Kastrup et al., 2018). That is why in 1930 James Jeans wrote that "the universe begins to look more like a great thought than a great machine" (Jeans, 1930 [2020]). Arthur Eddington (1939, p. 151) wrote that "The universe is of the nature of a 'thought or sensation in a universal Mind.'" Max Planck is reported to have said "I regard consciousness as fundamental. I regard matter as derivative from consciousness."[18] Erwin Schrödinger believed that "Consciousness cannot be accounted for in physical terms. For consciousness is absolutely fundamental. It cannot be accounted for in terms of anything else" (Moore, 1994, p. 181.) Lanza's concept of biocentrism suggests that "life and consciousness are fundamental to our understanding of the universe," and reality requires the presence of a conscious observer (Lanza, 2009, p. 2). These remarks sound remarkably like Vedāntic notions that Consciousness is the root and substance of reality. If human consciousness really is a major factor in the outcome of quantum experiments, we are inextricably connected to the reality we are trying to understand. However, the exact role of consciousness and the way it affects the outcome of the measurement remains uncertain.

Physicists often resist attributing an essential role to consciousness because they are trained to search for objective descriptions of the physical universe, without making claims about the nature of ultimate reality. There is a concern that if consciousness plays a crucial role in our experience of reality, it would be impossible to prove the existence of a real world outside the mind, raising the problem of solipsism, the difficulty of proving that there are other minds. It is arguable that if reality does not exist independently of the observer, we could each create our own universe, and shared knowledge would be harder to obtain. The alternative, preferred by most physicists, is adherence to scientific realism, the idea that science describes a literal, real world that exists independently of the mind, and scientific theories increasingly approach the truth about this world. Those who do believe that the experimenter's consciousness plays a part in the observation of quantum level events insist that the crucial importance of a conscious observer is consistent with the experimental evidence, which tells us that matter does not appear in a form independent of an observer.

Physicists who embrace the idea that the consciousness of the observer is important are often accused of being too mystical or anti-scientific, as if "science" automatically implies materialistic monism. However, since matter arises from the motion of quantum fields, if consciousness is a field one could speculate about a connection between matter and consciousness in the form of interacting fields, or that they are both aspects of a unified field such as the quantum vacuum. However, the nature of this interaction is unknown, and we have no idea how this field might transmit information, or, as some spiritual traditions believe, how consciousness manifests itself as the world.

An important possible connection between quantum physics and depth psychology is that the wave function is a potential form, and so is the archetype, which has led to the suggestion that they are both aspects of the same realm. Schäfer (2013) and Ponte and Schäfer (2013) refer to this as the realm of nonempirical, cosmic potentiality. It seems to correspond to Jung's notion of the unus mundus or the psychoid dimension, out of which synchronistic events emerge. It is as if events that emerge into spacetime originate in a dimension outside of spacetime. The correspondence between Jung's notion of the archetypes as pure forms that emanate from a unitary realm of existence is strikingly similar to the quantum physical idea that nonmaterial forms or wave functions emanate from a deeper reality in the form of physical reality. It is a short step to see an analogy between the archetype-as-such and the realm of quantum potential. These authors therefore describe the quantum wave function as the archetype underlying physical reality.

In summary, it seems at best not proven that human consciousness is responsible for the collapse of the wave function, not to mention the fact that we don't know what consciousness itself is, and it is impossible to imagine how consciousness could create physical reality. Nevertheless, a great deal of speculation has been built on this assumption.

Alternatives to the Copenhagen interpretation

Because the Copenhagen interpretation raised so many questions, a range of alternatives has arisen that try to explain quantum effects without sacrificing the accuracy of quantum measurements. There have been several attempts to get rid of the need for the role of consciousness in quantum mechanics, in order to maintain a physicalist ontology. One such attempt is the idea of hidden variables that have not yet been detected and may even be impossible to detect. Another is the many-worlds interpretation of quantum mechanics, which also eliminates the need for a conscious observer. In this model, although it appears as if a waveform collapses to form a particular outcome, there is actually no collapse into either a wave or a particle. All possible outcomes manifest themselves, branching deterministically into as many entirely new universes as there are possibilities. No observer is necessary for this to happen. This means that when the experimenter sees a particular result, in another universe there is a copy of that experimenter who sees the opposite result. However, we cannot detect these other worlds. What causes the universe to split is unknown. One advantage of this model is that it abandons the epistemological and metaphysical aspects of quantum theory and simply relies on mathematics. This model has many supporters, but its disadvantage is that it is entirely unprovable, and the idea that possibilities seem to branch into an infinite number of universes seems incredible. It means that people and objects are constantly dividing into innumerable copies, leading to questions about personal identity.

Purely epistemic interpretations of quantum waves only interpret them in terms of what we know about them, without postulating other worlds or hidden variables. An example is the approach known as quantum Bayesianism (aka QBism), which sees the wave function not as an objective reality but as a mathematical instrument used to describe the quantum world. The experimenter's choice describes the probability of what he or she will see and nothing more; the wave function is therefore a subjective property of the observer, so the subject is critically important. In a way, the wave function is a description of the observer's mental state. There is no fixed underlying reality that different observers could independently observe; there are only facts for each observer; quantum theory does not give us a direct description of reality. The experimenter cannot be separated from the experiment; reality is inherently interactive. The usual critique of this approach is that it veers towards idealism and does not account for the structure of reality.

A more recent approach to quantum physics is the relational approach (Rovelli, 2021), which is an alternative to the traditional metaphysics of individual substances and properties. Instead of an observer-independent system, the relational approach analyzes the network of relationships among quantum subsystems. The idea is to focus on the interaction between objects rather than on isolated objects. In fact, in this approach there are no individual objects; they are the way they interact, and their properties are the way they affect other objects. Thus, "there are no properties outside of interactions" (ibid., p. 79). An object can be "real with respect to one object and not with respect to another" (ibid., p. 82). Reality is a web of interactions and relationships. When an electron is not interacting, it has no position or velocity. The properties of two entangled particles exist only in relation to a third object that interacts with both. All physics exists in relationship to observers who are themselves quantum systems. Consciousness is not necessary in this approach. The cost of this approach is that there is no universal set of facts; a fact relative to one observer is not a fact in relation to another. Another difficulty is that it is hard to imagine relationships without objects that are related to each other, and it is not clear how these relations form coherent physical objects. If the world is only made up of relationships and relationships between relationships, an infinite regress seems a possibility.

Uncertainty and determinism

In the early years of quantum mechanics, a famous debate took place between Einstein and Bohr about the observation that some quantum events seem to be random or unpredictable or may have no definite cause. Einstein, who was a scientific realist, thought that the apparent randomness of quantum mechanics was due to our ignorance of the underlying mechanisms involved, while Bohr believed randomness to be an intrinsic feature of reality. Many theorists today adhere to Bohr's view, which contravenes a strictly deterministic view of reality. In contrast to classical physics, in which each event has a prior cause, quantum randomness means that at the quantum level there is no well-defined, necessary link between an event and previous event. For many theorists therefore, it seems that uncertainty is built into reality itself at the quantum level. Perhaps nature is truly indeterminate, probabilistic, and random prior to observation, or perhaps nature works in a precisely detailed manner but we simply don't understand exactly how it does so. If it is true that nature at its deepest level is not deterministic, this has implications for human psychology and human development, as well as for research into these fields. The well-known difficulty replicating psychological research[19] and the difficulty involved in assessing forms of psychotherapy may be connected to intrinsic randomness within the psyche and within reality overall.

Uncertainty at the quantum level is not simply an epistemological factor; it may also be a fact about the nature of reality. If uncertainty prevails at both the macro and micro level, we have to ask what organizing principle holds reality together to avoid chaos. If uncertainty is built into the quantum level of nature, it is a mystery how order then emerges at the macro level. On the surface it looks like causality carries out this function, but the principle of synchronicity, which is an acausal principle of explanation, makes the situation more complicated. It is possible that acausal correlations occur between psyche and matter of which we are unaware. Quantum mechanical experiments such as the famous double-slit experiment[20] suggest some kind of influence in the physical world that originates outside of space and time as we know them.

Analogies between psychotherapy and quantum mechanics

Quantum physics changes our concept of reality and makes it clear that our ordinary view of the world is fundamentally different than the deep nature of the world. The implications of this change for depth psychology and psychotherapy are important. Psychologists cannot afford to work within an obsolete view of reality; we have to move to a world view that takes into account what quantum mechanics tells us. One concept central to quantum mechanics that is a possible link to psychotherapeutic discourse is the importance of field effects in both these disciplines, although they use the word "field" in very different senses. In physics, the classical concept of a field describes an area of space in which a particular force is operating that affects objects at a distance from each other. Gravity, electromagnetism, and the nuclear forces within the atom are often described in terms of fields. Quantum field theory describes mathematically how particles interact with each other in a particular region.[21] However, although we use the term "intersubjective field" in psychotherapy, this does not mean that the fields described by field theory in physics are comparable to the relational field, which is a metaphor for the therapeutic interaction or the therapeutic space in which mutual influence takes place. The force of a relational field is the result of the psychological effects the participants have on each other, producing a field that is quite different than physical fields. The fact that the same word is used in physics and psychotherapy is a useful analogy but not a sameness.

Various authors have elaborated the idea that quantum interconnectedness in the microphysical world is analogous to the field relationship that occurs in psychotherapy (Mansfield & Spiegelman, 1996). The central metaphor of intersubjectivity theory in psychoanalysis is described by Stolorow et al. (1994, p. ix) as a field in which "psychological phenomena crystallize and in which experience is continually and mutually shaped." In this model, psychological phenomena are only understandable in their intersubjective context. Within the therapeutic field, the subjectivities of patient and psychotherapist fuse or merge, leading to mutual influence and shared unconscious fantasy. Ogden refers to the mutually created intersubjective state as the "analytic third" (ibid., p. 5). Empathic attunement and the transference-countertransference are also field effects. The field dynamics in psychotherapeutic situations are now well established, and they can emerge as imagery in the therapist's reverie or even in a shared active imagination (Schwartz-Salant, 1982, 1989; Spiegelman, 1996). One line of evidence for the autonomy of the therapeutic field is that the therapist and patient cannot predict what will emerge within a particular session—the material seems to happen to both participants as if the therapeutic field has a spirit of its own. Jungians assume that the therapeutic field is partly mediated by the interaction of the unconscious of both participants but also occurs within the field of the Self or the objective psyche, which can sometimes be sensed as a third presence in the consulting room acting as a deep medium of connection.

There is a further analogy between the relational approach to psychotherapy, based on the invariable influence of the therapist on the relational field, and Wheeler's idea that the physicist is a participant in his experiments rather than being an objective observer (Wheeler & Zurek, 1983). Like that of the quantum physicist, the intention of the psychotherapist, and his or her subjectivity, inevitably influence the dynamics of the therapeutic field. Perhaps unconscious material is in something analogous to a state of superposition until it is observed by the therapeutic dyad. Many psychoanalysts believe that the therapist's understanding of the patient's unconscious is more a question of interpretation than the excavation of objective material. Interpretation of psychological material, like the observation of quantum effects, is both creative and disruptive. The therapist's understanding of these dynamics may be best understood probabilistically. Heisenberg's uncertainty principle is very relevant to psychotherapy. Incidentally, the placebo effect, which significantly influences medical research and treatment, may be correlated with the observational effects of both the patient and the clinician who administers the placebo.

The interpersonal and the intrapsychic are complementary aspects of psychotherapy, analogous to the wave-particle descriptions of quantum mechanics, both of which are necessary to describe aspects of microphysical reality. The fact that the physicist cannot be precise about both the position and the momentum of a particle is analogous to the fact that it is impossible to focus both on the intrapsychic and the interpersonal situation at the same time. Entanglement has been seen as a loose analogy for empathy, but entangled particles are related physically, so at best that analogy can only be symbolic.

Bohm's implicate order, a realm of undivided wholeness out of which our ordinary world emerges, is analogous to Jung's notion of the psychoid dimension or the archetype-as-such prior to its symbolic manifestation. However, we must be cautious when we use quantum theory to support specific psychological theories, because it is not clear to what extent analogies from quantum mechanics can be applied to the psyche. Unlike the quantum realm, the psyche is not subject to mathematical description. However, notions such as the unbroken wholeness of reality, field dynamics, and the effects of observation on the observed, seem to be relevant to psychotherapy. The therapist is in the difficult situation of trying to understand the wholeness of the personality, knowing that this wholeness cannot be analyzed or broken into its constituents without reducing its unity.

Observation or measurement affects the behavior of a quantum level particle. If observation affects the psyche, this has implications for the mechanism of change in psychotherapy. Attention to thoughts, feelings, and memories may affect them in unknown ways. The way the therapist interacts with the client, and the observation of the material that emerges in therapy, have psychological consequences. Jung (CW 8, p. 229, fn. 130) notes the comment of Pauli that every observation of the unconscious "has an uncontrollable reactive effect on these same contents." The fact that observation of a quantum system selects one aspect of many possible outcomes or limits the state of the system also suggests an analogy to measurement in experimental psychology.

Bearing these analogies in mind, the psychologist has to avoid some of the more romantic, idiosyncratic, or forced applications of quantum theory that are sometimes appropriated by non-physicists who extend its concepts beyond what can be empirically justified. Einstein (1934) warned that "The present fashion of applying the axioms of physical science to human life is not only entirely a mistake but also has something reprehensible about it." We sometimes do need to look beyond our own field to cast light on it, but it is debatable how far such analogies between disciplines can be helpful. Analogies are suggestive but the processes they describe in quantum theory and psychotherapy are not identical. The extent to which quantum mechanical principles can be applied to the psyche remains to be clarified.

The question of free will

The issue of free will is sometimes raised in the context of quantum mechanical experiments because the observer can choose to design the experiment to show a photon as either a wave or a particle. The will of the experimenter therefore influences the physical outcome of the experiment, very much in contrast to classical mechanics, where observation could not have a physical effect on an experiment. Classical Newtonian physics is deterministic and does not allow free will since the mind is seen to be independent of the domain of physics. Physicalists assume that the brain operates according to physical laws, and neuronal mechanisms are responsible for decision making, so for some neuroscientists free will is illusory. In 1983 Benjamin Libet showed that the subjective decision to move a finger is preceded by brain waves (the readiness potential) that occur about 300–500 milliseconds before the conscious decision is made. Other experiments have shown that conscious awareness of the response to a stimulus comes several hundred milliseconds after a brain response has occurred, in which case conscious intention to perform an action is not primary. The brain initiates the action; our sense of choosing is our awareness of what the brain has already decided. According to some philosophers, this finding implies that consciousness is epiphenomenal and there is no free will (Wegner, 2002). The problem with these experiments is that the subjective awareness of exactly when we decide to move is not reliable. The unconscious may make the decision. Furthermore, it is not certain whether the readiness potential is related to the decision to move the finger or to attention to the finger itself. Later research suggested that the build-up of brain activity preceding voluntary movement may reflect background neural noise that may have many causes (Schurger et al., 2016).

Only hard determinists deny free will altogether; many philosophers assume that free will and determinism are somehow compatible. The uncertainty principle of quantum mechanics is sometimes said to undermine determinism because according to some interpretations of quantum mechanics, the result of a quantum measurement is not determined. Only the probable result can be determined, and there is no known mechanical cause for the actual outcome of a measurement that could have had other possible outcomes. However, this does not prove the existence of free will, because very small-scale quantum indeterminacies might be cancelled out in a macroscopic system such as the brain, so most authors believe they can be ignored for practical purposes. Also, even if quantum indeterminacy or randomness do occur in the neurons, the result might be a matter of chance and not free choice, possibly even undermining the possibility of free will.

The challenge to realism from quantum mechanics

Local realism assumes that an event in one place can only be affected by another event if there is enough time for a signal moving no faster than the speed of light to travel from one place to the other. Local realism was at the heart of Newtonian science until it was challenged by quantum mechanics. In classical Newtonian physics, measurement is not dependent on context; it reveals a pre-existing reality, but in quantum mechanics the context of an experiment is important because the physical properties of a quantum system depend on how they are observed. Prior to being observed, the properties of a quantum object are potentials or probabilities rather than firmly defined entities. From the realist point of view, the act of observation should not affect the properties of the object being observed. This situation, combined with the proven reality of nonlocality, the fact that one of a pair of quantum connected particles instantaneously changes when the other changes even when separated by large distances, challenges scientific realism, the doctrine that there is an external, objective physical world that exists independently of human observation. However, there are powerful arguments in favor of scientific realism, such as the success of science, its explanatory and predictive power, its invariant principles, and its ability to tell us about reality far beyond our ordinary perceptions. The facts of history are also in favor of realism rather than subjectivism. However, quantum mechanics offers challenges to realism not only because at the quantum level the outcome of an experiment may depend on the way it is carried out, but also because even if two identical quantum mechanical experiments are performed, they may not produce exactly the same results. These facts are a problem for realists, as is the difficulty of explaining how a photon can be both a wave and a particle. If local realism is finally shown to be illusory, it makes ordinary notions of space and time obsolete, or as the current speculation has it, space-time is "doomed," because space-time is not fundamental but emergent (Musser, 2017). This idea would have a radical effect on physics.

Some quantum physicists, such as Werner Heisenberg, Eugene Wigner (in his early but not later writing),[22] and Niels Bohr[23] (according to some readings of his work) took an anti-realist position that says that reality, at least at the microphysical level, only exists as a function of the way we observe and describe it. Henry Stapp (2011, 2017) is a recent proponent of the idea that either there is no objective real world at the quantum level, or it is impossible to describe reality at that level, so objectivity in the classical sense is unattainable.

Bohr pointed out that human beings are an integral part of the world science is trying to describe; therefore, the subject–object distinction is blurred. According to Bohr (1934, p. 18), the purpose of the physicist's description of nature "is not to disclose the real essence of phenomena but only to track down as far as possible relations between the multifold aspects of our experience." That is, he avoided ontological questions in favor of epistemological interpretations of quantum theory. Similarly, Heisenberg (1958a) believed that quantum physics tells us about "nature exposed to our method of questioning"; we only know the mathematics of elementary particles, not their objective nature. Because experience and knowledge of the quantum realm are affected by the mind of the observer, Stapp (2009) pointed out that quantum mechanics is dualistic at the operational level but ontologically mentalistic.

The unobservable parts of quantum mechanics are seen by scientific realists as real aspects of the world that have not yet been detected. Strict empiricists believe that only what is observable is real, and the unobservable parts of the theory are only useful concepts but not necessarily literal descriptions of reality.

Quantum and macroscopic levels of reality

It is possible that different physical laws apply at the quantum level and the macroscopic level, although most physicists would prefer to think that the quantum and classical realms operate according to the same physical laws.

The issue was raised by the paradox that the results of quantum experiments are probabilistic but the laboratory instruments used to detect them operate deterministically, according to classical physical laws, even though these instruments are themselves composed of quantum level phenomena that must obey the laws of quantum mechanics.

At times, quantum mechanical principles such as randomness seem to contradict what we observe in everyday reality, and the strangeness of the theory seems to defy common sense. To relate the strangeness of quantum mechanics to our everyday experience of the world, some physicists invoke the phenomenon of decoherence, which abolishes quantum effects at the macroscopic level, allowing ordinary reality to appear. However, it is not fully understood how the quantum behavior of elementary particles gives rise to classical behavior in the macroscopic world. The problem is how deterministic behavior at the macroscopic level emerges from non-deterministic behavior at the quantum level, how to reconcile the probabilistic aspects of the theory and its randomness with the ordinary behavior of macroscopic objects, which is largely predictable. However, Roland Omnès (2002) believes that the current interpretation of quantum mechanics is perfectly compatible with common sense and the uniqueness of reality. Although this uniqueness is not predicted by quantum principles, he believes it does not contradict them. As he puts it: "although the basic laws are quantum mechanical, the properties and phenomena occurring in the macroscopic world can be stated classically" (p. 161).

Philosophical issues raised by quantum mechanics

Is reality created by the observer?

The controversial role of consciousness in quantum mechanical experiments has re-enlivened the question of the relationship between our minds and our experience of reality, or between the nature of reality and our perception of it. Because the experimenter's choice affects the outcome of his experiment, quantum mechanics has raised the philosophical problem of whether phenomena exist independent of our observation of them, and if so how. If it were true that the quantum world cannot be explained independently of conscious observation, that would be an embarrassment to physicalism and determinism, and it would support an idealist metaphysics. The possibility that human consciousness actually causes the transition from a wave to a particle gave rise to the concept of observer-created reality. This is a once-popular idea (Wolf, 1981) that argues that an observer is necessary to bring the world into being because the observer seems to affect the outcome of an experiment by choosing to make a particular measurement, which causes a change in the quantum wave function so that it now has a definite quantifiable characteristic rather than being a probability. In this view, there is some kind of continuum between the physical world and consciousness. This leads some physicists to see the physical world as entirely contextual, meaning that its measurable properties do not exist until they are observed, which is a major challenge to realism. Henry (2005, p. 29) believes we must learn to perceive the world as quantum mechanical in nature. He suggests that the universe is "entirely mental," since there is no ontological ground outside the mind where the properties of the world could exist before being represented in the mind. For this idealist view, observation is synonymous with the physical world; it does not simply represent the world. However, although an early view of quantum physicists was that there was no actual particle in a specific place before it was observed, a typical modern view is that the observer does not cause a particle to exist in a particular position, but the observer finds the location of the particle. Therefore, observation by a conscious observer is not necessary for the particle to exist. Claims that "consciousness creates reality" are therefore greatly exaggerated; the fact that observation impacts a quantum system is only relevant to subatomic particles and not to macroscopic events.

Does quantum physics help our understanding of reality?

Although quantum mechanical predictions are very accurate mathematically, some of the underlying questions about how to interpret the experimental facts are unsettled. It is not clear what quantum mechanics says about the deep nature of reality that lies beyond our capacity to observe. Different interpretations of quantum mechanics suggest different ontologies. There is a range of interpretations about the meaning of quantum experiments (Herbert, 1987), and people chose interpretations according to their own preferred ontology. For many physicists, science itself does not provide any meaning; science only predicts what will be observed under particular conditions. To ask about meaning is to stray into psychology and philosophy. Nevertheless, questions remain about what is really going on at the quantum level. A much-debated question is whether quantum states are ontologically or physically real or whether they are purely epistemic, only mathematically useful predictors of experiments. However, given the success of quantum mechanics in many areas of technology, it seems likely to be describing a real world whose deep nature is not yet understood.

The experimental findings of quantum mechanics are themselves theory neutral. Each theoretical interpretation of these findings has a conceptual cost, forcing theorists to accept apparently strange realities. All of them suggest that our everyday worldview is fundamentally incomplete. Part of the difficulty may be that physicists construct measuring devices that correspond to human sensory systems and cognitive capacities, which served us well in our evolutionary history, but at a quantum level nature may not correspond to these limitations. At the moment, an individual physicist may adopt any interpretation of quantum mechanics that fits the experimental evidence.

One ontological question is whether ultimate reality is deterministic or indeterministic. Quantum mechanics and general relativity offer different ontologies, and it is not yet clear how these fundamental interpretations of reality relate to each other. There are debates about whether time is reversible or irreversible, and whether information can be transmitted from the future to the present. There are debates about whether causality is only something we experience or whether it is a universal law. The exact relationship between the nature of the world and our perception of it has long been debated in philosophy and is further debated in quantum mechanics.

The early founders of quantum mechanics such as Bohr and Heisenberg were well aware of the philosophical implications of quantum theory. They raised questions such as: to what extent does quantum mechanics tell us about the nature of ordinary reality? This question arose in part because quantum theory gives us accurate measurements but does not tell us the nature of what we are measuring. It does not necessarily say what a photon or a quantum field actually is, even though we know how they behave. Thus, science can be said to provide a description or representation of reality but does not necessarily tell us the nature of reality itself. We cannot give an account of reality independent of our means of observation of it. Some interpretations of quantum mechanics therefore involve philosophical speculation.

Quantum mechanics raises the question of whether or how quantum objects exist without being observed. Because they only exist as potentials before they are observed, for some philosophers, quantum theory supports idealism. In this view of reality, objects are seen as not distinct from the consciousness that observes them, and consciousness is primary and not an epiphenomenon of matter. In this view, matter is the way the world appears when we observe it, but we cannot know if anything exists "behind" that appearance, independently of our perception of it. Reality consists of a combination of observer and observed, who are not separable. We cannot prove the existence of an objective physical world outside our minds. Idealism is a minority view today, but it is advocated by Bernado Kastrup (2015; 2019), who interprets quantum mechanics in terms of objective idealism, which says that the world is a mental world, the result of the activity of consciousness.[24] It is as if the world is contained in and is the product of a cosmic Mind, of which the individual mind is a part. Kastrup's view is consistent with the Advaitic approach to Consciousness as the ground of reality. However, idealism is not necessarily the forced conclusion of quantum mechanics. Physicists who espouse metaphysical or scientific realism believe that quantum theory gives us objective knowledge of reality independently of the consciousness of the observer (Sepetyi, 2018).

Although the issue of what quantum theory tells us about the nature of reality is unsolved, quantum mechanics has important philosophical implications (Lewis, 2016). Quantum theory offers a radically different view of reality than classical physics. In the classical picture, based on atomism, physical reality consists of tiny, independent entities that move in time and space. These entities have intrinsic properties such as mass, motion, and charge that distinguish them from other entities. All the properties of objects in the world supervene on the basic properties of the atoms of which they are composed. Atoms and their constituents are ontologically fundamental. This approach to reality has been radically disrupted by the findings that quantum objects are not atomistic in the classical sense, and also by phenomena such as entanglement, in which two quantum particles are not independent of each other but maintain a correlation, so that if one changes its spin the other changes instantaneously, no matter how far apart they are or how long they have been separated, with no physical force applied. They behave like a single system, in that measurement of one of the quanta causes an immediate change in the other. The means by which they stay connected is not known, but they seem to transcend spacetime, as if the space and time between them does not exist, which violates the classical idea of locality. Entanglement is an epistemological feature of quantum systems, but the ontological implications of such quantum mechanical observations are controversial and difficult to grasp or imagine.[25] The entangled particles behave as if they were a unit rather than distinct individuals, suggesting a link to non-dual philosophical ideas about the unitary nature of reality. Perhaps the apparent separation of the particles is a product of the limitations of our brain and sensory systems, or it is a function of the experimental arrangement used to study it. It is possible that the two particles are connected in a quantum realm of reality that is not empirically demonstrable, outside our three-dimensional universe.[26] Alternatively, the particles are synchronistically connected, in which case entanglement may eventually prove to be a link between Jung's work and physics.

Quantum physicists acknowledge that their discipline is impossible to understand even though they know how to use it to describe physical reality (Gell-Mann, 1981). Richard Feynman (1994, p. 121) asserted that "I can safely say that nobody understands quantum mechanics." Not only is quantum theory abstract and heavily mathematical, the results of quantum mechanical experiments are puzzling, difficult to visualize symbolically, difficult to assimilate into everyday life, and seem to be remote from everyday psychological functioning. These are some of the reasons that quantum mechanics has not had much impact on our everyday "common sense" thinking even though much of our technology depends on it. Nevertheless, given quantum theory, we can no longer hold onto a folkloric view of reality based on classical physics.

Many physicists prefer to avoid the philosophical implications of their physics and try to remain pragmatic and instrumentalist. The philosophical puzzles raised by quantum mechanics are often ignored in favor of its enormous practical value—its predictions are highly accurate, and a large proportion of our economy depends on products based on them, such as transistors and lasers. From a philosophical and scientific point of view, one of the major unresolved debates is whether quantum mechanics is a complete theory about reality or whether it is only a partial or a statistical theory.

The physicist Bernard d'Espagnat (1983, 2006) describes the ontological characteristics of the subatomic level of matter using the term "veiled reality." He believes that everyday concepts and language are not suitable for describing reality as it is in itself, independently of the observer and the process of observation. Therefore, he sees most physicists as using purely practical, instrumental approaches that see quantum mechanics solely as a tool for organizing and predicting experiments. He points out that this approach does not distinguish between correct and incorrect theories about what actually happens at the quantum level. He believes that reality-in-itself exists; even if it cannot be precisely defined, we can get some knowledge of it empirically, but our models are only approximate, since reality remains behind a veil. Our models are then a matter of beliefs about reality. At the quantum level, objects have properties that depend on the way they are observed, but we do not know their properties before observation. His view of quantum reality is therefore similar to Kant's view of human knowledge; features such as space, time, and causality are properties of our knowledge of reality but not necessarily properties of veiled reality-as-it-is, which is inaccessible to direct empirical study and prior to the mind–matter split. d'Espagnat differs from Kant because he sees the veiled level as producing structures in phenomenal reality, just as Jung sees the noumenal level of the archetype-as-such producing symbolic material in consciousness. Pauli might say that the veiling described by d'Espagnat is due to the influence of the unconscious.

It would be a mistake to think that the foundational ontological questions raised by quantum mechanics are irrelevant to psychology. Mainstream psychology has presupposed philosophical realism and the possibility of stating something to be objectively true, but quantum physics at least calls this project into question.

Complementarity

A key problem in quantum mechanics has been to explain how a photon or an electron could travel in a wave form but be detected as a particle, depending on the experimental conditions. Bohr (1966) described the dual particle and wave aspects of a quantum entity as complementary, just as the two sides of a coin are complementary but both are properties of the coin. (The quantum entity may have other properties that are not understood.) Both descriptions are necessary even though they seem to be mutually exclusive; neither description alone can fully describe the entity, and Bohr thought we cannot see both aspects of it at once (this finding has been challenged recently). This paradox has to be accepted. Bohr believed that there is a reality behind the phenomena of wave/particle duality that is not accessible except in terms of mathematics. Words such as wave and particle are metaphoric or symbolic, not literal descriptions. It is possible that there is no real duality; a photon may only have one nature but may appear in different states under different conditions, just as water can appear as liquid, gas or solid.

Different types of measurements are complementary when both are necessary to provide a comprehensive account of a phenomenon, yet they are mutually exclusive and only one can be applied at any time. Complementary descriptions of a phenomenon unite apparently incompatible perspectives on it, although both descriptions are correct. It is as if we have to look at the situation in different ways to fully understand it. It seems impossible for both perspectives to be true, yet they are. Bohr determined various other epistemological implications of complementarity, which he thought reflects a universal principle that extends far beyond its original context. If this principle can be generalized, it may be true not only for physics but also for psychology, biology, and human knowledge in general (Holton, 1988). Bohr also wondered if complementarity might be a useful approach to mind–body duality. Complementarity is now thought to be central to the emerging field of quantum cognition, which applies principles of quantum theory to cognitive structures and processes (Wang et al., 2015). Jung (CW 8, fn. 130) approvingly quotes a suggestion of Pauli that consciousness and the unconscious are in a complementary relationship to each other.

Bohr realized that just as a subatomic particle is affected by a measurement, a mental content might be altered by our attention to it: "we must in general, be prepared to accept the fact that a complete elucidation of one and the same object may require diverse points of view which defy a unique description" (cited in Gieser, 2004, p. 105). Bohr understood that we cannot remove ourselves from our observations, blurring the distinction between subject and object. In a 1948 essay (Meier, 2001, p. 185), Pauli suggested that "one of the most important tasks for the Western mind" is to replace the idea of polar opposites with the idea of complementarity. In a 1953 letter to Jung (ibid., p. 91), written just as Jung was finishing *Mysterium coniunctionis*, Pauli talks about the use of complementarity in physics as a way to think of a *coniunctio* (union) between quantum physics and psychology.

The notion of complementarity may only be necessitated by our incomplete knowledge of quantum entities that do in fact have precise characteristics. The question is whether the photon's appearance as either a wave or a particle is purely a function of the instruments we use or whether this situation is intrinsic to the quantum realm even when it is not being observed. In the latter case, the quantum realm has its own principles. From the human perspective, it seems that a quantum level phenomenon only exists in the form in which it is measured. One problem with the idea of complementarity is the difficulty of knowing which of the possible descriptions should be chosen in a given situation; if the observer choses arbitrarily and freely, the experiment does not seem entirely objective or independent of the mind of the researcher. Because of the logical problem produced by complementarity—how can light be both a particle and a wave? —Bohr preferred not to talk about the quantum dimension except experimentally and mathematically. It is in a way unthinkable. This view is reminiscent of Kant's idea that the noumenal level of reality (reality as it is prior to our perception of it) is inaccessible. Bohr was reluctant to speak about the nature of reality—he had an aversion to anything that sounded mystical.

Quantum theory, New Age philosophy, and mysticism

It is often claimed by adherents to New Age philosophy that quantum physics supports a holistic view of the universe and shows that we are all connected within a supraordinate cosmic consciousness. This claim is roundly denied by skeptics (Stenger, 1993). Their concern is that to extend the principles of quantum physics beyond their usual domain of applicability leads to spurious conclusions based on previously held metaphysical assumptions. A typical critique is that New Age authors use quantum mechanical terms to make their arguments sound more scientific or to buttress their favorite theory, but in the process quantum mechanical language is stretched far beyond its original meaning, or it is taken out of context altogether (DeBakcsy, 2014; Mroczkowski & Malozemoff, 2019). Nevertheless, there has been a long-standing attempt to use quantum mechanics to support the mystical idea that consciousness creates reality (Marin, 2009), because of the presumed role of consciousness in quantum experiments. However, many physicists believe that the idea of observer-created reality is mistaken because in many approaches to quantum mechanics, consciousness is not needed to collapse the wave function; interaction with another macroscopic object such as a detector does so (Becker, 2018; Carroll, 2016; Nauenberg, 2007). However, on the basis of the importance of consciousness, misleading claims have been made about "quantum healing" that have no connection to the reality of quantum mechanics. This idea arose because the wave function is a probability wave or a potential state that is collapsed or localized by observation. Chopra (1993) therefore suggested that by means of the appropriate self-observation, one could "collapse" one's health to an improved state. However, Mroczkowski and Malozemoff (2019) point out that the sub-microscopic collapse phenomena cannot be extrapolated to the macroscopic level; objects as large as the human body do not exhibit quantum properties, not to mention the important fact that the result of such a collapse is random and unpredictable, so one cannot choose a particular outcome. This is not to deny the important effects of the mind–body connection, evidenced by the placebo effect and the use of imagery in healing, nor does it deny healing apparently brought about by spiritual means; it simply means that quantum level explanations are incorrect.

Many attempts have been made to relate quantum effects to psychological processes such as psi effects or states of mind reported by the world's mystics. Here we are on slippery ground, for several reasons. According to Richard Jones (2010), advocates of parallels between quantum level phenomena and mystical states distort both science and mysticism. These advocates use quantum level effects such as nonlocality and entanglement to explain mystical experience (Capra, 1986; Zukav, 1970). These authors focused on the inseparability of the observer and the observed, linking this connection to Eastern philosophical ideas that the world and our experience of it are a unity, and everything arises interdependently. For example, Capra (1986) says that "Like modern physicists, Buddhists see all objects as processes in a universal flux and deny the existence of any material substance" (p. 226). However, such comparisons have been roundly dismissed, in part because their proponents do not simply imply *analogies* between Eastern traditions and quantum mechanics but suggest an actual *identity* between them. Several of these proposed analogies fail on closer examination. Quantum theory does *not* say that subatomic particles are unreal; the process of actualizing a wave function into a particle makes something visible that was already real.

Mystics of many traditions claim that reality is a unified whole. Attempts have been made to relate this idea to the phenomenon of entanglement, as if this phenomenon means that all parts of reality are intimately connected— but it is not clear to what extent a phenomenon that applies at the level of subatomic particles can be generalized to the whole of macroscopic reality. Furthermore, while it is true that many Eastern religious traditions deny that the personal self is an entity and see the separation between the self and the world as an illusion, in quantum physics the role of the observer in the outcome of an experiment is sometimes crucial. New Age approaches often rely on the importance of observation in quantum mechanics, which links the experimenter and the experiment. This has given rise to philosophical conclusions such as the idea that there is no independently existing reality because subject and object are an essential unity. Justification for this view is found, for example, in the work of Heisenberg (1958a, p. 129), who wrote that "the idea of an objective real world whose smallest parts exist objectively ... independently of whether or not we observe them ... is impossible." He believed that "We can no longer speak of the behavior of the particle independent of the process of observation ... Nor is it any longer possible to ask whether or not these particles exist in space and time objectively" (Heisenberg 1958b, p. 15). Bohr and Heisenberg believed that physicists were not dealing with the particles themselves but with our knowledge of them. However, as noted earlier, a more modern view is that observation and measurement may be carried out by a mechanical instrument and not necessarily by a conscious observer. There is no experimental justification for privileging the Copenhagen interpretation (which itself has a range of interpretations) over any other, except personal preference to support one's favorite mystical ideas.

The view that the consciousness of the observer affects reality is at least consistent with the Advaitic view that matter results from the activity of Pure Consciousness. In that tradition, there is no mind–matter duality because only Consciousness is the ultimate reality. However, this comparison does not go far; Bohr and Heisenberg both believed there is no deep reality, a view that is inconsistent with the Advaitic ideas that the Ātman-Brahman is that deep ground. The popularity of such material seems to be related to the human need for a sense of unity and wholeness. However, the several interpretations of quantum mechanics that deny the role of consciousness have no connection to Eastern thought.

Possible connections between psi phenomena and quantum mechanics

The human mind is often reported to have paranormal modes of functioning that allow perception and knowledge beyond ordinary sensory processes, beyond what we ordinarily think the brain can do. These "anomalous mental phenomena" (May& Marwaha, 2014) are often known as psi or psychic experiences. They include phenomena such as telepathy, clairvoyance or remote viewing, mind–matter interaction or psychokinesis, pre-cognition, automatic writing, spirit communication through mediums, ghostly apparitions, the sense of being stared at, and out of body or near-death experiences. Telepathic communication within the therapeutic dyad is well documented (Totton, 2007). However, at the moment, phenomena such as remote healing (Radin et al., 2015) or communication between minds at a distance are impossible to explain because they imply connection and influence across time and space, for which there is no known mechanism within the parameters of contemporary materialist science (Radin, 2006, 2018). Many skeptics believe that such psi phenomena cannot be real because they are inconsistent with an objectivist, physicalist worldview. That ontology cannot imagine how mind to mind connections could occur, because physicalism is based on causality mediated by local physical processes. Precognition would violate various models of physical science based on our ordinary understanding of time. Therefore, if paranormal phenomena do occur, our existing descriptions of nature would have to be modified. However, psi phenomena cannot be ignored just because they cannot be explained. They have an important influence in popular culture, and they have been influential in the development of world religions and mythology (Kripal et al., 2014).

Research in this area is very controversial. Theorists on both sides of the debate have different views of reality. A large part of the dispute is based on the fact that psi phenomena transcend the usual boundaries of time and space, but conventional scientists have built their careers on physical models of reality, so anomalous experiences are unwelcome challenges that would force a re-evaluation of their views. Parapsychological phenomena seem to bridge minds or bridge matter and mind in a manner that is unacceptable to physicalists. Many mainstream scientists therefore tend to ignore, discount, or even ridicule these experiences, in spite of the large amount of evidence that they exist (summarized by Cardeña, 2018). Although the prevailing mainstream scientific consensus largely denies the possibility of psi phenomena, studies that demonstrate their reality are often of good quality (Bösch et al., 2006). They cannot be dismissed on purely ideological or philosophical grounds or in terms of the quality of the studies, the analysis of data, or in terms of fraud. Nevertheless, skeptics assume that even when research seems to indicate the reality of psi, there must have been some kind of experimental or statistical error that would account for the result. Or the skeptic is suspicious that the psi researcher is really trying to justify a religious belief. Thus, reductive explanations for mediumship suggest that the "spirits" that the medium claims to contact are merely relatively autonomous, unconscious aspects of the medium's own personality, or they are dissociative phenomena. These opinions are sometimes based on nothing more than prejudice. Prior convictions, expectations, confirmation bias, and the discomfort of cognitive dissonance[27] often overwhelm actual evidence. Often, the skeptic's personal metaphysical commitments do not allow the existence of psychic phenomena, and these beliefs are disguised as scientific objections. Thus, Reber and Alcock (2019) dismissed Cardeña's findings, not because of flawed methodology but because the psi data conflicts with contemporary physicalist science.

Research in this area is complicated by the fact that the laboratory setting does not reflect the conditions under which psi phenomena spontaneously appear in people's lives. They are most likely to occur between people with strong emotional bonds (Nachman, 2009); they tend to occur (or to be reported) during situations of threat, crisis, or loss. Laboratory studies are affected by the researcher's and subject's belief or disbelief in psi. Replicability of psi experiments in the laboratory is complicated by the observation that lack of interest or boredom on the part of the subject decrease its occurrence.[28] Even when psi experiments produce statistically significant results that cannot be dismissed as the result of chance or fraud, these effects are often not reproducible or replicable by others. (Replication, by the way, is a widespread problem in all psychological research; see note 19.) Furthermore, many laboratory trials show only a small statistical deviation from chance with no way to increase the strength of the effect; the evidence for psi does not seem to get stronger. Another of the main sources of resistance to these findings, even when they are statistically unassailable, is that no causal mechanism or field can be demonstrated to account for them, and there is no known medium through which these events could be mediated. The only plausible conceptual frameworks are either synchronicity, which requires us to abandon causality, and the idea of a transpersonal or non-local field of consciousness. Jung's idea of the collective unconscious is one such possibility since this links individual minds.

Because phenomena such as near-death experiences, death-bed communications, and mediumship do not fit within the boundaries of classical physicalism, these events tend to be ignored or discounted by mainstream psychology. This despite the fact that not only Jung but luminaries such as William James and William McDougall were interested in phenomena that suggest the survival of consciousness after death (Gauld, 1984). Because there is no known plausible mechanism for such phenomena within a physicalist framework, among mainstream psychologists there is considerable resistance to claims indicative of psychic ability, such as those demonstrated by Rhine (1934), since replicated numerous times (Radin, 2006). Experiments by Bem (2011) that seemed to demonstrate precognition caused considerable controversy when they were published in a mainstream psychology journal, although he used procedures and statistical methods used by many social psychologists. Scientific materialists cannot refute the statistics but cannot accept their implications, and therefore assume some kind of questionable research practices were involved. A similar situation obtains in the case of mediums who claim to be in touch with spirits (Beischel et al., 2015). Mainstream psychologists tend to reject reports of transpersonal or spiritual experiences, in part because the physicalist model of reality dominates the field, so numinous or mystical experiences "cannot" be real. However, the 2013 publication of an APA journal titled *Spirituality in Clinical Practice* offers some hope that the spiritual dimension of reality is being recognized by some mainstream psychologists.

It seems to some investigators that although psi effects are real, they are a type of phenomenon that is not amenable to ordinary methods of investigation. They are too capricious and difficult to control in a laboratory. However, the evidence suggests that human beings are connected in ways that are more fundamental or subtle than we can explain. At the moment, although there is no definitive theory that can explain psi phenomena, this is no reason to dismiss the large amount of experimental evidence that it exists. It is not unusual in the history of science for an observation to take years to be explained (the pros and cons of the argument about psi are summarized by Rabeyron, 2020). Metaphysical theories such as LeShan's "clairvoyant reality," in which apparent individuals are seen as linked parts of a unitary totality in which there is no separation between past, present, and future (LeShan, 2003), are intriguing but untestable.

The development of our understanding of quantum reality may eventually provide an explanation for psi phenomena (Nash, 1984). Some authors have suggested an analogy between telepathy and the phenomenon of quantum entanglement, the observation that elementary particles, no matter how far apart, may become connected in ways that cannot be explained in terms of

conventional interactions. At a non-local level, these spatially separate particles behave as if they are not independent of each other.[29] They are per-
manently correlated and behave as if they were a single entity. When one of a
pair of entangled particles changes, the other seems to "know" what has
happened and changes instantly, but this awareness is of a limited kind. The
two particles share the same superpositional state,[30] and when it is measured,
this state collapses instantaneously into values that conserve the original
quantity being measured, such as angular momentum or spin.[31] No signal or
influence seem to pass between entangled particles. This means that space
and perhaps time may not be as fundamental as they were previously
thought to be, just as some interpretations of quantum physics suggest that
mind and matter are also not absolutely distinct. However, such an explanation would invoke the problem of how these quantum-level phenomena
could be relevant to the macroscopic level and to the psyche. The collective
level of the psyche might provide a link between distant events, and so might
synchronicity, which acausally correlates phenomena. Non-local consciousness, which Aldous Huxley referred to as "mind at large," is often invoked as
an explanation for psi phenomena. Non-local connections between the ego
and the totality of Consciousness are often suggested as a link between
quantum phenomena, psychology, and spirituality (von Lucadou et al.,
2007). However, mainstream physicists believe that making such connections
between quantum mechanics and psi phenomena is a misuse and an over-
extension of quantum theory.

Theorists have suggested that two minds can somehow be entangled within
the same nonlocal consciousness, as if minds have a field property that can
connect them (Radin, 2006). If consciousness is truly nonlocal, that would
have profound implications for human relationships and might explain psi
effects. However, claims that connection between minds arises from quantum
entanglement are widely derided by physicists. They point out that the idea of
nonlocal mind is useful as a metaphor, but it cannot be taken as an exact
parallel to the nonlocality described by quantum mechanics, which concerns
entangled particles. As DeBakcsy (2014) notes, it makes no sense to see two
minds being in a superpositional state, and what measurement could cause the
"collapse" of a potential or probable mind state into a definite state? Entanglement is a mathematical correlation between quantum particles, and
although it is possible that consciousness is related to quantum level effects in
the brain, we cannot say that consciousness itself is composed of particles.
Whether the entanglement of particles in the quantum mechanical sense is
really relevant to the intersubjective field between people may be nothing more
than an analogy. Even if we grant that psi phenomena such as telepathy and
precognition exist, and the mind seems to have extraordinary abilities (Mayer,
2007), nonlocality and entanglement may not be the explanation for them.

In spite of the skeptics' reservations about psi phenomena, there are relevant data that cannot be ignored. In the last few decades, quantum

connections have been reported to operate within biological systems such as photosynthesis (Brookes, 2017) or between groups of neurons (Pizzi et al., 2004). The EEG patterns of separated individuals who have no sensory contact with each other have been shown to correlate (Wackermann et al., 2003). Emotional states such as depression seem to spread within social networks (Bond, 2008). These and other lines of evidence suggest that there is some kind of collective level of the psyche in Jung's sense, which links distant individuals, but the mechanism for this may not be entanglement in the quantum mechanical sense. The possibility of mind–mind interaction is one of the most challenging problems we can imagine. Klein (2017) suggests that understanding psi phenomena would help us understand the mind–brain question.

The zero-point field[32] or the quantum vacuum are candidates for non-local linkage between people, but this is speculative, and we have no idea how consciousness could interact with it—unless this field is synonymous with consciousness itself. Joachim Kepler (2020) has suggested that the zero-point field is an "immanently sentient medium" or substrate with which the brain interacts, allowing memory and phenomenal awareness. Another speculation is that the zero-point field, or the domain of the wave function, is the same as the archetypal realm of the psyche. In this vein, Kastrup (2019, p. 107) suggests that universal mind is the "ontological primitive" of quantum mechanics, and the quantum field is that mind. This is part of his idea that "existence consists of patterns of self-excitation of one universal mind" (p. 54), consistent with the Advaitic notion that the world is the activity of Consciousness.[33] It is supported by the idea that the universe contains a vast number of interpenetrating fields that interact with each other. Space is a plenum, filled with matter/energy, in which particles and antiparticles are continuously being created and destroyed in very short time periods and over very short distances. Matter is then an emergent phenomenon arising from a non-material source.[34] If the basis of the physical world is actually a realm of nonmaterial fields, this undermines a materialist ontology, suggests that everything in the world is connected at a non-empirical level of potential, which supports a non-dual ontology.

Psi phenomena suggest a particular set of metaphysical questions and assumptions, including a rejection of physicalist theories of consciousness. What science presently knows about the relationship between consciousness and reality seems to be incomplete. Because of psi effects and synchronistic events, we can no longer make a radical distinction between the inner and outer worlds, or between subjectivity and objective reality. Combined with observations from quantum mechanical phenomena and ideas such as Bohm's notion of the implicate order, it is possible to discern the emergence of a new ontology that suggests the existence of a level of unity, a ground state from which everything originates, which underlies the world of apparently separate objects.

Because of their physicalist bias, contemporary academic psychologists often see ideas about non-material levels of reality as anachronistic; they believe that such metaphysical notions have no place in psychology. Adherence to physicalism means that spirituality and religious experience must also be reduced to brain processes, with no reference to an objective spiritual reality, which has been omitted from the mind–body debate (Walach, 2007). Overall, although there are several organizations that study parapsychology (listed by White, 2011), this field is still regarded with suspicion by many psychologists and by most scientists, who tends to dismiss any kind of nonordinary psychic experience as the result of perceptual errors, deception, or social influences (French, 2003).

Reality and wholeness

The physicist David Bohm (1980, 1988) postulates a hidden, ontic realm of undivided wholeness at the ground of reality, which he calls the implicate (enfolded) order. This deeper reality is beyond either mind or matter. Out of this level, our three-dimensional world of separate objects emerges as the explicate (or unfolded) order, which has the grainy quality with which we are familiar. There is a constant interchange between the explicate and implicate orders, which Bohm refers to as the holomovement. "An essential part of this proposal is that the whole universe is *actively* enfolded to some degree in each of its parts" (Bohm, 1988, p. 66). Furthermore: "Because we are enfolded inseparably in the world, with no ultimate division between matter and consciousness, meaning and value are as much integral aspects of the world as they are of us" (ibid., p. 67).

Bohm is advocating a kind of neutral monism (described on p. 34). In his view of reality, which is consistent with a non-dual ontology, there are deep, non-local connections between what seem to be disparate objects. These connections are outside of space and time as we know them. In Bohm's words:

> One is led to a new notion of unbroken wholeness which denies the classical idea of analyzability of the world into separately and independently existing parts ... Rather, we say that inseparable quantum interconnectedness of the whole universe is the fundamental reality.
>
> (Bohm & Hiley, 1975)

, and "the mental and the material are two sides of one overall process ... separated only in thought and not in actuality." Bohm (1989) wrote that "We may well now ask whether the close analogy between quantum processes and our inner experiences and thought processes is mere coincidence ... a hypothesis relating these two may well turn out to be fruitful." Bohm (1980) believed that the structure of our language forces us to see the world as if it were made of fragments, and this problem makes it hard to describe the quantum level of reality. Our sensory systems also predispose to our seeing a world of differences and disconnections. Bohm's view is consistent with Jung's notion of the unus mundus and with ancient ideas of the pleroma.[35]

Barad (2007) believes that we cannot view the world exclusively through the lens of human experience. She therefore de-centers human beings but includes them as integral parts of the world. She sees human beings as "specific configurations" of becoming in the world (ibid., p. 352), which emerge through "intra-actions," which is Barad's neologism; each intra-action is part of an entangled world of which we are a part.[36] Intra-acting is distinguished from interacting, a verb that assumes the existence of pre-existing, independent entities. Instead, discourse and materiality are co-constituted and ontologically entangled; matter and meaning are "mutually articulated" (ibid., p. 152). She proposes a relational ontology in which phenomena emerge from the intra-action of matter, the body, and meaning, challenging the rigid subject–object dichotomy of traditional science. For her, entities are not ontologically distinguishable; they are constructed in relationships. Matter and meaning are entangled, and people are not independent entities with inherent properties: "Existence is not an individual affair … individuals emerge through and as part of their intra-relating" (ibid., p. ix).

Barad partly bases what she calls "agential realism" on the work of Niels Bohr, which she believes rejects "things" as ontologically basic discrete entities. She reads Bohr as saying that things do not have inherently determinate boundaries or properties. Whereas Bohr's work is often seen as an epistemological account of quantum mechanics, Barad articulates the ontological dimensions of his work. She believes that Bohr denies any subject–object distinction or the distinction between knower and known. For her, the object and the agent of observation are a whole; there is no meaningful distinction between them. The measuring instrument is not ontologically distinct from the object being measured. Together they form a phenomenon that we designate as a scientific object. We designate the difference between the instrument, the object measured, and the observer through an agentic cut that is constructed. This cut allows knower and known to be distinguished and rendered intelligible.

According to Barad, scientific practices are natural processes rather than external impositions on the natural world. For her, in quantum physics phenomena are not "things" or entities. A phenomenon is the inseparability of an observed object and the agent of observation, or the relationship of the quantum object and the experimental set-up. Only phenomena are fundamentally ontologically primary or real; they are the basic unit of existence, and only phenomena have properties. Intra-actions within phenomena produce the apparent separation of observed object and the observing apparatus, which are actually ontologically entangled; they are a non-separable whole. Barad (2007) believes that quantum mechanics therefore does away with "the metaphysics of individualism" (p. 195), meaning individual objects with pre-existent individual properties. Barad therefore questions the traditional subject–object and knower-known dualisms, suggesting they only come into existence as intra-actions within phenomena.

Perhaps the emphasis on wholeness that we see in some accounts of quantum mechanics and in Jung's psychology is a defense against our sense of social fragmentation and our urgent need to find some kind of unity.

Speculation about the field quality of consciousness

The philosopher David Chalmers has suggested that consciousness can be thought of as one of the primary building blocks of nature. This sounds speculative but it is consistent with the experience of the mystics of several traditions who describe the merger of their individual minds with a larger Consciousness or universal mind. In the Upaniṣadic tradition of India, it is believed that reality is constituted by the Consciousness of Brahman. In the West, William James (2010 [1890]) proposed that consciousness could be considered to be a field. He recognized that while the brain usually acts as a reducing valve to limit our cognition, transcendent experiences occur in which consciousness is extended beyond the usual limits. The evidence from psychotherapy that consciousness is a non-local field is based on phenomena such as projective identification, somatic countertransferences, and the accuracy of images arising in the therapist's reverie. These and phenomena such as out of body and near-death experiences suggest that consciousness is not limited to the brain. Other lines of evidence for a field theory of consciousness are psi effects, which remain controversial.

Suggestions have been made that the nature of the universe is mindlike (Schäfer, 2006). It would be culturally significant if we were able to stop radically separating matter and consciousness or matter and spirit. As David Bohm (1988) pointed out, this might lead to the joining of facts, values, meaning, and even morality, which at the moment science separates, which allows us to manipulate nature by claiming that science is morally neutral.

Conclusion

Quantum mechanics postulates a hidden dimension of reality that is not visible within our everyday three-dimensional and temporal reality. The deeper level may correspond to Jung's notion of the unus mundus, or to the psychoid realm or the realm of the archetype-as-such, prior to its manifestation as a symbol. This idea would be resisted by people who think it is too metaphysical and speculative, but our mental models of reality must evolve in concert with new discoveries. We do not know the extent to which the limitations of our perceptual and cognitive categories affect our understanding of the world, and we are not certain of the relationship between the psyche and matter. Whether consciousness plays a part in this relationship at the quantum level is still debated. Quantum mechanical experiments are difficult to visualize and seem to contravene common sense, but their implications for our understanding of reality cannot be ignored. The situation may be analogous to the historical change in perspective that occurred in the change from belief in a flat earth or an earth-centered universe to the modern view. Perhaps a confluence of quantum mechanics and depth psychology will provide such a new worldview.

Notes

1 It is comforting for the non-specialist that the physicist does not know *why* the mathematical procedures work—only that they do work. Experimentalists are sometimes like technicians who operate a machine correctly without understanding exactly how it works. Because of this, there are several different interpretations of quantum mechanics.
2 This comment is attributed to the physicist David Mermin.
3 A quantum is a packet of energy.
4 The wave function is symbolized by the Greek letter Ψ, or psi, which, perhaps synchronistically, is also used as an abbreviation for psychology because it is the first letter of the Greek word *psuche*, meaning mind or soul.
5 Quantum mechanical theory was developed in Copenhagen in the early twentieth century by Niels Bohr and Werner Heisenberg.
6 Instead of the word "collapse," the word "decoherence" is sometimes used to describe the way in which a wave function interacts with the macroscopic environment. Decoherence might be the way in which movement occurs between the quantum and macroscopic realms; it is part of the process that converts the quantum level into the macroscopic level. As quantum size objects become larger, they inevitably interact with their environment. This is one reason that some theorists believe that no conscious observers are necessary for quantum mechanics, and the physical world exists apart from our observation of it—a commitment to scientific realism, which insists on a correspondence theory of truth.
7 The idea that consciousness collapses the wave function to form matter sounds like psychokinesis.
8 Light seems to us to have a dual nature; sometimes it manifests itself as a discrete particle, sometimes as a continuous wave, depending on how it is measured. This quandary has not been completely resolved, perhaps because the way in which physics tries to categorize or think about light does not correspond to its real nature, which is not known. The apparent wave–particle duality may only be a function of the way we perceive light, which may not have a dual nature in itself; it may be something that can exist in different states. Particles and waves may only be ways of describing particular observations.
9 This theory, known as ontic structural realism, suggests that there are no objects, only relational structures. Or, objects only have relational properties but no intrinsic properties. This idea denies the atomistic structure of reality in which objects are composed of elementary building blocks. The idea is controversial (Berghoffer, 2018). A part of the problem is to explain how there can be relationships without actual objects that are in relation to each other.
10 The philosophy of logical positivism may have influenced the founders of quantum theory. Logical positivists insist that statements about things that cannot be observed have no meaning, so talking about what happens in a quantum event

when no one is observing it is meaningless. This idea was sometimes thought to be a fundamental insight about the nature of reality that had been introduced by quantum mechanics. Logical positivism was shown to be flawed by philosophers such as Kuhn. Many contemporary physicists embrace scientific realism, the idea that there is an objective world independent of our observation of it.

It is debatable whether Bohr was a positivist, but he is believed to have said that there is no quantum world unless we observe it. Heisenberg believed that the quantum world exists but behaves differently than the macroscopic world. He wanted to conceptually divide reality into a level that can be observed quantum mechanically and a level that can be observed classically.

11 However, Mermin (2004) points out that this is actually a quote from an essay by an associate of Bohr describing Bohr's view. It is not clear that Bohr himself held this view.

12 Barad (2007) believes that the indeterminate nature of the natural world is the foundational issue in quantum mechanics. She believes that Heisenberg's uncertainty principle is epistemic, but Bohr's indeterminacy principle is an ontic principle in which rather than the observer being ignorant, indefiniteness belongs to the object itself. But if the act of measurement creates the phenomenon it describes, it may be that no firm distinction between ontology and epistemology can be made.

13 Pauli was a believer in the symmetrical properties of matter, the idea that a physical system that is a mirror image of another system would behave identically. He was shocked by the discovery that the parity principle of particles and anti-particles and weak interactions in the atomic nucleus was invalid.

14 The uncertainty principle says that we can never know the precise position of a quantum level particle such as an electron. It may not even be in the atom with which it is associated. Heisenberg argued that we should not assume the existence of a quantum level reality we cannot observe; we can only describe our observations of it. In his 1958 *Physics and philosophy* he takes a Platonic position, suggesting that the quantum level particles are more like ideas than ordinary physical objects, and they can only be expressed mathematically. He believed that ordinary language is not adequate to describe the quantum level.

15 Kepler believed that the planets produce tones as they orbit the sun.

16 Time dilation refers to the fact that a clock on a rocket moving near the speed of light records time slowly from the point of view of an observer on the earth. Each observer would see the other clock as slow.

17 Religious traditions would point to a cosmic or transpersonal Consciousness that observed the universe prior to the existence of humanity—an ultimate Subject. This would of course be entirely outside the domain of physical science.

18 From an interview in *The Observer*, Jan. 25, 1931, p. 17, column 3.

19 The replication crisis in psychological research came to attention about 10 years ago, when earlier experimental findings often could not be replicated even when they were repeated using the same procedures. This problem is greater in psychology than in other areas of research because of the complexities of human nature. It may be due to a degree of randomness in the psyche.

20 In the double slit experiment, which is the archetypal demonstration of quantum mechanical strangeness, photons behave like particles when detectors are present, but they behave like waves if they are not being detected. Photons behave differently depending on whether they pass through one slit on a screen or through two slits. If only one slit is open, they behave like particles. If two slits are open, they behave like waves, passing through both slits to produce a wave interference pattern. Importantly, an interference pattern appears even when only one photon at a

time is sent towards the two slits, as if the photon passed through both slits at once and then interfered with itself as if it were a wave. Photons behave like waves unless a measurement is made to determine which slit the photons went through. If a measurement is made, the photons appear as particles that appear in a single position. Measurement forces the particles to appear at one or the other slit; if the experimenter can detect exactly which of the two slits the photon went through, the interference pattern is destroyed. If the experimenter cannot tell, the interference pattern reappears. The photons seem to "know" which aspect of their nature is demanded by the experimental setup, almost as if they know they are being observed. The problem is to discover how the preference is controlled at the individual level. Bohm's pilot wave theory answers this by saying that the particle that passes through one slit is given information by the pilot wave about whether the other slit is open, and the particle choses its trajectory accordingly. There is thus a rudimentary mind-like quality present even at the quantum level.

One question raised by this experiment is how much of reality the experimenter is discovering and how much is he creating.

21 Quantum field theory is a theory of the subatomic, quantum dimension in which solid matter is replaced by excitations of field energy. Mass or solidity is an emergent phenomenon out of the quantum field. Quantum fields are carried in the quantum vacuum, an ocean of potential whose nature is unknown. The vacuum contains many interwoven fields; it is not empty. Particles and waves are really quantum fields; the matter of the universe is made of fields. Points in the field that have higher energy states are interpreted as particles, and as energy moves or oscillates through the field it looks like the particle is moving. Particles cannot be separated from the field around them.

22 Later in his life, Wigner changed his opinion about the necessity for a conscious observer, because of the difficulty of fitting the role of consciousness into the prevailing Western duality between mind and matter. As well, if consciousness is the ultimate reality, the possibility arises that there is no real, external reality outside of our consciousness. His further concern was the difficulty of disproving solipsism, the idea that only personal consciousness exists. Physicists who are committed to materialism insist that consciousness must arise from the brain, and many dislike the idea that consciousness could have an active role in their experiments.

23 Einstein wanted to remove the influence of the human observer from the results of experimentation, while Bohr thought the observer and the experiment are inseparable. Einstein was committed to scientific realism. Because Bohr is reported to have stressed the experimenter's subjectivity, in the 1920s Einstein accused Bohr of introducing mysticism into quantum physics in a way that is incompatible with science. Bohr adamantly denied this charge, and he distanced himself from the importance of consciousness. At least one biographer of Bohr says that he tried to preserve objective descriptions of atomic-level phenomena (Pais, 1991).

24 This view is different than subjective idealism, as proposed in the eighteenth century by Bishop Berkeley, which says that the world only exists to the extent that it is perceived. This view is difficult for many scientists and philosophers to accept. One critique is that idealism makes it difficult to account for intersubjective agreement between different observers. Another problem is that there was a universe before there were minds present to observe it. However, idealist philosophers with a spiritual bent postulate the existence of a universal Mind that has always existed, like the Brahman of the Upaniṣads.

25 Einstein proposed that hidden variables explain this simultaneity without violating locality, so that something is missing from quantum theory. However, Bell's

theorem proved that local hidden variables do not account for entanglement; the quantum world is indeed non-local.

26 The recent theory of modular spacetime suggests that spacetime does not exist independently of the objects within it. If space and time emerge from the quantum world, the two particles are closer at that level rather than in the ordinary physical sense.

27 Confirmation bias is the tendency to interpret data in terms of one's pre-existing beliefs. Cognitive dissonance occurs when information and evidence contradict one's existing beliefs.

28 In this context, Jung also noted that synchronistic events during mantic procedures are more likely to occur when they are connected to "interest, curiosity, expectation, hope, and fear" (CW 8, para. 912).

29 This finding is a serious problem for materialist realism, which would prefer to hold onto locality. It is not a problem for an idealist interpretation of reality, in which nonlocal consciousness simultaneously affects both particles (Goswami, 1989).

30 The term superposition means the potential or sum of all probabilities. Measurement turns the potential into an actuality.

31 This means that if two connected particles have a total spin of zero, and then fly off in opposite directions, each particle has spin of one-half, and if one spins in one direction the other spins in the opposite direction. Whichever way one particle changes, the other instantly changes in an equal and opposite way that conserves angular momentum, no matter how far apart they are. It is as if each particle instantly "knows" the spin of the other, although there is no time for information to pass between them. This conservation of spin is also found if measurement is made at different times. Somehow, the measurement of one particle fixes the result of the other. This is an example of nonlocality.

32 The zero-point field is a universal, all-pervasive background, an ocean of energy that contains electromagnetic waves and particles that spontaneously emerge into existence and disappear. Its name derives from the fact that fluctuations in the field are detectable even at temperatures of absolute zero, the lowest possible energy state.

33 Incidentally, the Indian tradition is much more accepting of psi phenomena than is the West. The spontaneous appearance of these phenomena was observed long ago. It is mentioned in Patañjali's *Yoga sūtras*, which are at least 2000 years old. In the Indian tradition, *siddhis*, or psychic abilities, are well known.

34 It is tempting to postulate that the quantum field out of which matter arises is synonymous with the field of non-local consciousness, which would be consistent with the claim of non-dual spiritual traditions that matter arises as the activity of consciousness. However, this is the kind of speculation that would be derided by may physicists because it verges on "quantum mysticism."

35 The word Pleroma means fullness. Jung used the word to refer to a dimension beyond time, space, and causality, a state of absolute unity or potential out of which anything might arise.

36 Barad believes that by making an agential cut we do not discover facts about independently existing things; rather, we bring these "things" into existence. This approaches a nondual view in which no things exist separate from anything else. From a non-dual point of view there are no individual subjects or agents or doers separate from the totality; each apparent choice and action is the result of the totality acting.

There are various interpretations of Bohr's philosophy. I should note here the claims by Faye and Jaksland (2021) that Barad is misreading Bohr. They point out that although agential realism is consistent with quantum mechanics it actually dissents from Bohr's own views and from other interpretations of quantum mechanics, even though it may be useful in social theorizing. Thus, Barad claims that "according to Bohr, "the central lesson of quantum mechanics is that we are part of the nature that we seek to understand" (p. 247). But Faye and Jaksland point out that Bohr believes it is not possible for the observer to influence the events that may appear under the experimental conditions he has arranged; "the experimenter has nothing to do with how the atomic object appears" (ibid., p. 8241), so that Barad's interpretation "finds no counterpart in Bohr's interpretation of quantum mechanics" (ibid.). There is controversy about whether Bohr was an entity realist or an antirealist—whether or not he believed that atomic objects are real entities in themselves but unknowable to the physicist except as they appear in their interaction with instruments. Bohr often claimed that the wave function only has a symbolic character, not necessarily an objective physical state. Faye and Jaksland deny Barad's claim that Bohr questions the subject–object or knower-known dualisms, which they see as "at the foundation of Bohr's interpretation of quantum mechanics" (ibid., p. 8246). They also claim that Barad's ontological use of the word "phenomena" does not correspond to Bohr's epistemological usage.

Chapter 4

The question of the Self
Jungian, Western, and Eastern approaches

Is there a self? If so, what is it?

The nature of the self, and the source of the sense of having a self, are much debated in both the Eastern and the Western religious and intellectual traditions (Siderits et al., 2010; Ganeri, 2012). The problem is to explain how it is that we experience a private inner world and a feeling of personal identity. It is easier to believe that we have a self than to explain its nature. It is easier to say *that* I am than it is to say exactly what or who I am. The problem is to explain the nature of the subject who thinks, feels, plans, and remembers, and to explain why we feel a core sense of continuity across time.

There seems to be a kind of subjective mental "space" into which our awareness of reality emerges, a kind of center of what it feels like to exist, and an internal locus of intention and agency. We can give an auto-biographical account of ourselves if we are asked who we are, and we can reflect on ourselves. In fact, the capacity for self-reflection is sometimes said to bring the self into being, in a strange loop (Hofstadter, 2008).[1] However, it has been difficult to know whether there is an ontological self that is carrying out these psychological functions or whether the combination of these functions constitute what we refer to as a self, which is then purely phenomenal, not necessarily an ontological entity.

One of the main issues is whether the word "self" refers to a spiritual or metaphysical principle, such as the Ātman of the Upaniṣadic tradition or Jung's Self as the "God within." In contrast, postmodern philosophers and many psychologists deny any essence to the personality and see the sense of self as constructed by a combination of language, narrative, relationships, neural activity, and culture. For some theorists the self is a fiction rather than an essential, stable, bounded, coherent entity. The self is often seen as an emergent phenomenon, constantly being re-formed (Gergen, 1991). Psychotherapists use the term "self" as a convenient way of thinking about personality and to describe clinical phenomena, but they may not have a commitment to any particular ontological theory of the self, which for practical purposes can be treated phenomenologically.

DOI: 10.4324/9781032618456-4

In Western psychology, William James (2010 [1890]) sparked an interest in the self because of his long chapter on this subject in his *The principles of psychology*. Here, he discussed the self as the origin of agency within the personality. He distinguished between various senses of the self; the "me" refers to one's experience of oneself and feelings that one attributes to oneself. In contrast the "I" is a core self, the knower and doer, the focus of experience that is most intimately ours; it includes our moral sensibility, conscience, and will. James thought that it was not necessary for psychology to study the "I," which could be relegated to philosophy. He asserted that "thought is itself the thinker, and psychology need not look beyond" (James, 1950 [1890], p. 401). James also recognized a material self, including the body, possessions, home, and family, a social self that refers to the way others see us, and a spiritual self containing emotions and desires. James believed that the "pure ego" is a puzzling feature of the self, which allows it to recognize its own thoughts and brings them together. (James by the way was not happy with the concept of the unconscious, which he thought was a whimsical idea that could be used to prove anything.) Most subsequent Western psychologists focused on what James called the self as the sense of "me," which can be an object of knowledge.

Because the self is always changing, Western philosophers often prefer the idea of a constantly evolving self, making it a process rather than an entity, so that over time it is the same in some ways yet also different. Psychologists such as Erickson emphasize that one's sense of identity may change at different stages of life, but identity and the sense of self are not synonymous.[2] The self may be different than the person's identity, which is affected by factors such as nationality, culture, gender, ethnicity, economic status, and other demographic factors. Some of these may change during a lifetime, while the sense of being a continuous self may not.

Ideas about self-fulfillment, self-determination, and self-actualization are widespread in popular culture, and they are very appealing. Accordingly, the sense of a self-as-subject plays a major role in Western society. Even though the nature of the self and the means by which it is developed remain controversial, we have an intuitive sense of its persistent existence, although this is denied by several theorists who see the self as illusory, only a folkloric idea.

The Western tradition's emphasis on self-development, exemplified by Maslow's (1971) concept of self-actualization and Jung's notion of individuation, imply an intrinsic and characteristic individuality. These theories imply that the self gradually grows and improves, and its essential nature becomes clearer. The overall emphasis in the West is therefore largely on becoming than on Being itself, which is much more characteristic of traditions such as Vedānta, which emphasize the eternal sameness of the Ātman or the spiritual Self at the core of the personality, which is not born and does not die. For this tradition the "who am I" question is better stated as "what am I," since the pronoun "who" sounds personal, but the ultimate subject, the transpersonal Self or the Ātman, is considered to be impersonal.

Even the body participates in selfhood; immunology tells us that certain parts of the body are recognized as belonging to the body-self, while anything that is perceived as non-self, such as an invading microorganism, is attacked, so there seems to be a sense of self at the cellular level. The brain also participates in this recognition, as evidenced by a neurological condition known as asomatognosia, usually due to parietal lobe damage, which makes the individual not recognize parts of his body as belonging to him. The psychological effects of split-brain surgery also raise the question of the relationship of selfhood to the brain, since division of the corpus callosum may produce the sense of two sub-selves with different attitudes, although in some such cases there remains one dominant sense of self. For the materialist who believes that the brain produces consciousness, the brain organizes experiences in a way that constitutes or expresses the self. The philosopher Derek Parfit (1986, p. 273) believes that "what I really am is my brain ... I am essentially my brain." In his view, there are only brains and bodies; there is no other source of personal identity.

Many philosophers are skeptical about the existence of a self, following the example of the eighteenth-century philosopher David Hume, who noted that when he searched inside his mind, all he found was a collection of rapidly changing feelings and perceptions; he could not find a self that was distinct from them, although this does not prove it does not exist. To whom do these experiences occur? What holds the bundle of experiences together?

Psychotherapeutic views of the ego and self

The self became central to the practice of psychotherapy with the advent of humanistic psychology, psychoanalysis, and especially psychoanalytic self-psychology. Humanistic psychology was concerned with the search for personal identity, authenticity, and self-actualization, or the fulfillment of all the potentials of the self. Carl Rogers believed that people have an "actualizing tendency," or an innate wish to realize the full potentials of the self. The person in therapy wants to "become more and more himself ... trying to discover something more basic, something more truly himself" (Rogers, 1961, p. 109). Perhaps Rogers was thinking about Shakespeare's admonition: "This above all—to thine own self be true" (*Hamlet*, 1, iii, 75).

The terms ego and self are taken for granted in much contemporary psychoanalytic thought, but the meaning of these terms has varied a good deal. Freud used the German noun *das Ich*, which literally means the "I," the person we feel ourselves to be, but sometimes this word was subsequently understood to mean the self, the person as a whole, and sometimes to refer to the ego. Freud rarely used the German term "Das Selbst." In his early writing, he sometimes used the term ego to refer to the total self, and sometimes to refer to a group of ideas, some of which are allowed to become conscious while others are repressed because they are unacceptable. After 1923, Freud redefined his idea of the ego as one of the three subdivisions or structures within the mental apparatus (in contrast to the id and superego). The ego mediates between the instinctual demands of the id and the moral demands of society and the superego. Freud decided that some of the ego's operations are automatic and unconscious, especially its defensive operations. A disagreement subsequently arose between psychoanalytic theorists who saw the self as a sub-function of the ego and those who saw the self as the whole person. In some psychoanalytic literature, the term self refers to a group of self-representations in the mind, the concept one has of oneself. Or it may refer to an internal agent, a center of personal values and autonomous striving. Other authors use the terms ego and self as synonyms. Usually today the ego refers to a set of functions such as perception, attention, planning, adaptation to reality, object relations, integration of the personality, and language. It is sometimes reified and referred to as if it were an executor of behavior.

For Jung, the term ego refers to the field of consciousness. It is the "subject of all personal acts of consciousness" and the "center of the field of consciousness" (CW 9ii, para. 1), in contrast to the Self, which he sees as the center of the whole personality and a deeper level of identity than the ego. He sees the ego as "a highly complex affair full of unfathomable obscurities" (CW 14, para. 129). He believed that the ego is supremely important "in bringing reality to light" (ibid., para. 130), as if the ego's awareness of reality is a kind of second creation. Jung believed that the Self or the unconscious uses the ego as a reflecting mirror to become conscious of itself; it is a "divine instrument" (ibid., para. 132). In the Jungian literature, the word ego is often used to refer to the empirical personality. Roughly speaking, in much of the contemporary psychoanalytic literature the word "self" is similar to Jung's use of the term "ego." Jung does not discuss ego defenses in the manner of the Freudian tradition. His classification of ego functions and his typology, which divides people into introverts and extraverts and the individual's preference for thinking, feeling, sensation, and intuition, has been developed into the Myers–Briggs Type Indicator, which has been helpful in managing relational and organizational differences.

In her *New ways in psychoanalysis*, Karen Horney described a "spontaneous individual self" (Horney, 1939, p. 9) that could not be analyzed into instinctual components. Its main characteristic is genuineness. She believed that alienation from oneself is at the core of neurosis, and the therapeutic goal is to "restore the individual to himself … and find his center of gravity in himself" (ibid., p. 11). In her 1950 *Neurosis and human growth*, the self becomes central to her theory; she speaks of the self as a "central inner force common to all human beings and yet unique in each, which is the deepest source of growth" (ibid., p. 17). For her, the real self is not truly analyzable.

The concept of a true rather than false self is important to Winnicott (1965); his idea presupposes a pre-verbal self that exists prior to any interaction with others. This true self, which develops given a psychologically supportive environment, is spontaneous, natural, and not constrained. If it is not allowed to express itself, the individual develops a false self, which is compliant, inhibited, and forced to behave in accord with the wishes of others. However, whether the "false" self is really not part of the individual's true self is debatable, and sometimes the distinction requires a value judgment about what aspects of the personality are preferred. The self we believe ourselves to be is prone to self-deception, distortions, and defenses designed to protect its vulnerability.

Kohut (1971), the founder of psychoanalytic self-psychology, does not define the self clearly, in part because he believed that the essence of the self is not knowable; we only see its manifestations. The self is the person's experience of him- or herself as a whole, as a person continuous over time. Kohut refers to the self as a "center of initiative and a recipient of impressions" (Kohut, 1977, p. 99). The self for Kohut is not a representation in the mind or a concept of oneself in one's mind, as it was in earlier psychoanalytic theory. The self is a supraordinate structure, the entire psychological system of a person, and also an internal experience that has continuity in time and space. Kohut believed that the personality has a nuclear program or innate design that unfolds to form a sense of self, which is built up in development as a result of interaction with others. The development of a healthy sense of self requires the presence of an empathic, responsive milieu in childhood, in which the child is valued and mirrored in an emotionally attuned way. The child also needs idealizable caregivers who can soothe the child and provide a sense of direction. For Kohut, pressure from the nuclear self to express its talents and abilities provides an inborn motivation to realize its potentials during development. One of the primary conflicts in development is the tension between the unfolding of the nuclear self in an authentic way and the environmental pressures that may not allow it to do so. The self in psychoanalytic self-psychology became central to understanding both normal development and psychopathology.

From soul to self

Soul

Many cultures believe that human beings have a spiritual essence, often described as a soul, which religions typically see as an immaterial, immortal principle within the person. People in radically different religious cultures, both historically and geographically, believe that mind, body, and soul are somehow distinct, although the exact relationship of soul and body is argued. Religious traditions typically privilege the soul over the personal self, and they believe the soul gives us our permanent sense of identity, whereas the body is changing all the time. For the ancients, the true self was the soul.

Before Descartes, the soul was regarded as the agent of both bodily functions and also cognitive functions such as thinking. In the mid-seventeenth century, Descartes decided that physiological functions were purely material and were separate from the soul, which is entirely immaterial, independent of the body, and without a physical location. He regarded the soul as the province of all mental faculties that could not be understood mechanistically, such as beliefs, feelings, and free will.

Until the early eighteenth century, the existence of the soul was largely taken for granted, but after the Enlightenment the idea gradually became secularized. By the end of the nineteenth century, the emerging discipline of psychology had replaced the soul with the mind and adopted a radically dualistic distinction between mind and body. Thanks to the influence of behaviorism in the early years of twentieth-century psychology, notions of soul, mind, and consciousness seemed to be off limits to empirical inquiry, in contrast to personality, the body, and observable behavior. Today, the word soul is used in religion, in folk psychology, and colloquially in phrases such as "a lost soul," but it is virtually a taboo in mainstream academic psychology because of this field's materialist bias. Jung is an exception to this neglect; for him, the soul is a reality. He speaks of the soul as "the living thing in man, that which lives of itself and causes life" (CW 9i, par. 56). He constantly maintained the importance of the idea of the soul, using it to convey the sense of a deeper level of subjectivity than the ego. He sees the soul as the source of dream images and the imagination, and the home of "supreme values," possessing an innate religious function (CW 12, para. 14). Sometimes he used the word as a synonym for the psyche as a whole, sometimes as a kind of intrapsychic organ that links or bridges consciousness with the depth of the psyche. Jung's concern for the soul has continued in the work of subsequent theorists within the Jungian world, for whom the soul is of primary concern. In the Jungian literature, the term "soul" is typically used to refer to the mystery of human nature, which cannot be reduced to simple terms because of its links to the transcendent dimension.

James Hillman (1975, pp. 67–70) believes that soul cannot be defined rigorously; it is "a perspective rather than a substance, a viewpoint towards things rather than a thing itself. The soul makes meaning possible, turns events into experiences, is communicated in love, and has a religious concern." In his work, soul is our capacity for imagination, that which recognizes all realities as primarily symbolic or metaphorical. Evangelos Christou (1976) suggested that what we refer to as body, mind, and soul are different orders of reality. Each has its own perspective. The body is concerned with sense perceptions and physicality, the mind with ideas and concepts. The soul deals with what really matters to us, the discovery of meaning in life, how we reflect on our mental and physical states and integrate them into our lives, and our capacity to develop the imagination. Wolfgang Giegerich (2012b) sees the soul as the core concept of psychology. He does not see the soul in its traditional metaphysical sense, as a substantial agent or entity or substance, and he complains that Jung did not fully let go of a metaphysical approach to the soul. For Giegerich the use of this word is purely mythological language with no single meaning. The soul exists, it is real, it is indispensable, the essence of Jung's psychology, but it should not be reified. He points out that the word soul is used differently in different contexts. The soul is about the sphere of shared meaning generated by specific cultural communities. The soul is about human interiority and subjectivity, quite separate from the biological organism. The soul is the productivity of the mind such as fantasies, dreams, or art, or however the mind formulates what deeply moves us. Soul is also manifest outside the person in communities and cultural institutions such as religions. The soul "comprises consciousness as such as well as the world as a whole" (ibid., p. 74). Giegerich uses the term "the logical life" of the soul to mean not its rules of reasoning but its internal structures, complexity, and relationships. The soul has its own dynamics, necessities, and ways of unfolding and changing over time. The origin of the soul is itself.

With the exception of Jungian writers, modern psychology has no need for the soul. Stress on the mind or the self has entirely replaced the soul or relegated it to the province of religion. For materialistic psychology, everything attributable to the soul is now a function of the brain. This kind of psychology has contributed to the virtual erasure of concern with the soul for the majority of people in contemporary Western cultures, leading to preoccupation with conscious concerns, ignoring what in *The red book* Jung referred to as the Spirit of the Depths.

What is the self?

The question of how to account for the individual's sense of selfhood and sense of continuous identity over time is ancient and unresolved (Sorabji, 2006). We sense the presence of an "I" that remembers, thinks, and experiences, but it is difficult to explain exactly what carries out these functions. Part of the problem is to explain how the combination of our sensory information in five different modalities produces a unified, synchronized field of awareness, the so-called "binding" problem. Binding occurs in the brain in a way that fuses perceptions such as color, sound, size, shape, and mass, all of which are processed differently and at different speeds, but which seem to arise within our awareness at the same time. This function is important because it contributes to the sense that we have a unified self that is the subject of experience. Without binding, we would experience a flow of perceptions, thoughts, and feelings as a stream of separate events rather than a unity within an apparent center of consciousness.

Notions about the self, especially whether there is such a thing as a true self, an essential or core self, are controversial in academic psychology (Strohminger et al., 2017; Leary & Tangney, 2012). This controversy is especially true of notions of a transpersonal[3] Self, as we find in Jung and the Upaniṣadic tradition. For some writers, the self is a purely empirical, psychological concept, socially and developmentally achieved. Klein (2010) suggests that rather than being an entity, the self may be a set of multiple, interrelated processes and systems, such as a combination of memory and knowledge of the facts of one's life. He suggests that much of the confusion in the literature results from a failure to distinguish between two metaphysically separable aspects of the self (Klein, 2012). The epistemological self is based on a collection of neural activity that provide features such as memory and various aspects of the personality. The ontological self can be conceived of as single, subjective, unified awareness. The epistemological self and its neurology are empirically testable, without the difficulties that accompany ontological questions about the nature of the self. When psychologists focus on the self, they are usually investigating the epistemological self and the neural systems that underpin it. Klein thinks that the epistemological self is at least in part responsible for providing the ontological self with knowledge of who and what it is. The epistemological self is an object we can investigate, while the ontological self is a subject, and has largely been ignored. (It would correspond in some ways to Jung's Self and the Upaniṣadic Ātman). For Klein, the ontological and epistemological selves are not reducible to each other, and he cites several cases in which the epistemological self is lost because of brain damage but the sense of subjective self-awareness, or ontological selfhood, is preserved. He points out that the ontological subject cannot be reduced to an object of inquiry and study without stripping it of its status as a subject; it cannot be an object to itself, and it cannot be observed directly as an object of self-reflection. Klein therefore approaches the Vedāntic idea that the Self is the ultimate Subject and can never become an object.

In Klein's view, the ontological self is not reducible to neurological functioning. He endorses the transmission theory of consciousness, which is that the brain does not create the ontological self but enables its expression (Kelly et al., 2009). This view, however, maintains a dualistic matter-mind split and runs into the problem of how consciousness and the brain interact, so at best it can only be a metaphor. From a non-dual, Vedāntic point of view, there is no "relationship" between brain and personal consciousness since they are two aspects or manifestations of the same Pure Consciousness, seen from different frames of reference or perspectives.[4] From the Vedāntic point of view, although empirically there are two levels of consciousness, one Absolute and one relative or personal, there is ultimately no division between an ontological self and an epistemological self because consciousness cannot be divided. The epistemological self is one of the manifestations of the more fundamental, irreducible ontological Self, which is Pure Consciousness. This Self cannot be found on brain scans or by any other scientific means (Ruby & Legrand, 2007) because it is not material. However, as Klein (2012) points out, the scientific method does not exhaust our ways of knowing reality; there may be aspects of reality that are not amenable to the scientific method, and there are levels of existence that cannot be captured using constructs such as matter, energy, or universal laws.

To describe the self, it has been tempting to imagine a homunculus fantasy of a little person in the head who is doing the remembering, thinking, perceiving, and all the other activities of the self, as if there is a spectator in an inner theater. But this does not solve the problem of who is the spectator, and leads to an infinite regress, since it requires another homunculus in the head of the homunculus, and so on ad infinitum. So, is there some kind of self-entity that initiates behavior and makes decisions? There are a range of contemporary theories of the self.

Theories of the nature of the self

Typical of materialistic theories of the self, Damasio (2010, p. 8) believes that the brain constructs the mind and consciousness, and ultimately the self is "a dynamic collection of integrated neural processes" (p. 10). For him, the self is a process, not a thing, that is present whenever we are conscious. Damasio believes we have an autobiographical self, which consists of lasting long-term memories, personality characteristics, life experiences, and behavioral traits, but we also have a core self that is transient, constantly being recreated for each object with which the brain interacts.

Typical of experiential theories of the self, Zahavi (2005, 2014) sees the self as a mental thing, the subject of experience, and an integral part of our consciousness. He believes that the experience of the sense of self constitutes the self; consciousness is self-consciousness, which is many-layered, including functions such as self-reflection, agency, and decision making. The feeling of the subjective ownership of an experience is a property of the self; each experience has a first-person character, or what-it-is-like-for-me-ness, which allows an experience to feel like mine rather than belonging to another. This first-person characteristic remains the same through each experience, producing a continuous sense of self. Perhaps the weakness of this theory is that it does not address how the continuity of the self is maintained over time. Ratcliffe (2017) has a similar, experiential theory of the self but stresses the importance of interpersonal relationships in the development of the self and subjectivity. He sees the self as developed and sustained interpersonally and continually dependent on other people, even in adulthood.

Strawson's "minimal self" theory sees the self as a distinct mental entity (Strawson, 1997, 2011). Each self *is* the structure of its experiences; the self is not a thing separate from the experience. He suggests that the self is brief and episodic rather than continuous; it exists from milliseconds up to a few seconds with the end of each short-lived experience, and it is constantly being replaced. We constantly return to consciousness from momentary unconsciousness or absences, whereupon the self and consciousness restart. For this author there is no self or experiencing subject without an experience. The self is therefore distinct from personality, personhood, and agency, or other psychological features we attribute to people. The qualities of the person are not the same as the qualities of the self. There is no good explanation for how these other qualities interact with the self. For Strawson, many selves will exist during a person's lifespan. We have the impression of long-term continuity, but that does not mean that the self is a continuous mental thing. The sense of continuity that some people have is a narrative perspective that is constantly being updated. Strawson believes that there are other people beside himself who do not have much sense of the mental presence of an "I" that exists over time—they are naturally episodic, with little interest in the past. Strawson's view of the self depends on the view that mental phenomena are ultimately neurologically based.

Postmodern views of the self view it as largely the result of the accretion of social interactions, with no essential aspect. Ryan and Rigby (2015) believe that the self exists in the form of a self-schema, a fixed mental image based on early learning, roles, skills, and habits. This schema changes over time. Narrative theories of the self argue that the self is a story we develop that links experiences that would otherwise be episodic. In this view, the self is constructed by means of memories and storytelling, using self-reflection and language to form a sense of personal identity. The self is then a fiction rather than a mental thing, or the story is itself the self. Dennett (1992) sees the self as a purely fictional product; the self is an abstraction or an idea, an illusion, neither a mental nor a physical thing. For him, we invent the self using language. The self is a figurative center of gravity where the individual's stories meet to form an autobiography; one is the main character in a book of one's own making. The self constantly changes to incorporate new experiences. Notably, approaches to the self based on the idea that it is constructed rather than innate may not adequately explain the ineradicable, subjective sense of "I am," which may account for the persistence of the idea of a core self.

Is there a core or true self?

With a few exceptions (Taylor, 2012), many contemporary philosophers and psychologists do not believe there is an ontological or core self (Carruthers, 2011; Weger et al., 2016; Weger & Herbig, 2019; Schlegel et al., 2013), especially if this is conceived of as non-material, in part because we would then have the problem of how a non-material entity could interact with the physical body. Physicalism sees the self, if it exists at all, as a function of brain activity. All human subjectivity is then reduced to neural activity, and the notion of an ontological self is seen as an anachronistic, folkloric idea. Ryle (1949) suggests that thoughts and feelings are simply what the brain does; mind or the self is an activity of the brain, not an entity or a "ghost in the machine." Baggini (2011) is typical of contemporary writers who deny that there is any core self, in spite of our sense of continuity. For him, the apparent unity of the self is due to an organized collection of individual functions, combined with our memories, experiences, and learning. The self is not a thing independent of its constituents. In a similar vein, Metzinger (2009) suggests that the self is an illusion or model created by the brain.

Critics of the notion of an essential or true self deny the idea that the individual has an inborn identity. Expressions such as "be yourself" or "be true to yourself" are seen as merely colloquial terms or folk psychology. However, folk psychology is here to stay, and psychotherapists must take it into account all the time. People who believe in a true self see it as a kind of kernel of authenticity within the personality that outlasts impermanent aspects of the self. However, it is not always clear what "authentic" means; it may suggest that we express our deepest nature in our behavior, acting without deception in a way that is true to our real beliefs and values. Authenticity may mean being true to our innate temperament, dispositions, and talents. However, this idea does not consider the necessity for a social persona and the inevitability of concealing shadow material, both of which are also part of the self. Furthermore, one might feel comfortable with the self one has, even if its potentials have not been realized.

A typical example of the idea that we have a true self arises in situations of inner conflict. For example, a fundamentalist Christian may be torn between homosexual impulses, which he feels reflects his true nature, and biblical notions that this behavior is wrong, an idea that he has internalized as a result of his environment, so that it too seems to be a part of his sense of self. In such cases, we may ask whether one or other pole of the tension is more authentically a part of the true self, and how we would know which is which. The outcome of decisions of this kind is sometimes seen as the result of contact with a "core" self. In their review of the concept of the true self, Strohminger et al. (2017) suggest that "What counts as part of the true self is subjective and strongly tied to what each individual person herself most prizes" (p. 557). Furthermore, the observer's assessment of the attitude of the person's true self depends on the observer's values. If the observer thinks that homosexuality is wrong, he or she will believe that the desire to resist these feelings represents the true self. Strohminger et al. believe that the notion of a true self is really a "hopeful phantasm" because hidden properties may be assumed or attributed to it that may contradict the available data about the person, as when a manifestly evil person is deemed to be good "deep down." Therefore, they believe that because the idea of a true self is radically subjective and unverifiable, it cannot be a scientific concept, although it may be a "useful fiction," even as it remains a fiction. Rather than being an innate set of properties, what we consider to be the true self can also be seen to be a function of the individual's acquired values combined with those of the social environment.

Baumeister and Bushman (2013) ask why, if the inner self is different than the way the person usually acts, we should necessarily consider the inner one the "true" self? Sparby et al. (2019) point out that it may be unwarranted to posit a true self that exists so deeply within the structure of the personality that it never appears in reality. They suggest that the true self is an essence that is difficult to investigate using conventional philosophical and psychological means because these are based on external observation. However, they believe that the true self can be studied from a first-person perspective. Weger and Herbig (2021) point out that because it is so subjective, the self cannot be a subject of academic inquiry if this inquiry is practiced in its current form. Many academic psychologists subscribe to the view that the existence of a true self is only a posit, not provable. Nevertheless, the self is a convenient convention whose existence is often taken for granted, especially by psychotherapists.

The problem of multiple personality complicates the issue of whether there is a true self. In the case of multiple personality, the self spontaneously splits, and any sub-personality may become the dominant one, temporarily displacing the host personality. Often, each sub-personality is a complex in Jung's sense. This disorder reveals how potentially fluid the self may become. All the sub-personalities are authentic parts of the self; they all belong. Even people who are not suffering from this difficulty know that their personality has different aspects to it. Sometimes we find ourselves acting in a way that is contrary to our usual personality, for example when we are possessed by an emotionally powerful complex. In dreams, we see many unknown characters that are assumed to be aspects of the dreamer, all components of the same self.

Jung on the Self

Jung's view of the transpersonal Self is a radically different idea than notions of the personal self used by mainstream academic and psychoanalytic psychology. The most important distinction is that Jung believes that the Self is an a priori image of the divine within the psyche, which he refers to as the God within (CW 7, para. 399). This presence accounts for the ubiquity of religion in all human cultures, where the Self is projected onto whatever is the local name for divinity.

In the English language Jungian literature, the word "Self" is often written with an upper-case letter "S" to distinguish it from the personal self or the empirical personality, although this convention was not adopted in Jung's *Collected Works,* perhaps because the editors did not want to give the impression that Jung was writing about spirituality. However, it seems an essential distinction given the development of psychoanalytic self-psychology, which concerns the development and vicissitudes of the personal self.

For Jung, the term "Self" describes both the center of gravity of the psyche and also the totality of consciousness and the unconscious, the "whole range of psychic processes in man. It expresses the unity of the personality as a whole" (CW 6, para. 789; CW 12, paras. 20 and 44). The Self is also the psyche's organizing principle, the guide of the individuation process, and the archetypal source of the empirical personality. Jung points out that when talking about the Self he is describing something "essentially unknown and expressing it in terms of psychic structures which may not be adequate to the nature of what is to be known" (CW 11, para. 956). The Self can be recognized in dream imagery that manifests numinosity, a sense of wholeness, or the union of opposite qualities. Jung insisted that this kind of imagery is empirically demonstrable, so the existence of the Self is not a merely metaphysical or theological assertion. He is willing to accept a much wider range of Self symbols than would traditionally be accepted as images of the sacred. At times therefore, the Self appears in dream symbols that are radically different than images of the divine found in the theistic traditions. The following is a dream image of the Self, reported by Corbett (2021):

> I was surrounded by a fine mist. I sensed a presence, as if someone was coming towards me. The mist opened to reveal a gigantic blue eye, about three feet across. I felt penetrated by its gaze as I stood there in awe and fascination. The contours of the eye became red, orange, and gold. The eye came closer, until I was only aware of the round iris, which became square, then round, then square again, continuing to change in this way. The eye now seemed like a huge window or door, beyond which I could see a world of light, and into which I could now enter. I was excited by this landscape, yet also frightened by the sense of infinity, boundlessness, and eternity I saw. The light beyond the door was unlike any light I have ever seen; it was silvery and cold, but also warm, soft, and colorless. I felt as though I was falling into it.

The eye is a maṇḍala,[5] one of the important ways in which the Self appears in dreams.

Here are two further surprising manifestations of the Self in dreams, reported by Mansfield and Spiegelman (1989):

> I am in a European city, crossing a Renaissance bridge to a futuristic city. This bridge is quite beautiful, with sculpture along the sides, but it is also paved in the modern way. As I walk across the bridge, I see a figure corning toward me. He is a crippled beggar with only half a body, rolling on a kind of skateboard. As he approaches me, I greet him, and he informs me that he is God. Surprised but not astonished, I nod and offer

him a drink at a kiosk at the side of the bridge. He accepts and now has a full body, rather large, in fact. We drink wine in a mutual toast to each other. He now holds his hands over my own and there pours, from his fingers on to my palms, a great number of gold and silver coins from every nation and every time.

I am informed that God is a great worm whose body constitutes the matter of the entire universe. All the galaxies are his organs, and all the living forms are cells within these organs. The worm doubles back on itself, head to tail, like the uroboros, and undergoes a vast pattern of inhalation and exhalation. Those creatures fortunate enough to be located at the regions of the body where this breathing occurs can have mystical experiences.

Obviously, the Self as a giant eye, a great worm, or a crippled beggar with half a body would not be accepted as manifestations of the divine by many traditional theists who advocate a transcendent divinity. However, because of the numinosity and emotional power of these images, for Jung they are manifestations of the archetypal level of the psyche and hence ultimately of the Self. Each such symbol is only a partial manifestation of the Self, which cannot be fully known because it includes both consciousness and the unconscious, and the unconscious can never be known in its totality.

Jung thought we cannot decide the exact relationship of dream images of the Self to the metaphysical God of the theistic traditions, but he assumed that there is some kind of psychological relationship between them, and that "there is an original beyond our images" (CW 18, para. 1589). An important distinction between Jung's approach and traditional theological notions of divinity is that Jung sees the manifestations of the Self as emerging from the archetypal level of the psyche rather than from the heavenly or transcendent realm described by theology. For Jung, the experience of transcendence is synonymous with the experience of the objective psyche, which is the source of the gods and goddesses of all religious and mythological pantheons.

Human images of God have evolved since antiquity, and Corbett (2021) sees Jung's approach as a further step in this evolution, essentially the emergence of a new myth of God. Corbett points out that Jung's approach to the Self has the advantage of being based on personal experience and does not require belief in a sacred text, an institution, or adherence to a creed. A further advantage is that Jung avoids the anthropomorphic images of God typical of the theistic traditions, and he by-passes some of the philosophical issues raised by traditional theological descriptions of the divine. Importantly for Jung, images of the divine may evolve or transform as we penetrate further and further into the unconscious (Jung, 1975, p. 314). A further important difference between Jung's notion of the Self and traditional theistic God-images is that Jung accepts each experience of the Self as a form of personal revelation, a possibility that many religious traditions deny.

Jung insists that his notion of the Self is based purely on observations of its appearance in the psyche, and the existence of an intrapsychic God-image says nothing positive or negative about the existence of God in the traditional metaphysical sense (CW 12, para. 15). However, Jung often speaks of God in a way that goes beyond the notion of an intrapsychic God-image, for example in his *Answer to Job*. In this text, Jung asserts one of his most controversial ideas, suggesting that the divine has a dark side that causes evil and suffering. According to Jung, the God-image of the biblical story was unconscious of its dark side and needed human consciousness to become aware of it. Extending this idea, Jung believes that the Self, or the transpersonal unconscious, is a totality containing all the opposites, such as good and evil, and can only become conscious by differentiating itself within the human psyche. For Jung, this implies a process of mutual transformation between humanity and divinity. This and the seamless continuity of the human and transpersonal levels of the psyche allows Jung to speak of the "relativity" of God (CW 6, para. 412), meaning a process of reciprocal relationship rather than an absolute separation of the human and the divine realms.

Although Jung sees the Self as the "God within," he goes on to say that he is not trying to create a "God substitute." He is simply empirically demonstrating the "existence of a totality supraordinate to consciousness," which the ego experiences as something numinous. "This 'self' never at any time takes the place of God, though it may perhaps be a vessel for divine grace" (CW 10, para. 874).

Individuation and the Self

Jung believes that individual ego consciousness or the empirical personality arise from the unconscious, within which it was contained as a potential (CW 9i, para. 503). The personality emerges out of an original wholeness, in which it begins in a germinal state that gradually unfolds during the individuation process (CW 7, para. 186). Fordham (1976) referred to this state as the primary Self.[6] Jung's notion of individuation suggests that the empirical personality gradually incarnates or incorporates more and more of the innate potentials of the a priori Self throughout the life span. For Jung, this process is guided by the Self, which acts as a blueprint for the evolution of the personality, so that the Self is the archetypal basis of the development of the ego. This is similar to Kohut's notion that the personal self has a kind of innate program that it is trying to fulfill but requires responsive social interactions in childhood to develop firmly. However, Kohut's self does not have the spiritual (*imago dei*) quality of Jung's Self.

Jung believes that individuation means embracing our "incomparable uniqueness ... becoming one's own self ... 'coming to selfhood' or 'self-realization'" (CW 7, para. 266.) It is as if the Self "wants" to realize and differentiate itself, using human consciousness as a vehicle for this purpose. In fact, this process occurs whether or not the ego cooperates consciously. Jung (1965, p. 3) describes his own life as the "self-realization of the unconscious. Everything in the unconscious seeks outward manifestation, and the personality too desires to evolve out of its unconscious condition and to experience itself as a whole." One of the ways this process manifests itself is by means of constant pressure from the unconscious to become conscious, for example in dreams but also in symptoms.

Eastern views: the Self in the Upaniṣadic tradition

The issue of the self is particularly important, indeed central, in the traditions that arose out of the Upaniṣads, the sacred scriptures of the Hindu traditions.[7] Here, a central question is the search for absolute spiritual reality. Whereas traditional Western approaches to the self typically rely on quantitative or qualitative research methods or psychotherapeutic evidence, Eastern approaches to the Self (or no-Self in Buddhism) are based on practices such as Yoga and meditation, although self-inquiry is also prominent. There is general agreement in many Eastern traditions that because of our cognitive limitations the empirical reality that we experience is not the ultimate reality, and the knowledge we have of the world is not the ultimate truth. The empirical personality is not the core or essence of the person, which has to be realized by means of spiritual practices, which offer the potential for freedom from the limitations of empirical existence even when one is still embodied. The wide range of Eastern traditions have conflicting views about how this liberation can be attained, and they differ on the question of whether or not there is a divine Self or anything permanent within the person. I have chosen two contrasting approaches to illustrate some of these different approaches to the self: the tradition of Advaita Vedānta and some features of Buddhism.

The Self in Advaita Vedānta

In the tradition of Advaita Vedānta, the substrate of reality is described as Pure Consciousness, which I write here with an upper-case letter "C" to distinguish it from the personal, heavily conditioned consciousness of the empirical personality. These are only separable conceptually, since Consciousness is seen as indivisible (Indich, 1980). This universal Consciousness is a single, unitary, non-dual, principle, known as Brahman, which underlies or is the same as the entirety of empirical reality. Brahman is the unifying ground of all states of consciousness, a kind of universal cosmic soul, the essence of the entire universe. The personal psyche, or the apparently individual mind, is a local function of Pure Consciousness, which is entirely independent of human mental processes. Within each apparent individual lies the

Ātman, the eternal, spiritual Self, which is identical to the supreme Consciousness of Brahman, the infinite, divine spirit of creation (Aitareya Upaniṣad I.2.1). According to Śaṅkara, the (eighth century) important exponent of this tradition, the existence of the Ātman is self-revealing in the awareness that one exists, in the felt sense of "I am." The Ātman is the ultimate Subject of awareness, and so cannot become an object. Strictly speaking, one cannot say anything about it, but for pedagogic and discussion purposes we use language while we recognize the limitations of language. The task of spiritual development is the sublation of the empirical self and the realization of the Ātman.

The Vedāntic Self or the Ātman is entirely impersonal. It is the ground or source of the individual's consciousness. Our awareness of the Ātman is obscured by the superimposition onto it of personal psychological material such as conceptual thought, one's self-image, feelings, desires, memories, bodily sensations, language, and our sense of personal identity. This personal level of consciousness conceals the Ātman in a way analogous to the way the clouds obscure the sun, which is always present. Another metaphor is to see the personal mind as a wave or eddy within the ocean of Totality, inseparable from it. If the personal material of the psyche were like a movie playing on a screen, in this metaphor the screen represents Pure Consciousness, or the Ātman, which is not affected by the movie, which is analogous to personality factors coloring the screen. This divine Self is non-dual; there is no other. The Ātman is unlimited by anything finite and unmodified by the personality. When we use the word "me" we superimpose personality characteristics onto the Ātman. This misappropriation of the properties of the personal self onto the Ātman is a basic error, resulting from *avidyā*, or ignorance. In meditation, one gets "behind" the personal contents of consciousness to That which is aware of the contents, as if one were looking at the screen on which a movie is played rather than the movie itself. In meditation, the apparent self is lost and becomes identical with Pure Consciousness itself.

The Ātman is the only source of consciousness; it illumines the perceptions, thoughts, and behavior of the empirical personality. The unchanging Ātman is responsible for the underlying unity of the personality in spite of its constantly changing mental and physical states. This Consciousness is self-luminous, as if, like the sun, it is a light that illumines itself and everything else (Bṛhad-āraṇyaka Upaniṣad, IV.3.9).

The empirical personality or jīva is thought of as the Ātman shrouded in ignorance or limited by the mind. The jīva is a kind of mask worn by the Ātman. This situation is sometimes described metaphorically as two birds in a tree. One eats of the fruit of the tree and tastes both its sweet and bitter fruits, while the other calmly looks on without eating (Muṇḍaka Upaniṣad, III.1.2). The active bird represents the apparent individual engaged with the world, while the other remains aloof. It is the "unseen Seer, the unheard Hearer, the unthought Thinker ... the Self" (Bṛhad-āraṇyaka Upaniṣad

III.7.23). Whereas the phenomenal consciousness of our ordinary mental states is usually directed towards an object, the Ātman or Pure Consciousness is non-intentional. Whereas the empirical personality is an active agent striving towards its goals, the Ātman is pure subjectivity or witness Consciousness that observes the personal mind but is distinct from it. In meditation, the ego may dissolve into it. Importantly: "The wise man beholds all beings in the Self, and the Self in all beings" (Īsha Upaniṣad VII, 6; Bhagavad-Gītā 13.27).

Ātman-Brahman cannot be fully described within a dualistic, verbal framework since it is beyond conceptual categories. It is sometimes said to have no attributes, but sometimes it is endowed with descriptors such as absolute existence, absolute Consciousness, and absolute bliss or fullness (Saccidānanda). Or is described as Satya (Truth), Jñāna (Knowledge) and Ananta (Infinity). These are simply terms that express the ways in which Ātman-Brahman is experienced by human beings and formulated by the mind; they are not adjectival in the limiting sense. Ātman-Brahman is unlimited, and within it there are no distinctions or qualities. Ātman/Brahman is sometimes spoken of as a center of peace and happiness within us, but again, it is a mistake to attribute qualities to it. Because Brahman cannot be described in words or thoughts, the Upaniṣads describe it in terms of negation—it is not-this, not-this (Bṛhad-āraṇyaka Upaniṣad, II.3.6). According to Śaṅkara, Brahman "has no distinguishing mark such as name, or form, or action, or heterogeneity, or species, or qualities" (quoted in Indich, 1980, pp. 23–24).

The Advaitic tradition is non-dual; it sees reality as undivided at the absolute level. Our perception of a world of apparently separate objects, subjects, and individuals is seen as the result of māyā, which is thought of as the creative power of Brahman to appear as the phenomenal world of multiplicity and conditioned existence. We mistakenly take this appearance to be real.[8] The world has phenomenal reality, but it is illusory in the sense that it is not what it seems to be. Its actual nature is the infinite Brahman. Śaṅkara's metaphor is that a rope may look like a snake until we realize its true nature; the erroneous perception is an example of māyā. The illusion occurs because we have superimposed our knowledge and memory of the snake onto the rope, but this mistake is corrected, or sublated, when we see the reality. Analogously, knowledge of the phenomenal world is sublated by knowledge of Brahman, which cannot be contradicted. The activity of Brahman is self-revealing as the manifest universe; it produces the appearance of the phenomenal world. From the point of view of the world, the world can be said to emerge from Brahman, but from the non-dual point of view there is no world separate from Brahman. All such appearances and apparent dualities are constructed by the mind and its sensory organs. The nature of the relationship between the non-dual reality of Brahman and the phenomenal world of apparently separate objects is attributed to the effects of māyā, and it is an indescribable mystery (Radhakrishnan, 2008 [1923], vol. 1).

The Ātman is unthinkable by the mind. It is: "Birthless, eternal, everlasting, and ancient, it is not killed when the body is killed" (Kaṭha Upaniṣad, I.2.18). There is no experience without the Ātman; according to Śaṅkara, it is "by nature the very essence of perception itself" (commentary on the Brahma-Sūtra, III, iii, 54). It is that which allows us to be conscious of the world. The Ātman cannot be perceived by the sense organs because it is the ultimate perceiving Subject or knower of experience (Bṛhad-āraṇyaka Upaniṣad I.4.14). The senses are only the instruments through which perception happens. The Ātman is that which sees through the eyes and hears through the ears: "You cannot see that which is the witness of vision: you cannot hear that which is the hearer of hearing" (ibid., III.4.2). The Self cannot become an object of thought because it is unlimited. More strictly speaking, at the non-dual level, pure Consciousness is neither a subject nor an object; it only knows itself because there is only itself. Accordingly, it cannot be conceptualized, qualified, or defined. We only know the Ātman implicitly by being aware of being aware, and through the felt sense of "I am."

For Śaṅkara, the Ātman and the empirical personality are radically different than each other. The Ātman is the ultimate Subject, unchanging, eternal, without parts, without pleasure or pain. It is beyond the karmic sphere of action and reaction, whereas the personality has components, it has a body, it changes continuously, and it suffers and dies. In this tradition, only what is permanent and unchanging is absolutely real.

Coward (1984) points out that traditions such as Vedānta are somewhat similar to the via negativa of Christian theology, because the Advaitic devotee is taught to systematically negate wrong perceptions or concepts of the Ātman, using the approach of *neti neti*, a Sanskrit term meaning it is not this and not that, until the true experience of the Self arises. As a result of meditation and the practice of self-inquiry, asking the "who am I?" question, both the sense of being a separate self and the reality of ordinary sense perception and discursive thought are negated, leading to intuitive awareness of the Self. To realize the Ātman requires the shedding of all historical and personal attributes, including identification with one's body, mental states, biographical details, and personality traits, because the Self is not the body and not the senses or the mind. The empirical self has to be sublated, negated, or deconstructed, in order to reveal the essential Self. The empirical self who has lived a life and has a personal autobiography seems to be real because of its association with the mind and body, but it disappears when it realizes its identity with the Ātman. Śaṅkara understands the Upaniṣadic statement "Thou art that" to mean the identity of the Ātman and the personal self.

The Ātman and Jung's Self: similarities and differences

Jung's notion of the Self links Western psychology with Eastern religious traditions. Jung believes that his notion of the Self is comparable to the

Ātman of the Upaniṣadic tradition and the Puruṣa of Patañjali's yoga philosophy (CW 9i, para. 248). In Jung's words, the Ātman forms "an exact parallel to the psychological idea of the self" (CW 16, para. 474).[9] Jung also speaks of the Self as a "that particular configuration of Eastern ideas which is condensed in the *Brahman-Ātman* teaching of India" (CW 6, para. 188). If Jung is correct, he has discovered and brought into his psychology an ancient truth.

Jung writes that the Ātman:

> speaks through me ... Not through me alone, but through all; for it is not only the individual Ātman but Ātman-Purusha, the universal Ātman, the pneuma, who breathes through all. We use the word "self" for this, contrasting it with the little ego. From what I have said it will be clear that this self is not just a rather more conscious of intensified ego ... What is meant by the self is not only in me but in all beings, like the Ātman, like Tao. It is psychic totality.
>
> (CW 10, para. 873)

The Ātman is Pure Consciousness and the totality. Given Jung's equation *psyche = consciousness* (CW 8, para. 380; emphasis in original), combined with his notion that the Self is the totality of the psyche, it is reasonable to believe that his idea of the Self is in some ways synonymous with the Upaniṣadic Ātman. Jung has discovered some ways in which the Ātman personifies itself within the psyche in the form of numinous symbols. I suggest that numinous symbol of the Self – such as those we see in dreams – correspond to the experience of what the Upaniṣadic tradition refers to as Saguṇa Brahman, or the divine with attributes, also referred to as Īśvara, the personal God or the relative or creative and expressive level of Brahman (Corbett, 2023). Saguṇa Brahman is analogous to theistic descriptions of God as having qualities such as love or mercy. This is one of two levels of Brahman described by the Upaniṣads. The absolute level is called Nirguṇa Brahman, the divine beyond name, concept, and form. This level has no attributes and cannot be described. It is not experienceable by an ego—that would be like a teacup trying to contain the ocean. It corresponds to what Jung refers to as the "unknowable metaphysical background" of our God-images (CW 11, para. 558), or perhaps the archetype-as-such.

Although Jung equates his idea of the Self with the Ātman, some authors deny this compatibility (Whitney, 2017, 2018; Whitfield, 2009; Sachdeva 1978). One of the main points of contention arises from Jung's notion that the Self is unconscious of its own dark side, a notion Jung derived from the biblical story of Job. In this story, Yahweh is an image of the Self. Jung believed that because Yahweh was not conscious of his dark side, Job experienced considerable evil and suffering. Because Job was able to maintain his integrity and insist that he did not deserve his suffering, he acted as a reflecting consciousness for Yahweh, forcing him to become conscious of his dark side, of which he was hitherto unconscious. Jung's larger point is that the Self is a totality, within which the opposites such as good and evil are not divided. The opposites are not differentiated until they become conscious within a human being, who then suffers the tension of such opposites. The individual thereby acts as a reflecting consciousness for the Self, thus allowing the Self to differentiate itself by becoming conscious of the opposites within its own nature.

However, can the Self actually be partly unconscious, as Jung claims? In a 1959 letter to Jung, Erich Neumann pointed out that "If the Self contemplates you as the ego, then the Self is not unconscious" (Jung & Neumann, 2015, p. 344). Corbett (2021) pointed out that the Self cannot be unconscious of itself if it *is* Consciousness itself. Jung's idea that the Self needs human consciousness to become conscious is also incompatible with his idea that the Self is the totality of the psyche, both conscious and unconscious. It therefore cannot be unconscious of part of itself. Whitney (2018) also focuses on Jung's idea that the Self needs human consciousness to act as a reflecting consciousness for itself, pointing out that this is a very different image than the self-illuminating Ātman or Puruṣa of the Upaniṣadic tradition, which is pure Consciousness, and so cannot be unconscious. The Upaniṣadic Ātman does not require another consciousness to become conscious, because Consciousness is its nature. A further difference is that the non-dual Vedantic Self is beyond the opposites of good and evil, which are seen as the mind's conditioned reactions to experience. Pure Consciousness itself has no qualities. On balance, it seems that Jung's claim that the Self could be partially unconscious is an overreach.

In both Vedānta and Jungian psychology, the experience of the Self is extremely important—it is perhaps the highest value. In both these traditions, the Self is the divine essence within the empirical personality. Yet there are major differences in the way these traditions describe how the Self manifests itself, and differences in the way the Self is to be realized. The Upaniṣadic tradition assumes the existence of the Self based on the testimony and authority of ancient seers and texts and insists that this realization is available to others willing to practice and inquire in particular ways, typically under the guidance of a guru. In contrast, for Jung, the path to the Self is a psychological process, involving the understanding of numinous imagery and symbols of wholeness that spontaneously arises from the unconscious. Jung tries to remain an empiricist or a phenomenologist, without speculating about the metaphysical background or source of images of the Self. The traditional guru attaches no importance to the kind of numinous material that is important to Jung, while Jung does not value meditative states, which he regards as akin to unconsciousness because of their associated loss of ego. In a further stark contrast, the traditional Indian guru typically sees ego-consciousness as a form of bondage and sees the ego itself as illusory; at best the ego only reflects the Consciousness of the Self but has no light of its own. However, for Jung the ego is essential, because without it we are unconscious. Jung believes it is important to maintain a healthy ego in relation to the Self, and the ego must not be assimilated by the Self, even as the ego is relativized by the Self.

In contrast to the traditional Indian way of the seer or the guru, Jung believes that "The claim to authority is naturally not in itself sufficient to establish a metaphysical truth" (CW 14, para. 785). Jung acknowledges that the testimony of an inspired person is the experience of a "will transcending his consciousness," and naturally this is felt to be divine (ibid.) However, he "cannot see that it proves the existence of a transcendent God." Jung asserts that it is wiser "not to drag the supreme metaphysical factor into our calculations ... but, more modestly, to make an unknown psychic or perhaps psychoid factor" responsible for such inspirations (CW 14, para. 786). As evidence, Jung points to the divergence of inspiration among different religious traditions, each insisting on its own unique rightness. For Jung, although the religious individual is free to "accept whatever metaphysical explanations he pleases" about the origin of numinous images, Jung sees himself as a scientist who "cannot take heaven by storm" but must abide within the bounds of scientific interpretation (CW 12, para. 16). Jung obviously felt obliged to speak the language of empirical science in order for his psychology to be taken seriously. By claiming the mantle of empirical science, he was also attempting avoid major entanglements with the custodians of traditional religion, although in this he did not fully succeed, since notables such as Martin Buber accused him of straying out of the territory of psychology into theology. However, Jung believed that his work is based on empirical observation of numinous imagery rather than on stories derived from sacred texts and historical traditions. He advocates a psychological approach to the spiritual dimension that enables each person to find his or her personal experience of it.

For the Vedāntic system, knowledge of the Self is a matter of recognition of the Pure Consciousness that is the ground of experience. This requires that we realize that thoughts, feelings, and other mental contents come and go, so they are not the essence of who we are, but Pure Consciousness always remains and never changes. That Consciousness is not affected by mental contents, and it cannot be analyzed because it is never an object. It is referred to variously as our "true nature," as Awareness, Being, and so on. We become aware of it when we stop superimposing personal material, conditioned thoughts and feelings, onto it. It is arguable that psychotherapeutic work assists in this process by reducing the intensity of such conditioning. However, constant attention to intrapsychic material also runs the risk of intensifying our identification with our personal history, complexes, traumas, memories, and so on. If we see the ephemeral nature of such conditioned material, we discover That which has no content or quality. Jung has an inkling of this level when he talks about a "higher consciousness" that looks on while we are affected by emotional storms, which "prevents one from becoming identical with the affect" (CW 11, para. 17). This would correspond to the Vedāntic Ātman-Brahman or Pure Consciousness, which is not affected by psychological turmoil. Jung does not discuss the concept of Pure Consciousness as the substrate of psychological material; he largely focuses on the contents of consciousness and the unconscious, whereas in non-dual philosophy these contents and the way we relate to them are not thought to be fundamental. From a non-dual point of view, to focus on the contents of the mind rather than the background Consciousness would be like attending to the crests of the waves while ignoring the ocean from which they arise.

As well as his emphasis on the importance of the ego, there are some other areas in which Jung's work is incompatible with the non-dual traditions. Jung seems to have believed that consciousness evolved. In a letter he says that "warm-bloodedness and a differentiated brain were necessary for the inception of consciousness" (Jung, 1975, p. 494). Also, "the psychic structure must, like the anatomical, show traces of the earlier stages of evolution it has passed through" (CW 15, para. 152). In the Upaniṣadic view, Consciousness did not evolve; it is eternal, with no beginning. However, Jung might be referring to the evolution of the contents of the psyche, especially its personal levels, rather than the psyche itself. In his early work, Jung speaks of the collective unconscious as the repository of repeated human experience that took eons to form (e.g., CW 7, para. 151), but later he says that we do not know the origin of the psyche or its archetypal level. He believes that the question of whether the psyche "originated" is a metaphysical problem that cannot be answered (CW 9i, para. 187); he suggests that the psyche arose "with life itself" (CW 11, p. 149, note 2). This latter opinion is consistent with the Advaitic belief that absolute Consciousness transcends evolution. Indich (ibid., p. 94) makes the further point that Jung's theory of the collective unconscious or the Self includes its teleological function, guiding the individual through the process of individuation, in contrast to the Advaitic notion that "the goal of human life entails the transcendence of the stages of life ... and the phenomenal world itself." The Vedāntic tradition does not describe the unconscious in Jung's sense because, in that tradition, Consciousness is all, so it cannot be unconscious of itself. The word unconscious would only be meaningful at the empirical or ego level. Perhaps the nearest Vedāntic equivalent is the term *avidyā*, which is often translated as a lack of vision, misperception, or more broadly as ignorance (Chapple, 2008).[10]

A further important difference between Jung and traditions such as Vedānta is that they offer the possibility of the transcendence of suffering, whereas Jung believed that: "Complete redemption from the suffering of this world is and must remain an illusion" (CW 16, para. 400). For Jung, the only ways to deal with suffering are to discover its meaning, to endure it (Jung, 1973, p. 236) or to outgrow it. In contrast, the Indian traditions generally agree that suffering is the result of a misunderstanding of the true nature of reality and so can be alleviated through spiritual practice. Furthermore, whereas the individuation process is never fully completed because complete wholeness cannot be attained and the unconscious can never be fully assimilated, the Vedāntic tradition offers a final end point, the attainment of liberation.

Individuation or enlightenment?

For Jung, the individuation process involves increasing consciousness of the Self, and the progressive embodiment of the Self, in the form of the realization of its potentials within the personality. At the same time as the ego maintains an ongoing relationship with the Self, ideally the ego is not assimilated by the Self and does not identify with it. This is obviously a different goal than the experiential realization of the Self in meditation with the concomitant loss of the ego or the sense of being a separate self, in states such as samādhi. While individuation requires more and more assimilation of the unconscious, for Vedānta knowledge of the Ātman is a matter of recognition that we have superimposed personal material onto it. Liberation requires knowledge or realization of oneself as the Self; it is attained through meditation and inquiry, not through relationship to the unconscious. The Ātman reveals itself when ignorance is removed. Realization of the Self occurs "through hearing, reflection, and meditation" (Bṛhad-āraṇyaka Upaniṣad II.4.5) and through spiritual intuition, but not by means of conceptual thought. Non-dual approaches are not concerned with the detailed analysis of the contents of the mind, whereas Jung believes that it is important to pay attention to the psyche's numinous images, which are manifestations of the Self. In this way, he believes that the empirical personality is strengthened and made more comfortable with itself, and its consciousness is broadened and deepened. This approach is quite different than the approach to the Self through meditation, which ignores psychological contents and leads to the direct recognition of Pure Consciousness. Non-dual traditions do not consider numinous experiences and exotic states of mind as particularly important.

The approaches of Vedānta and Jung have different aims and methods and consequently attain different results. The Vedāntic idea of liberation is clearly not the same as Jung's idea of individuation. In the Vedāntic tradition, the liberated sage or jīvanmukta is a person who realizes that he is actually the Self and who sees all beings as the Self. That is, unlike the individuation process, for Advaita, Self-realization is impersonal, beyond individuality and personal will; it transcends any form of modified consciousness. These approaches complement each other and may overlap, but they are not identical. From the Advaitic point of view, one might be relatively well balanced psychologically but still enveloped in ignorance of one's true nature. The notion of liberation or *mokṣa* in Advaita is therefore different than the Western notion of psychological health. Importantly, it is clear from the behavior of some Eastern spiritual teachers who have exploited their students that spiritual realization does not necessarily improve mental health or lead to personality integration. Clinical experience also confirms that years of meditation do not necessarily lead to the softening of painful complexes. On the other side of this coin, psychotherapeutic work is valuable because it makes the personality more comfortable, healthy, and integrated, but does not lead to liberation.

According to Vedānta, at the ultimate non-dual level, even the attempt at detachment from phenomenal activity by means of spiritual practice is an activity grounded in ignorance, since it involves an apparent subject trying to achieve a goal that is already present. In Śaṅkara's metaphor, it is like searching for the necklace that is around one's neck (Indich, 1980, p. 107). According to some teachers, the only true liberation occurs with the transcendence of all forms of duality in nirvikalpa samādhi, a state of total absorption in Brahman. However, Śaṅkara does not believe that the attainment of samādhi is enough to eradicate identification with mental contents and prevent the superimposition of personal material onto the Ātman, which are the real causes of bondage. For him, samādhi is not enough for liberation because we return from samādhi to ordinary consciousness.

Bridging Jung's Self and the Upaniṣadic tradition

Jung (CW 11, para. 773) warned against building "false and dangerous bridges over yawning gaps" between East and West. He believed that Westerners should not simply imitate Eastern philosophy; he wanted the West to discover Eastern truths in the way of the West, which he believed would "produce its own yoga" (CW 11, para. 961) in the course of time. One of Jung's major concerns was the healing of the Western psyche, and he did not think that the adoption of Eastern religious practices would do so. He thought that Western people are not suited to Eastern practices and the Western God-image has to evolve in its own way.

In spite of this caveat, as we have seen there are some obvious similarities between the Ātman and Jung's notion of the Self, for example when Jung describes the Self as the "God within," which is consistent with the Upaniṣadic understanding of the Ātman. As noted above, although the symbolic, intrapsychic manifestations of the Self that Jung describes are not discussed in the Upaniṣads, it is reasonable to assume that the numinosity of Jung's Self-symbols indicate that they are manifestations of what the Upaniṣadic tradition calls Saguṇa Brahman, or God with attributes. Although it may be useful for devotional and psychological purposes to see the Ātman in these symbolic forms, symbols are by their nature limited, and we do not wish to attribute limitations to the unlimited. However, symbols remind us that they point to a deeper reality. We cannot use imagery or language to talk about the nature of the Self, since language always requires a subject and object, and the Self transcends the subject-object differentiation, so language and imagery would always mis-represent the situation.

The Upaniṣads do not discuss the psychological effects and manifestations of the Ātman with anything like the level of detail in which Jung describes symbols of the Self. The Upaniṣads assert the presence of the Ātman based on the testimony of seers, ṛṣis or advanced sages who realized or perceived or heard this truth in meditation. Jung provides empirical evidence for the existence of the Self by describing its manifestations within the psyche, which are often relevant to personal material. The Upaniṣadic tradition does not describe these kinds of images, and it sees the Self as impersonal. However, in the Upaniṣads, Consciousness is said to be self-revealing, and it is entirely possible that the Self symbols that Jung describes are part of a process of self-revelation of aspects of the Self as it manifests itself in human consciousness. This is important because the notion of the Ātman-Brahman may lead to a rather impersonal spirituality. It may feel difficult to relate to the Absolute with no characteristics. Therefore, a focus on the individuation process and the symbolic appearances of the Self are important reminders of the human dimension.

The individuation process involves increasing consciousness of the objective psyche, which Jung believes contains *saṁskāras*, a Sanskrit term that refers to latent impressions or imprints on the mind from previous lives. For Jung, *saṁskāras* refer to the individual's archetypal endowment (Jung, 1996, p. 74). These are not incompatible views if one's archetypal endowment is acquired by karma, and indeed Jung suggests that karma "is essential to a deeper understanding of the nature of an archetype" (CW 7, p. 77, n. 15). Coward (1984) makes the point that Jungian scholars have downplayed the importance of karma in Jung's thought, apparently because acknowledging it would make his psychology even less acceptable to mainstream Western psychology.

Jung often speaks of psychological work such as attention to dreams and synchronicities as ways to experience the Self, but Advaita suggests that knowledge of the Self more a matter of letting go of false beliefs, such as reference to a "me," and recognizing what is real. In the Advaitic tradition, realization of the Self is hidden by ignorance and by personal material, but the Self is always present, like the sun hidden by clouds. When ignorance (the clouds) is gone, the Self is realized. An obvious problem is how to bridge the gap between the two orders of reality, between the phenomenal, egoic realm and the transcendent level of Consciousness. Advaita assumes that this radical discontinuity is only a problem for the human ego. Jung's approach to the numinous symbolic manifestations of the Self may act as such a bridge, although I suspect the strict Advaitin might deny the possibility of any such possibility on the grounds that the Ātman itself has no quality of the kind found in a symbol.

Jung is consistent with the Upaniṣadic tradition when he sees the Self as a priori, "pre-existent to consciousness," and having an "incorruptible" or "eternal" character (CW 11, para. 401). Jung writes that the Self is a construct that "serves to express an unknowable essence which we cannot grasp as such, since, by definition, it transcends our power of comprehension" (CW 7, para. 398). This attitude to the Self is again consistent with the Upaniṣadic view. However, Jung's belief that aspects of the Self can be experienced symbolically (CW 9i, para. 315), for example in dreams, contrasts with the Advaitic view that the Self can never be experienced as an object because it is the ultimate Subject of all experience.

The approach to the dream in Jung and Advaita

Indich (1980) points out that there are at least six different analyses of the nature and origin of dreams in classical Indian thought. An important difference between Jung and Advaita is that Jung values dreams very much, while Advaitic thinkers emphasize the superiority of the waking state over dreams, which they believe represent the experience of vague consciousness in which the mind "functions in a disorderly manner with little thought and many conflicting, unstable, and unreliable images" (ibid., p. 64). The Advaitic approach to dreams therefore does not emphasize their importance for communicating between the Self and empirical consciousness. Advaitic thinkers prefer the logical thinking and self-conscious will of the waking state. Advaita argues that the dreamer remains "involved in the causal or karmic order" as a result of his identification with the dream content (ibid., p. 82). Thus, consciousness in dreams is as bound to ignorance as it is in waking experience.

Jung insists that because the psyche is real, its images are images of something real, even if they are transient. However, in the Advaitic view dream images are only apparently real but cannot be ultimately real since that which is truly real is eternal. Advaita sees the dream as a product of the jīva, the individual soul, which is a blend of the Self and not-Self. Furthermore, dream images are essentially dualistic because they are specific and limited. Vedānta therefore attaches no special importance to the kind of symbolic dream material on which Jung focuses. Eastern traditions rely on meditative techniques to realize the Self; meditation and self-inquiry are thought to lead to direct knowledge that erases the distinction between knower and known. During meditation, imagery is allowed to simply flow through the mind without paying attention to it, but Jung saw the approach through meditation as an avoidance of the need to dialog with the unconscious, which he regarded as essential for the West. Rather than simply observing the mind without engaging the unconscious, Jung preferred that Westerners use attention to dreams and active imagination as a form of meditation and connection to the Self. Jung believed that the Self must be translated into psychological terms "in order to make it perceptible at all" (CW 18, para. 1538), which is why attention to its imagery is important. In contrast, for a strict non-dual approach, dream imagery can be seen as no more important than any other *vṛitti*, or modification of the mind that must be stilled to experience the Ātman.

The empty self or no-self in Buddhism

The doctrine of no-self, *anātman* (Sanskrit) or *anattā* (Pali) is fundamental to many schools of Buddhism. They deny the existence of any metaphysical Self or Ātman in the sense of an enduring entity or an essential, a priori, self-existent reality. The notion of a substantial self is seen as illusory or an ontological fallacy (MacKenzie, 2010). Although the personal self is acknowledged to be real from an empirical, conventional, and experiential point of view, it is thought to be not ultimately real because it consists of an aggregation of more basic processes such as memory, mental contents, perceptions, attention, personality traits, bodily functions, and so on. The idea of no-self means that we misidentify these components of the personality as if they indicate the existence of a self as a substantial entity, but this is imaginary, producing harmful thoughts of "me" and "mine" with corresponding attachments, cravings, aversions, hatred, and ill-will. The Buddha saw clinging to the idea of a fixed self as the core of suffering.

The denial of a fixed self is asserted because everything in nature is constantly changing, so nothing is permanent. From the Buddhist perspective, everything that seems to be stable and lasting is in fact in constant flux. Furthermore, nothing is separate from the totality of reality; everything has components, so all apparently separate objects and selves are composites rather than fixed or self-existent entities. Much Buddhist practice is therefore directed towards the transcendence of the notion of the self. Not only is the self seen to have no intrinsic essence, reality itself is described as empty or void (Ryan & Rigby, 2015). Nevertheless, some Mahāyāna Buddhist schools talk of the Buddha-nature, which can be understood to be the essential nature of all sentient beings, what we actually are rather than something we possess. The idea of a Buddha Nature seems to imply the existence of an essence that has the potential for growth into Buddhahood. This doctrine seems to contravene the idea that beings are empty of any essence. Some Buddhist scholars admit that there is an apparently stable, witness consciousness in the movement of experience, even in meditation (Albahari, 2006).

The Buddhist notion of the self as a collection of aggregates such as materiality, feelings, perceptions, impulses, mentation, and consciousness, contrasts with essentialist theories of the Self such as the Vedāntic Ātman. The Buddhist idea is similar to the Western philosophical bundle theory, which accepts the idea that objects have properties but denies that this implies an underlying substrate to account for these properties, which are in a contingent relationship to each other. All talk of a self or an ego is then only a mental construction. However, the Buddhist view raises various questions: what holds the aggregates of the personality together? If the Ātman is denied, and if there is no permanent soul that survives death, how does a causal chain of events produce karma that continues from one birth to another? One possible response is that a continuous stream of consciousness links life after life.

Whereas Vedānta teaches that Brahman or ultimate reality is permanent and changeless, Buddha's essential insight was that nothing is permanent, so this doctrine seems to have arisen in direct contrast to the Upaniṣadic view of the Ātman-Brahman. Buddhists believe that belief in the Ātman is purely psychological and speculative (Prasad, 2000), the product of culture, religious conditioning, and faith in *śruti*, literally that which was heard by the ancient rishis who are said to have directly experienced the truth. Buddhists prefer the notion of dependent origination, a process view of reality that teaches that everything that happens is the result of prior causes; there is no fundamental ground or Brahman. Everything, including the apparent self, is dependent on everything else, which incidentally rules out the idea of a creator God who is self-existing.

In the early Vedic literature, the word Ātman was sometimes used to refer to the personal self. Later, in the Upaniṣads, it became the divine Self at the core of the personality. Because of this variation in translation, there has been some debate about whether the Buddha only denied the existence of a personal self or the ego and its processes, or whether he denied the metaphysical Ātman of the Upaniṣads. When the Buddha was directly asked whether or not there is a self, he remained silent, presumably to avoid responding in a manner that would have led to wrong views; he believed that the question is not a useful one. He may have been implying that the true nature of a person is beyond affirmation or negation, neither self nor no-self, sometimes referred to in the Zen tradition as No-Self, which cannot be conceptualized and is beyond affirmation or negation (Abe, 1985). While the Upaniṣadic thinkers were concerned with what is eternal and unchanging, the Buddha seems to have been more concerned with empirical reality and its fluctuations. All these traditions recommend meditation as a way to deconstruct the ego, in contrast to Western psychologies that want to reinforce it.

Jung's partial non-duality

Non-dual philosophy asserts that reality is an undivided unity (Loy, 1997), not a collection of discrete objects and separate selves, which is how it seems to be conventionally. Things that seem to be separate are inseparable aspects of totality. In fact, there are no separate "things" or separate selves, despite appearances, and subject and object are inseparable. What seems to be a separate object is really a concept constructed by means of thought, our sensory systems, and the use of language, which combine to superimpose the experience of separateness onto a whole. However, non-duality seems to be incompatible with the everyday way we understand and experience the world. We feel separate from the totality because of our body, our social conditioning, and the development of an ego and a personality with which we identify. Social convention also tells us that we are separate individuals, but convention is not necessarily a good guide to truth.

The attempt to describe non-duality, especially the experience of it, runs into the paradox that it cannot be adequately described using language or conceptual thought, since these are intrinsically dualistic. For this reason, the *Tao te jing* says that the Tao that can be named is not the true Tao. Another difficulty is that there are several versions of non-duality, which is found in traditions such as Advaita Vedānta, Mahāyāna Buddhism, and Taoism. Non-dual thought is also seen among some Sufi, Jewish, and Christian mystics and philosophers. These traditions describe versions of non-duality in their own ways, or they stress different aspects of non-duality. Notably however, non-duality has never found much favor in the West.

Jung's stress on the importance of wholeness and his preference for monistic philosophy are clear throughout his writing. At times he also approaches a sensibility reminiscent of the non-dual traditions, but he never commits himself fully to this philosophy. Traces of a non-dual approach to reality are seen in Jung's work in statements such as:

> At times I feel as if I am spread out over the landscape and inside things, and am myself living in every tree, in the plashing of the waves, in the clouds and the animals that come and go, in the procession of the seasons.
>
> (Jung, 1965, pp. 225–226)

Also: "this self is the world, if only a consciousness could see it" (CW 9i, para. 46). Jung sees the Self as "the hypothetical summation of an indescribable totality" (CW 14, n. 66 p. 107). Furthermore: "all creation … consists of nothing but God, with the result that man, like the rest of creation, is simply God become concrete" (CW 11, p. 402). The idea that humanity is God made "concrete" would be no surprise to the non-dual Upaniṣadic traditions. Similarly: "It was only quite late that we realized (or rather are beginning to realize) that God is Reality itself and therefore—last but not least—man. This realization is a millennial project" (CW 11, p. 402). (That is, it will take a long time.) In contrast, for the nondual traditions, realizing that God is reality itself and that humanity is inseparable from God is not a long-term project; it is expressed in famous Upaniṣadic sayings such as "Thou art That" (*Chāndogya Upanishad* VI, 8, 7). Different schools of Vedānta interpret this phrase differently. Typically, the word "thou" means the apparently individual or personal self, which is actually That, the divine Self or the Ātman, which is the same as Brahman, or ultimate reality. The non-dual approach is thus very different than traditional Judeo-Christian ways of thinking about the divine, which make a clear distinction between God and humanity. Classical theism often treats the divine as a kind of superior Personality, but non-dual thinking sees the divine as impersonal at its absolute level.

As much as Jung sometimes verges on a non-duality sensibility, he never fully releases his Western dualistic bias, and he rarely overcomes the subject-object division. His stress on the importance of increasing consciousness through the individuation process insists on the importance of the ego, but from a non-dual point of view the ego is not a distinct entity but simply another object of Consciousness like any other of its contents. For the non-dual traditions, what we call the ego is a psychological concept that can be deconstructed, but for Jung the ego is essential. He felt that consciousness is "inconceivable without an ego ... If there is no ego there is nobody to be conscious of anything. The ego is indispensable to the conscious process" (CW 11, para. 774). Thus, Jung believes that if one abolishes the ego, as in Eastern meditative practices, one creates unconsciousness, and the supreme Consciousness of the Ātman is "not one we could possess. Inasmuch as it exists, we do not exist" (Jung, 1973, p. 247). In contrast, in the Vedāntic tradition, we do not "possess" consciousness since we *are* consciousness; the Ātman is the source and content of the sense of "I." The Ātman is the only source of consciousness; it illumines the ego or whatever state the conditioned mind is in, analogously to the way the sun illumines the moon.

Notes

1 A strange loop is a hierarchy of levels or stages linked to each other such that as we move through the levels, even though we feel we are moving upwards in the hierarchy, we eventually return to the starting point in a closed cycle. An example is Escher's *Drawing Hands*.

2 The philosopher John Locke (1975 [1689]) believed that our sense of personal identity is based on our memory of continuity between our present sense of self and the earlier self that we are now remembering. However, the memory criterion is now seen to be circular, since it means that we would have to prove that the person who has the memories now is identical with the person who had the experiences described in the memories, meaning we have to first establish the identity that the memory itself was supposed to establish. Furthermore, it may be impossible to distinguish true from false memories. We are clearly more than our memories; the connection between the self and autobiographical memory has proven to be very complex (Guerini et al., 2019). Some features of the self are preserved in patients with dementia (Ben Malek et al., 2019), so they may for instance recognize themselves in photographs. It may be that we identify more with our body than with our memories.

3 The word transpersonal can be used in a variety of contexts. The term was first suggested in 1968 by Abraham Maslow, who held that the self may move beyond

being purely biographical, personal, and egoic towards becoming collective, communal. and even cosmic. This view approaches Jung's view that there is a transpersonal level of the psyche.

4 Rather than seeing the brain as the source of consciousness, Bernado Kastrup (2014) sees the brain as the way subjective experience looks when viewed from the outside.

5 For Jung, maṇḍala imagery represents the unity of the psyche; it is the empirical equivalent of the unus mundus. The center of the maṇḍala suggests the meeting place of the archetypal and the phenomenal worlds, or the totality of both worlds. Hence, the maṇḍala is an image of the Self.

6 The existence of an early neurological structure that provides the potential for the infant's responses to the environment has been confirmed by neuroscientific findings; Panksepp (1998) refers to it as the core self, while Damasio (2010) uses the term nuclear self or proto-self, from which the autobiographical self emerges. These latter are physicalist approaches, only relevant to the personal self.

7 The Upaniṣads contain the essence and culmination of the earlier Vedic texts. They are considered to contain knowledge of ultimate reality revealed to sages who transmitted them orally until they were written down, beginning perhaps as early as 1500 BCE. They are the foundation of many of the later religions and philosophies of India. There is a range of interpretations of these texts; commentators tend to project or find within them the interpreter's own philosophical preferences. I rely largely on the interpretations of Saṇkara and his non-dual metaphysics.

8 The subject-object distinction presumably evolved to allow early hominins to survive by differentiating self from non-self. This distinction is therefore deeply ingrained, but it can be dissolved in meditation, when consciousness only knows itself.

9 In the English edition of the *Collected works*, the word "self" is not capitalized, but here I follow the practice in much subsequent English language literature that uses an upper case "S" to distinguish Jung's Self from the personal self or the empirical personality.

10 Perhaps *avidya* is the result of a combination of the limitations of our sensory systems combined with the heavy conditioning that results from our personal history.

References

Abe, M. (1985). The self in Jung and Zen. *The Eastern Buddhist*, 18(1), 57–70.

Addison, A. (2009). Jung, vitalism and "the Psychoid": an historical reconstruction. *Journal of Analytical Psychology*, 54, 123–142.

Addison, A. (2017). Jung's psychoid concept: an hermeneutical understanding. *International Journal of Jungian Studies*, 9(1), 1–16.

Albahari, M. (2006). *Analytical Buddhism: the two-tiered illusion of self.* Palgrave Macmillan.

American Psychiatric Association. (2022). *Diagnostic and statistical manual of mental disorders* [DSM], 5th edition. American Psychiatric Association.

Anderson, D. (2021). The soul's logical life and Jungian schisms. *Psychological Perspectives*, 64(1), 37–53.

Arthur, A.R. (2001). Personality, epistemology and psychotherapists' choice of theoretical model: A review and analysis. *European Journal of Psychotherapy, Counseling & Health*, 4(1), 45–64.

Atmanspacher, H. (2012a). Dual-aspect monism a la Pauli and Jung. *Journal of Consciousness Studies*, 19, 96–120.

Atmanspacher, H. (2012b). Dual-aspect monism à la Pauli and Jung perforates the completeness of physics. *AIP Conference Proceedings*, 1508(1), 5–21.

Atmanspacher, H., & Fuchs, C.A. (2014). *The Pauli–Jung conjecture and its impact today.* Imprint Academic.

Atmanspacher, H., & Fach, W. (2013). A structural-phenomenological typology of mind-matter correlations. *Journal of Analytical Psychology*, 58(2), 219–244.

Atmanspacher, H., & Primas, H. (1996). The hidden side of Wolfgang Pauli. *Journal of Consciousness Studies*, 3, 112–126.

Atmanspacher, H., & Rickles, D. (2022). *Dual aspect monism and the deep structure of meaning.* Routledge.

Aurobindo, S. (1996). *The synthesis of Yoga.* Lotus Light Publications.

Ayer, A.J. (Ed.). *Logical positivism.* Free Press.

Aziz, R. (1990). *C.G. Jung's psychology of religion and synchronicity.* University of New York Press.

Babbage, D.R., & Ronan, K.R. (2000). Philosophical worldview and personality factors in traditional and social scientists: Studying the world in our own image. *Personality and Individual Differences*, 28(2), 405–420.

Baggini, J. (2011). *The ego trick: what does it mean to be you?* Granta Books.

Barad, K. (2007). *Meeting the universe halfway: quantum physics and the entanglement of matter and meaning.* Duke University Press.

Barzegar, A., Taqavi, M., & Shafiee, A. (2021). Zeilinger on Information and Reality. *Foundations of Science,* 26 (4), 1007–1019.

Baumeister, R.F., & Bushman, B.J. (2013). *Social psychology and human nature.* Cengage Learning.

Beauregard, M., Trent, N.L., & Schwartz, G.E. (2018). Towards a postmaterialist psychology: theory, research, and applications. *New Ideas in Psychology,* 50, 21–33.

Becker, A. (2018). *What is real? The unfinished quest for the meaning of quantum physics.* Basic Books.

Beischel, J., Boccuzzi, M., Biuso, M., & Rock, A.J. (2015). Anomalous information reception by research mediums blinded conditions II: Replication and extension. *EXPLORE: The Journal of Science & Healing,* 11, 136–142.

Bem, D. (2011). Feeling the future: experimental evidence for anomalous retroactive influences on cognition and affect. *Journal of Personality and Social Psychology,* 100, 407–425.

Ben Malek, H., Philippi, N., Botzung, A., Cretin, B., Berna, F., Manning, L., & Blanc, F. (2019). Memories defining the self in Alzheimer's disease. *Memory,* 27(5), 698–704.

Berghoffer, P. (2018). Ontic structural realism and quantum field theory: are there intrinsic properties at the most fundamental level of reality? *Studies in History and Philosophy of Science,* 62, 176–188.

Bohm, D. (1980). *Wholeness and the implicate order.* Routledge & Kegan Paul.

Bohm, D. (1986). A new theory of the relationship of mind and matter. *Journal of the American Society for Psychical Research,* 80(2), 113–115.

Bohm, D. (1988). Postmodern science and a postmodern world. In D.R. Griffin (Ed.), *The re-enchantment of science* (pp. 57–68). State University of New York Press.

Bohm, D. (1989 [1951]). *Quantum theory.* Dover.

Bohm, D., & Hiley, B. (1975). On the intuitive understanding of nonlocality as implied by quantum theory. *Foundations of Physics,* 5(1), 93–109.

Bohr, N. (1934) *Atomic physics and the description of nature.* Cambridge University Press.

Bohr, N. (1966). *Causality and complementarity: essays 1958–1962 on atomic physics and human knowledge.* Vintage.

Born, M. (1949). *Natural philosophy of cause and chance.* Oxford University Press.

Bond, M. (2008). Three degrees of contagion. *New Scientist,* 201(2689), 24–27.

Bornstein, R. F. (2001). The impending death of psychoanalysis. *Psychoanalytic Psychology,* 18, 3–20.

Bösch, H., Steinkamp, F., & Boller, E. (2006). Examining psychokinesis: the interaction of human intention with random number generators: a meta-analysis. *Psychological Bulletin,* 132, 497–523.

Broekaert, J., Basieva, I., Blasiak, P., & Pothos, E. M. (2017). Quantum-like dynamics applied to cognition: a consideration of available options. *Philosophical Transactions of the Royal Society A: Mathematical, Physical & Engineering Sciences,* 375 (2106), 1–30.

Brooke, R. (1991). *Jung and phenomenology.* Routledge.

Brooks, R.M. (2011). Un-thought out metaphysics in analytical psychology: a critique of Jung's epistemological basis for psychic reality. *Journal of Analytical Psychology,* 56(4): 492–513.

Brookes, J. C. (2017). Quantum effects in biology: golden rule in enzymes, olfaction, photosynthesis and magnetodetection. *Proceedings of the Royal Society A: Mathematical, Physical & Engineering Sciences*, 473(2201), 1–28.

Brown, D. (1991). *Human universals*. McGraw Hill Humanities.

Bruza, P.D., Wang, Z., & Busemeyer, J.R. (2015). Quantum cognition: a new theoretical approach to psychology. *Trends in Cognitive Sciences*, 19(7), 339–383.

Bunge, M.A. (2006). *Chasing reality*. University of Toronto Press: Scholarly Publishing Division.

Burde, J.K., & Shama Rao, A.H. (2011). Self-actualization from an Eastern perspective—a preliminary exploration. *Psychological Studies*, 56(4), 373–377.

Burr, V. (1995). *An introduction to social constructionism*. Routledge.

Buber, M. (1952). *The eclipse of God*. Harper.

Capra, F. (1986). *The tao of physics*. Flamingo.

Card, C. (1991a). The archetypal view of C.G. Jung and Wolfgang Pauli. *Psychological Perspectives*, 24(1), 19–33.

Card, C. (1991b). The archetypal view of C.G. Jung and Wolfgang Pauli, part 2. *Psychological Perspectives*, 25(1), 52–69.

Cardeña, E. (2018). The experimental evidence for parapsychological phenomena: a review. *American Psychologist*, 73(5), 663–677.

Carnap, R. (1936). Testability and meaning. *Philosophy of Science*, 3, 419–471.

Carruthers, P. (2011). I do not exist. *Trends in Cognitive Sciences*, 15, 189–190.

Carpenter, R.H.S., & Anderson, A. J. (2006). The death of Schrödinger's cat and of consciousness-based quantum wave-function collapse. *Annales de la Fondation Louis de Broglie* 31(1), 45.

Carroll, S. (2016). *The big picture: on the origins of life, meaning, and the universe itself*. Dutton.

Carter, R. (2010). *Mapping the mind*. University of California Press.

Chalmers, D.J. (1995). Facing up the problem of consciousness. *Journal of Consciousness Studies*, 2, 200–219.

Chalmers, D.J. (1996). *The conscious mind*. Oxford University Press.

Chalmers, D.J. (1997). Moving forward on the problem of consciousness. *Journal of Consciousness Studies*, 4(1), pp. 3–46.

Chalmers, D. J. (2010). *The character of consciousness*. Oxford University Press.

Chapple, C. K. (2008). *Yoga and the luminous: Patañjali's spiritual path to freedom*. State University of New York.

Chibbaro, S., Rondoni, L., & Vulpiani, A. (2014). *Reductionism, emergence, and levels of reality*. Berlin: Springer.

Chomsky, N. (2023). The false promise of ChatGPT. *The New York Times*, March 8. www.nytimes.com/2023/03/08/opinion/noam-chomsky-chatgpt-ai.html

Chopra, D. (1993). *Ageless body, timeless mind: the quantum alternative to growing old*. Crown.

Christou, E. (1976). *The logos of the soul*. Spring Publications.

Churchland, P. M. (1979). *Scientific realism and the plasticity of mind*. Cambridge University Press.

Churchland, P.S. (1996). The Hornswoggle problem. *Journal of Consciousness Studies*, 5–6, 402–408.

Colman, W. (2011). Synchronicity and the meaning-making psyche. *Journal of Analytical Psychology*, 56(4), 471–491.

Colman, W. (2017). Soul in the world: symbolic culture as the medium for psyche. *The Journal of Analytical Psychology*, 62(1), 32–49.

Colman, W. (2018). Are archetypes essential? *Journal of Analytical Psychology*, 63(3), 336–346.

Corbett, L. (2011). *The sacred cauldron: psychotherapy as a spiritual practice*. Chiron Publications.

Corbett, L. (2019). *Psyche and the sacred*. Routledge.

Corbett, L. (2021). *The God-image: from antiquity to Jung*. Chiron Publications.

Corbett, L. (2023). Jung's Self and the Ātman of the Upaniṣads. In L. Stein (ed.), *Eastern practices and individuation: essays by Jungian analysts*. Chiron Publications.

Cousins, L.S. (1981). The Paiihana and the development of the Theravadin Abhidhamma," *Journal of the Pali Text Society*, 9, 22–46.

Coward, H. G. (1984). Jung and Hinduism. *The Scottish Journal of Religious Studies*, 5(2), 65–88.

Crick, F., & Koch, C. (1990). Towards a neurobiological theory of consciousness. *Seminars in the Neurosciences*, 2, 263–275.

Dafermos, M. (2021). The metaphysics of psychology and a dialectical perspective. *Theory & Psychology*, 31(3), 355–374.

Damasio, A.R. (2002). How the brain creates the mind. *Scientific American*, 12(1), 4–9.

Damasio, A. (2000). The feeling of what happens. *Body, emotion, and the making of consciousness*. Vintage.

Damasio, A. (2010) *The self comes to mind: constructing the conscious brain*. Pantheon Books.

DeBakcsy, D. (2014). Stop Heisenberg abuse! Three outrageous misappropriations of quantum physics. *Skeptical Inquirer*, 38(3), 40–43.

Dennett, D.C. (1991). *Consciousness explained*. Penguin Books.

Dennett, D.C. (1992). *The self as a center of narrative gravity*. In: F. Kessel, P. Cole, & D. Johnson (eds.), *Self and consciousness: multiple perspectives*. Erlbaum.

DeRobertis, E. (2005). Metaphysics and psychology: a problem of the personal. *Journal of Theoretical and Philosophical Psychology*, 25(2), 101–119.

d'Espagnat, B. (1983). *In search of reality*. Springer-Verlag.

d'Espagnat, B. (2006). *On physics and philosophy*. Princeton University Press.

de Voogd, S. (1984). Fantasy versus fiction: Jung's Kantianism appraised. In R.K. Papadopoulos & G. S. Saayman, (Eds.), *Jung in modern perspective*. University of Michigan: Wildwood House.

Downing, J. (2000). *Between conviction and uncertainty: philosophical guidelines for the practicing psychotherapist*. SUNY Press.

Drob, S.L. (2017). *Archetype of the absolute: the unity of opposites in mysticism, philosophy, and psychology*. Fielding University Press.

Eccles, J.C. (1994). *How the self controls its brain*. Springer.

Eddington A.S. (1939). *The philosophy of physical science*. Macmillan.

Edelman, G. (2004). *Wider than the sky: the phenomenal gift of consciousness*. Yale University Press.

Einstein, A. (1934). *Essays in science*. Philosophical Library.

Erwin, E. (1997). *Philosophy and psychotherapy*. Sage Publications.

Faye, J., & Jaksland, R. (2021). Barad, Bohr, and quantum mechanics. *Synthese* 199, 8231–8255.

Fear, R., & Woolfe, R. (1999). The personal and professional development of the counsellor. the relationship between personal philosophy and theoretical orientation. *Counselling Psychology Quarterly*, 12(3), 253–262.

Feynman, R. (1994). *The character of physical law*. Penguin Books.

Fodor, J.J.A. (1983). *The modularity of mind: an essay on faculty psychology*. MIT Press.

Fordham, M. (1976). *The self and autism*. Karnac.

Frank, A. (2017). Minding matter. *Aeon*, March 13. https://aeon.co/essays/materia lism-alone-cannot-explain-the-riddle-of-consciousness

Frank, D.J. (1972). Common features of psychotherapy. *Australia and New Zealand Journal of Psychiatry*, 6, 34–40.

Frank, D.J., & Frank, J.B. (1993). *Persuasion and healing: a comparative study of psychotherapy*. Johns Hopkins University Press.

Frankish, K. (2016). Illusionism as a theory of consciousness. In K. Frankish (Ed.), *Illusionism as a theory of consciousness* (pp. 13–48). Imprint Academic.

Frattaroli, E. (2001). *Healing the soul in the age of the brain*. Penguin Books.

French, C.C. (2003). Fantastic memories: the relevance of research into eyewitness testimony and false memories for reports of anomalous experiences. *Journal of Consciousness Studies*, 10(6–7), 153–174.

Gadamer, H. (1982). *Truth and method*. Crossroads.

Ganeri, J. (2012). *The self: naturalism, consciousness, and the first-person stance*. Oxford University Press.

Gauld, A. (1984). *Mediumship and survival: a century of investigations*. Academy Chicago Publishers.

Gell-Mann, M. (1981). Questions for the future. In: J.H. Mulvey (Ed.), *The nature of matter*. Oxford University Press.

Gergen, K.J. (1991). *The saturated self: dilemmas of identity in contemporary life*. Basic Books.

Gieser, S. (2004). *The innermost kernel: depth psychology and quantum physics. Wolfgang Pauli's dialogue with C.G. Jung*. Springer.

Giegerich, W. (2008). *The soul's logical life: towards a rigorous notion of psychology*, 4th edition. Peter Lang.

Giegerich, W. (2012a). A serious misunderstanding: synchronicity and the generation of meaning. *Journal of Analytical Psychology*, 57(4), 500–511.

Giegerich, W. (2012b). *What is soul?* Spring Journal Books.

Glover, E. (1991). *Freud or Jung*. Northwestern University Press.

Goodman, N. (1984). *On minds and other matter*. Harvard University Press.

Goodwyn, E.D. (2019). Jung and the mind–body problem. In J. Mills (Ed.), *Jung and philosophy* (pp. 67–85). Routledge.

Goswami, A. (1989). The idealistic interpretation of quantum mechanics. *Physics Essays*, 2(4), 385–400.

Grotstein, J.S. (1981). *Splitting and projective identification*. Jason Aronson.

Grünbaum, A. (1986). *The foundation of psychoanalysis: a philosophical critique*. University of California Press.

Guerini, R., Marraffa, M., Meini, C., & Paternoster, A. (2019). Self and memory: a multidisciplinary debate. *Frontiers in Psychology*, 9.

Guggenbühl-Craig, A. (2015). *Power in the helping professions*. Spring Publications.

Gupta, B. (2003). *Cit: consciousness*. Oxford University Press.

Gupta, M. (2014). *Is evidence-based psychiatry ethical?*Oxford University Press.

Gusnard, D.A., & Raichle, M.E. (2001). Searching for a baseline: functional imaging and the resting human brain. *Nature Reviews Neuroscience* 2: 685–694.

Haber, H.F. (1994). *Beyond postmodern politics: Lyotard, Rorty, Foucault.* Routledge.

Hameroff, S.R., & Penrose, R. (2014). Consciousness in the universe: a review of the "Orch OR" theory. *Physics of Life Reviews*, 11(1), 39–78.

Hansson, S. (2006). Falsificationism falsified. *Foundations of Science*, 11(3), 275–286.

Hanson, N.R. (2018). *Perception and discovery: an introduction to scientific inquiry*, 2nd edition. Springer.

Hartelius, G. (2017). Taylor's soft perennialism: psychology or New Age spiritual vision? *The International Journal of Transpersonal Studies*, 36(2), 136–146.

Haule, J.R. (1984). From somnambulism to the archetypes: the French roots of Jung's split with Freud. *Psychoanalytic Review*, 71(4), 635–659.

Hayes, S.C. (1993). Analytic goals and varieties of scientific contextualism. In S.C. Hayes, L.J. Hayes, H.W. Reese, & T.R. Sarbin (Eds.) *Varieties of scientific contextualism* (pp. 11–27). Context Press.

Hearnshaw, L.S. (2020). *The shaping of modern psychology.* Routledge.

Heisenberg, W. (1958a). *Physics and philosophy.* Harper & Row.

Heisenberg, W. (1958b). *The physicist's conception of nature.* Trans. A. Pomerans. Harcourt Brace.

Henderson, D. (2010). The coincidence of opposites: C.G. Jung's reception of Nicholas of Cusa. *Studies in Spirituality*, 20, 101–113.

Henry, R.C. (2005). The mental universe. *Nature*, 436(7047), 29.

Herbert, N. (1987). *Quantum reality: beyond the new physics.* Anchor Books.

Hibberd, F.J. (2014). The metaphysical basis of a process psychology. *Journal of Theoretical and Philosophical Psychology*, 34(3), 161–186.

Hillman, J. (1975). *Re-visioning psychology.* Harper & Row.

Hobson, A. (2013) There are no particles, there are only fields, *American Journal of Physics*, 81(3), 211–223.

Hoeller, S. (1982). *The Gnostic Jung and the seven sermons to the dead.* Quest Books.

Hofstadter, D. (2008). *I am a strange loop.* Basic Books.

Hogenson, G.B. (2019). The controversy around the concept of archetypes. *Journal of Analytical Psychology*, 64(5), 682–700.

Holowchak, M.A. (2014). Psychotherapy as science or knack? A critique of the hermeneutic defense. *Journal of the General Philosophy of Science*, 45(2), 223–238.

Holton, G. (1988). The roots of complementarity. *Daedalus*, 117(3), 151–197.

Hölzel, B.K., Carmody, J., & Vangel, M., *et al.* (2011). Mindfulness practice leads to increases in regional brain gray matter density. *Psychiatry Research: Neuroimaging*, 191(1), 36–43.

Horney, K. (1939). *New ways in psychoanalysis.* W.W. Norton.

Hughes, H.S. (2002). *Consciousness and society.* Transaction Publishers.

Hume, D. (1748). *Philosophical essays concerning human understanding.* A. Millar.

Hunsley, J. (2007). Addressing key challenges in evidence-based practice in psychology. *Professional Psychology: Research and Practice* 38(2), 113–121.

Indich, W.M. (1980). *Consciousness in Advaita Vedānta.* Motilal Banarsidass Publishers.

Indick, W. (2002). Fight the power: the limits of empiricism and the costs of positivistic rigor. *The Journal of Psychology*, 136(1), 21–36.

James, W. (1898). *Human immortality. the supposed objections to the doctrine.* Riverside Press.

James, W. (1950 [1890]). *The principles of psychology,* vol. I. Dover.

James, W. (2003 [1907]). *Pragmatism: a new name for some old ways of thinking.* Barnes & Noble.

James, W. (2010 [1890]). The self and its selves. In C. Lemert (Ed.), *Social theory: the multicultural readings* (pp. 161–166). Westview Press.

Jeans, J. (2020 [1930]). *The mysterious universe.* Minkowski Institute Press.

Jones, E. (1959). *The life and work of Sigmund Freud.* Basic Books.

Jones, R.H. (2010). *Piercing the veil: comparing science and mysticism as ways of knowing.* Jackson Square Books.

Jones, R. (Ed.). (2014). *Jung and the question of science.* Routledge.

Jonkisz, J. (2012). Consciousness: a four-fold taxonomy. *Journal of Consciousness Studies,* 19(11), 55–82.

Jung, C.G. (1928). *Contributions to analytical psychology.* Kegan Paul.

Jung, C.G. (1954–1990). *Collected works.* Ed. H. Read, M. Fordham, & G. Adler. Trans. R.F.C. Hull. Princeton University Press/Routledge. Cited as CW.

Jung, C.G. (1964). *Man and his symbols.* Doubleday.

Jung, C.G. (1965). *Memories, dreams, reflections.* Random House.

Jung, C.G. (1988). *Nietzsche's Zarathustra: notes of the seminar given in 1934–1939 by C.G. Jung,* vol. 1. Ed. J.L. Jarrett. Princeton University Press.

Jung, C.G. (1973). *Letters,* vol. 1. Ed. G. Adler & A. Jaffe. Trans. R.F.C. Hull. Princeton University Press.

Jung, C.G. (1975). *Letters,* vol. 2. Ed. G. Adler & A. Jaffe. Trans. R.F.C. Hull. Princeton University Press.

Jung, C.G. (1976). *The visions seminars.* Spring Publications.

Jung, C.G. (1996). *The psychology of Kundalini Yoga.* Princeton University Press.

Jung, C.G., & Neumann, E. (2015). *Analytical psychology in exile: the correspondence of C.G. Jung and Erich Neumann.* Ed. M. Liebscher. Trans. H. McCartney. Princeton University Press.

Jung, C.G., & Pauli, W. E. (1955). *The interpretation of nature and the psyche. 1. Synchronicity: an acausal connecting principle. 2. The influence of archetypal ideas on the scientific theories of Kepler.* Trans. R.F.C. Hull. Pantheon Books.

Kant, I. (1950 [1787]). *Critique of pure reason.* Humanities Press.

Kant, I. (2004 [1772]). *Prolegomena to any future metaphysics that will be able to come forward as science: with selections from the critique of pure reason.* Trans. G. Hatfield. Cambridge University Press.

Kastrup, B. (2014). The "brain as receiver": comments on Steven Novella's post. www.bernardokastrup.com/2014/06/the-brain-as-filter-metaphor-comments.html (retrieved December 13, 2022).

Kastrup, B. (2015). *Brief peeks beyond: critical essays on metaphysics, neuroscience, free, skepticism and culture.* Iff Books.

Kastrup, B. (2019). *The idea of the world: a multi-disciplinary argument for the mental nature of reality.* John Hunt Books.

Kastrup, B. (2021). *Decoding Jung's metaphysics.* John Hunt Books.

Kastrup, B., Stapp, H.P., & Kafatos, M.C. (2018). Coming to grips with the implications of quantum mechanics. *Scientific American,* May 29.

Katz, S.T. (Ed.). (1978). *Mysticism and philosophical analysis.* Oxford University Press.

Kaufman, S.A. (2010). *Reinventing the sacred: a new view of science, reason, and religion*. Basic Books.

Kelly, E.F., Kelley, E.W., Crabtree, A., Gauld, A., Grosso, M., & Greyson, B. (2009). *Irreducible mind*. Rowman & Littlefield Publishers.

Kelly, E.F., Crabtree, A., & Marshall, P. (2019). *Beyond physicalism: toward reconciliation of science and spirituality*. Rowman & Littlefield Publishers.

Kepler, J. (2020). The common basis of memory and consciousness: understanding the brain as a read-write head interacting with an omnipresent background field. *Frontiers in Psychology*, 10, 2968.

Kime, P. (2018). Psychological empiricism and naturalism. In C. Roesler (Ed.), *Research in analytical psychology: empirical research* (pp. 11–26). Routledge.

King, T. (1999). *Jung's four and some philosophers*. Notre Dame University Press.

Klein, S.B. (2012). The self and its brain. *Social Cognition*, 30(4). 474–518.

Klein, S.B. (2010). The self: as a construct in psychology and neuropsychological evidence for its multiplicity. *Wiley Interdisciplinary Reviews: Cognitive Science*, 1 (2), 172–183.

Klein, S.B. (2015). A defense of experiential realism: the need to take phenomenological reality on its own terms in the study of the mind. *Psychology of Consciousness: Theory, Research, and Practice*, 2(1), 41.

Klein, S.B. (2016). The unplanned obsolescence of psychological science and an argument for its revival. *Psychology of Consciousness: Theory, Research, and Practice*, 3(4), 357–379.

Klein, S.B. (2017). Using psychic phenomena to connect mind to brain and to revise quantum mechanics. *Cosmos and History: The Journal of Natural and Social Philosophy*, 13(2), 34–46.

Klemm, D.E., & Klink, W.H. (2008). Quantum physics and beyond: consciousness and quantum mechanics: opting from alternatives. *Zygon*, 43(2), 307–327.

Knox, J. (2003). *Archetype, attachment, analysis: Jungian psychology and the emergent mind*. Routledge.

Knox, J. (2004). From archetypes to reflective function. *Journal of Analytical Psychology*, 49(1), 1–19.

Koch, C. (2014). Is Consciousness universal? A "complex" theory of consciousness. *Scientific American*, January 1. www.scientificamerican.com/article/is-consciousness-u niversal/.

Kohut, H. (1971). *The analysis of the self*. International Universities Press.

Kohut, H. (1977). *The restoration of the self*. International Universities Press.

Kistler, M. (2020). New trends in the metaphysics of science. *Synthese*, 197, 5.

Kripal, J., Jain, A., Prophet, E., & Anzali, A. (2014). *Comparing religions*. Oxford University Press.

Kuhlmann, M. (2013). What is real? *Scientific American*, 309(2), 40–47.

Kuhn, T.S. (1962). *The structure of scientific revolutions*. University of Chicago Press.

Laing, R.D. (1961). *The self and others*. Tavistock Publications.

Lakoff, G., & Johnson, M. (1999) *Philosophy in the flesh: the embodied mind and its challenge to Western thought*. Basic Books.

Lanza, R. (2009). *Biocentrism: how life and consciousness are the keys to understanding the true nature of the universe*. Benbella Books.

Latour, B. (1988). *Science in action: how to follow scientists and engineers through society*. Harvard University Press.

Laurence, S., & Macdonald, C. (Eds.). 1998. *Contemporary readings in the foundations of metaphysics*. Blackwell Publishers.

Laurikainen, K.V. (1987). Wolfgang Pauli's conception of reality. In P. Lahti & P. Mittelstaedt (Eds.), *Symposium on the foundations of modern physics: the Copenhagen interpretation*, pp. 209–228. World Scientific.

Laurikainen, K.V. (1990). Atoms and consciousness as complementary elements of reality. *European Journal of Physics* 11, 65–74.

Leahey, T.H. (2001). *A history of modern psychology*, 3rd edition. Prentice Hall.

Leary, M.R., & Tangney, J.P. (Eds.). (2012). *Handbook of self and identity*. Guilford Press.

LeShan, L. (2003). *The medium, the mystic, and the physicist: towards a general theory of the paranormal*. Helios Press.

Lewis, P.J. (2016). *Quantum ontology: a guide to the metaphysics of quantum mechanics*. Oxford University Press.

Lichtenberg, J.D., & Slap, J.W. (1973). Notes on the concept of splitting and the defense mechanism of the splitting of representations. *Journal of the American PsychoAnalytic Association*, 21(4), 772–787.

Lincoln, Y.S., Lynham, S.A., & Guba, E.G. (2017). Paradigmatic controversies, contradictions, and emerging confluences, revisited. In N.K. Denzin & Y.S. Lincoln (Eds.), *The Sage handbook of qualitative research*, 5th edition (pp. 108–150). Sage Publications.

Locke, J. (1975 [1689]). *An essay concerning human understanding*. Ed. P.H. Niddich. Oxford University Press.

Loy, D. (1997). *Nonduality: a study in comparative philosophy*. Humanity Books.

MacKenzie, M. (2010). Enacting the self: Buddhist and enactivist approaches to the emergence of the self. In M. Siderits, E. Thompson, & D. Zahavir (Eds.), *Self, no self? Perspectives from analytical, phenomenological, and Indian traditions* (pp. 239–273). Oxford University Press.

Main, R. (1998). *Jung on synchronicity and the paranormal*. Princeton University Press.

Main, R. (2004). *The rupture of time: synchronicity and Jung's critique of modern Western culture*. Brunner-Routledge.

Main, R. (2007). *Revelations of chance: synchronicity as a spiritual experience*. State University of New York Press.

Main, R. (2013). Secular and religious: the intrinsic doubleness of analytical psychology and the hegemony of naturalism in the social sciences. *Journal of Analytical Psychology*, 58(3), 366–386.

Main, R. (2022). *Breaking the spell of disenchantment: mystery, meaning, and metaphysics in the work of C.G. Jung*. Chiron Publications.

Majorek, M. (2012) Does the brain cause conscious experience? *Journal of Consciousness Studies*, 19, 121–144.

Manousakis, E. (2006). Founding quantum theory on the basis of consciousness. *Foundations of Physics*, 36(6), 795–838.

Mansfield, V. (1995). *Synchronicity, science, and soul-making*. Open Court Publishing.

Mansfield, V., & Spiegelman, J.M. (1989). Quantum mechanics and Jungian psychology: Building a Bridge. *Journal of Analytical Psychology*, 34(1), 3–31.

Mansfield, V., & Spiegelman, J.M. (1991). The opposites in quantum physics and Jungian psychology. I. Theoretical foundations. *The Journal of Analytical Psychology*, 36(3), 267–287.

Mansfield, V., & Spiegelman, J.M. (1996). On the physics and psychology of the transference as an interactive field. *Journal of Analytical Psychology, 41(2)*, 179–202.

Marcus, P., & Rosenberg, A. (Eds.). (1998). *Psychoanalytic versions of the human condition*. New York University Press.

Marin, J.M. (2009). "Mysticism" in quantum mechanics: the forgotten controversy. *European Journal of Physics*, 30(4), 807–822.

Marmodoro, A. & Mayr, E. (2019). *Metaphysics: an introduction to contemporary debates and their history*. Oxford University Press.

Maslow, A.H. (1971). *The farther reaches of human nature*. Viking Press.

Masson, J. (1993). *Against therapy*. Common Courage Press.

May, E.C., & Marwaha, S.B. (Eds.) (2014) *Anomalous cognition: remote viewing research and theory*. Jefferson, NC: McFarland.

Mayer, E.L. (2007). *Extraordinary knowing: science, skepticism, and the inexplicable powers of the human mind*. Bantam Books.

McGuire, W., & Hull, R.F.C. (1977). *C.G. Jung speaking*. Princeton University Press.

McGinn, C. (1999). *The mysterious flame: conscious minds in a material world*. Basic Books.

Meier, C.A. (Ed.) (2001). *Atom and archetype: the Pauli/Jung letters, 1932–1958*. Princeton University Press.

Mermin, N.D. (2004). What's wrong with this quantum world? *Physics Today*, 57(2), 10–11.

Messer, S. B., & Winokur, M. (1984). Ways of knowing and visions of reality in psychoanalytic therapy and behavior therapy. In H. Arkowitz & S. B. Messer (Eds.), *Psychoanalytic therapy and behavior therapy: is integration possible?* (pp. 53–100). Plenum Press.

Messer, S. B., & Woolfolk, R. L. (1998). Philosophical issues in psychotherapy. *Clinical Psychology: Science and Practice*, 5(2), 251–263.

Metzinger, T. (2009). *The ego-tunnel: the science of the mind and the myth of the self*. Basic Books.

Mills, J. (2013). Jung's metaphysics. *International Journal of Jungian Studies*, 5(1), 19–43.

Mills, J. (2014). Jung as philosopher: archetypes, the psychoid factor, and the question of the supernatural. *International Journal of Jungian Studies*, 6(3), 227–242.

Mills, J. (2019). Philosophizing Jung. In J. Mills (Ed.), *Jung and philosophy*, pp. 1–14. Routledge.

Mills, J. (2002). Reexamining the psychoanalytic corpse: from scientific psychology to philosophy. *Psychoanalytic Psychology*, 19(3), 552–558.

Michell, J. (1999). *Measurement in psychology: a critical history of a methodological concept*. Cambridge University Press.

Michell, J. (2003). The quantitative imperative: positivism, naïve realism and the place of qualitative methods in psychology. *Theory & Psychology*, 13(1), 5–31.

Mohanty, (1994). *Essays on Indian philosophy: traditional and modern*: Oxford University Press.

Moore, W. (1994). *A life of Erwin Schrödinger*. Cambridge University Press.

Morawski, J. G. (Ed.). (1988). *The rise of experimentation in American psychology*. Yale University Press.

Mossbridge, J., Tressoldi, P.E., & Utts, J. (2012). Predictive physiological anticipation preceding seemingly unpredictable stimuli: a meta-analysis. *Frontiers in Psychology*, 3, 390.

Mroczkowski, J.A., & Malozemoff, A.P. (2019). Quantum misuse in psychic literature. *Journal of Near-Death Studies*, 37(3), 131–154.

Musser, G. (2017). Spacetime is doomed. In S. Wuppuluri & G. Ghirardi (Eds.), *Space, time, and the limits of human understanding* (pp. 217–227). Springer Publications.

Nachman, G. (2009). Clinical implications of synchronicity and related phenomena. *Psychiatric Annals*, 39(5), 297–308.

Nagel, E. (1979a). *Teleology revisited and other essays in the philosophy and history of science*. Columbia University Press.

Nagel, T. (1979b). *Mortal questions*. Cambridge University Press.

Nagel, T. (1998). What is it like to be a bat? In N. Block, O. Flanagan, & G. Güzeldere (Eds.), *The nature of consciousness*. The MIT Press.

Nagel, T. (2012). *Mind and cosmos: why the materialist neo-Darwinian conception of nature is almost certainly false*. Oxford University Press.

Nagy, M. (1991). *Philosophical issues in the philosophy of C.G. Jung*. State University of New York Press.

Nash, C.B. (1984). Quantum physics and parapsychology. *Parapsychology Review*, 15 (3), 4–6.

Nauenberg, M. (2007). Critique of "Quantum enigma: physics encounters consciousness." *Foundations of Physics* 37, 1612–1627.

Nida- Rümelin, M. (2016). The illusion of illusionism. In K. Frankish (Ed.), *Illusionism as a theory of consciousness* (pp. 200–214). Imprint Academic.

Niikawa, T. (2021). Illusionism and definitions of phenomenal consciousness. *Philosophical Studies*, 178(1), 1–21.

Norcross, J. C. (2011). *Psychotherapy relationships that work: evidence-based responsiveness*, 2nd edition. Oxford University Press.

Ogden, T. H. (1994). *Subjects of analysis*. Rowman & Littlefield.

Ogden, T. H. (2019). Ontological psychoanalysis or "what do you want to be when you grow up?". *The Psychoanalytic Quarterly*, 88(4), 661–684.

Omnès, R. (2002). *Quantum philosophy: understanding and interpreting contemporary science*. Princeton University Press.

Orange, D. (2010). *Thinking for clinicians: philosophical resources for contemporary psychoanalysis and the humanistic psychotherapies*. Routledge.

Pais, A. (1991). *Niels Bohr's times, in physics, philosophy, and polity*. Oxford University Press.

Panksepp, J. (1998) *Affective neuroscience: the foundations of human and animal emotions*. Oxford University Press.

Papadopoulos, R.K. (2006). Jung's epistemology and methodology. In R.K. Papadopoulos (Ed.), *The handbook of Jungian psychology* (pp. 7–53). Routledge.

Parfit, D. (1986). *Reason and persons*. Oxford University Press.

Parker, I. (2015). (Ed.). *Handbook of critical psychology*. Routledge.

Parnia, S., Spearpoint, K., & Fenwick, P.B. (2007). Near death experiences, cognitive function, and psychological outcomes of surviving cardiac arrest. *Resuscitation*, 74 (2), 215–221.

Pauli, W. (1955). The influence of archetypal ideas on the scientific theories of Kepler. In C.G. Jung & W. Pauli, *The interpretation of nature and the psyche*. Pantheon Books.

Pauli, W. (1994a [1950]). The philosophical significance of the idea of complementarity (R. Schlapp, Trans.). In C.P. Enz & K. von Meyenn (Eds.), *Writings on physics and philosophy* (pp. 35–42). Springer-Verlag.

Pauli, W. (1994b [1954]). Matter. In C.P. Enz & K. von Meyenn (Eds.), *Writings on physics and philosophy* (pp. 27–34). Springer-Verlag.

Peat, F.D. (1987). *Synchronicity: the bridge between matter and mind.* Bantam Books.

Penrose, R. (1987). Minds, machines, and mathematics. In C. Blakemore & S. Greenfield (Eds.), *Mindwaves: thoughts on intelligence, identity, and consciousness.* Blackwell Publishing.

Perlovsky, L.I. (2016). Physics of the mind. *Frontiers in Systems Neuroscience*, 10, 84.

Pietikainen, P. (1998). Archetypes as symbolic forms. *Journal of Analytical Psychology*, 43(3), 325–342.

Pilecki, B.C., Clegg, J.W., & McKay, D. (2011). The influence of corporate and political interests on models of illness in the evolution of the DSM. *European Journal of Psychiatry*, 26(3), 194–200.

Pizzi, R., Fantasia, A., Gelain, F., Rossetti, D., & Vescovi, A. (2004). Nonlocal correlation between separated human neural networks. In E. Donkor, A.R. Pirick, & H.E. Brandt (Eds.), *Quantum information and computation II* (pp. 107–117). Society of Photo-Optical Instrumentation Engineers.

Ponte, V.D., & Schäfer, L. (2013). Carl Gustav Jung, quantum physics and the spiritual mind: A mystical vision of the twenty-first century. *Behavioral Sciences*, 3(4), 601–618.

Popper, K.R. (1968 [1934]). *The logic of scientific discovery.* Hutchinson & Co.

Popper, K. (1972). *Objective knowledge.* Oxford University Press.

Popper, K. (1977). Materialism criticized. In K. Popper & J. Eccles (Eds.), *The self and its brain. An argument for interactionism* (pp. 51–99).

Praetorius, N. (2003). Inconsistencies in the assumptions of constructivism and naturalism. *Theory & Psychology*, 13(4), 511–539.

Prasad, H.S. (2000). Dreamless sleep and soul: a controversy between Vedānta and Buddhism. *Asian Philosophy: An International Journal of the Philosophical Traditions of the East*, 10(1), 61–73.

Raabe, P.B. (2014). *Philosophy's role in counseling and psychotherapy.* Jason Aronson.

Rabeyron, T. (2020). Why most research findings about psi are false: the replicability crisis, the psi paradox, and the myth of Sisyphus. *Frontiers in Psychology*, 11, 2468.

Radhakrishnan, S. (1994). *The principle Upaniṣads.* Oxford University Press.

Radhakrishnan, S. (2008 [1923]). *Indian philosophy.* Oxford University Press.

Radin, D. I. (2006). *Entangled minds: extrasensory experiences in a quantum reality.* Paraview Pocket Books.

Radin, D. (2018). *Real magic: ancient wisdom, modern science, and a guide to the secret power of the universe.* Harmony.

Radin, D., Schlitz, M., & Baur, C. (2015). Distant healing intention therapies: an overview of the scientific evidence. *Global Advances in Health and Medicine*, 4 (Suppl), 67–71.

Ratcliffe, M. (2017). Selfhood, schizophrenia, and the interpersonal regulation of experience. In C. Durt, T. Fuchs, & C. Tewes (Eds.), *Embodiment, enaction, and culture: Investigating the constitution of the shared world* (pp. 149–171). MIT Press.

Ratner, K. (1997). *Cultural psychology and qualitative methodology: theoretical and empirical considerations.* Springer Science & Business Media.

Rao, K.R. (2005). *Consciousness studies: cross cultural perspectives.* McFarland.

Rao, K.R. (2016). *Psychology in the Indian tradition.* K.K. Printworld.

Reber, A.S., & Alcock, J.E. (2019) Searching for the impossible: parapsychology's elusive quest, *American Psychologist*, 75(3), 391–399.

Rhine, J.B. (1934). *Extra-sensory perception*, 4th edition. Branden Publishing Company (1997).

Rieff, P. (1973). *The triumph of the therapeutic: uses of faith after Freud*. Penguin.

Rivera, J. (2016). God and metaphysics in contemporary theology: reframing the debate. *Theological Studies*, 77(4), 823–844.

Robinson, D.N. (2007). Theoretical psychology: what is it and who needs it? *Theory & Psychology*, 17, 187–198.

Roesler, C. (2012). Are archetypes transmitted more by culture than biology? Questions arising from conceptualizations of the archetype. *Journal of Analytical Psychology*, 57, 223–246.

Roesler, C. (2018). The effectiveness of Jungian psychotherapy. In A. Kuzmicki & I. Blocian (Eds.), *Contemporary influences on Jung's thought*. Brill.

Rogers, C.R. (1961). *On becoming a person*. Houghton Mifflin.

Rorty, R. (1999). *Philosophy and social hope*. Penguin Books.

Rosenblum, B., & Kuttner, F. (2011). *Quantum enigma: physics encounters consciousness*. Oxford University Press.

Rovelli, C. (2021). *Helgoland: Making sense of the quantum revolution*. Riverhead Books.

Ruby, P., & Legrand, D. (2007). Neuroimaging the self? In Y. Rossetti, P. Haggard, & M. Kawato (Eds.), *Sensorimotor foundations of higher cognition* (pp. 293–318). Oxford University Press.

Russell, B. (1992 [1927]). *Analysis of matter*. Routledge.

Ryan, R. M., & Rigby, C. S. (2015). Did the Buddha have a self? No-self, self, and mindfulness in Buddhist thought and Western psychologies. In K. Brown, D. Creswell, & R. Ryan (Eds.), *Handbook of mindfulness: theory, research, and practice* (pp. 245–265). Guilford Press.

Ryle, G. (1949). *The concept of mind*. Peregrine Books.

Saban, M. (2014). A response to Jon Mills' paper, "Jung's metaphysics". *International Journal of Jungian Studies*, 6(3), 205–216.

Saban, M. (2022). Two Jungs: two sciences? *International Journal of Jungian Studies*, 1, 1–21.

Sachdeva, I.P. (1978). *Yoga and depth psychology*. Motilal Banarsidass.

Sattin, D., Magnani, F.G., Bartesaghi, L., Caputo, M., Fittipaldo, A.V., Cacciatore, M., Picozzi, M., Leonardi, M., & Leisman, G. (2021). Theoretical models of consciousness: a scoping review. *Brain Sciences*, 11(5), 535.

Schäfer, L. (2006). Quantum reality, the emergence of complex order from virtual states, and the importance of consciousness in the universe. *Zygon*, 41(3), 505–532.

Schäfer, L. (2013). *Infinite potential*. Deepak Chopra Books.

Schlegel, R.J., Smith, C.M., & Hirsch, K.A. (2013). Examining the true self as a wellspring of meaning. In J.A. Hicks (Ed.), *The experience of meaning in life: classical perspectives, emerging themes, and controversies*. Routledge, C. Springer Netherlands.

Schurger, A., Mylopoulos, M., & Rosenthal, D. (2016). Neural antecedents of spontaneous voluntary movement: a new perspective. *Trends in Cognitive Science*, 20, 77–79.

Schwartz-Salant, N. (1989). *The borderline personality: vision and healing*. Chiron Publications.

Schwartz, J.M., & Begley, S. (2002). *The mind and the brain: neuroplasticity and the power of mental force*. Harper Collins.

Schwartz, J.M., Stapp, H.P., & Beauregard M. (2005). Quantum physics in neuroscience and psychology: a neurophysiological model of mind-brain interaction. *Philosophical Transactions B: Biological Sciences*, 360(1458), 1309–1327.

Schwartz-Salant, N. (1982). *Narcissism and character transformation*. Inner City Books.

Seager, W. (1997). Consciousness, information, and panpsychism. In J. Shear (Ed.), *Explaining consciousness: the "hard problem"* (pp. 269–286). MIT Press.

Searle, J. (2005). *Mind: a brief introduction*. Oxford University Press.

Segal, R.A. (2014). On Mills' "Jung's Metaphysics". *International Journal of Jungian Studies*, 6(3), 217–222.

Segal, R.A. (2018). Is Jungian analysis scientific? In A. Kuzmicki & I. Blocian (Eds.), *Contemporary influences of C.G. Jung's thought*. Brill.

Sepetyi, D. (2018). Quantum mechanics and consciousness: no evidence for idealism. www.researchgate.net/publication/327594187_Quantum_Mechanics_and_Consciousness_No_Evidence_for_Idealism.

Shamdasani, S. (2003). *Jung and the making of modern psychology: the dream of a science*. Cambridge University Press.

Shean, G.D. (2013). Controversies in psychotherapy research: epistemic differences in assumptions about human psychology. *American Journal of Psychotherapy*, 67(1), 73–85.

Shedler, (2010). The efficacy of psychodynamic psychotherapy. *The American Psychologist*, 65(2), 98–109.

Shedler, J. (2015). What is the evidence for "evidence-based" therapy? *The Journal of Psychological Therapies in Primary Care*, 4, 47–59.

Siderits, M., Thompson, E., & Zahavi, D. (2010). *Self, no self? Perspectives from analytical, phenomenological, and Indian traditions*. Oxford University Press.

Simon, C. (2019). Can quantum physics help solve the hard problem of consciousness? *Journal of Consciousness Studies*, 26(5–6), 204–218.

Skrbina, D. (2017). *Panpsychism in the West*. MIT Press.

Slife, B.D., & Williams, R.N. (1995). *What's behind the research? Discovering hidden assumptions in the behavioral sciences*. Sage Publications.

Solms, M. (2021). *The hidden spring: a journey to the source of consciousness*. W.W. Norton.

Sorabji, R. (2006). *Self: ancient and modern insights about individuality, life, and death*. University of Chicago Press.

Sparby, T., Edelhäuser, F., & Weger, U. (2019). The true self. critique, nature, method. *Frontiers in Psychology*, 10, 2250.

Spence, D.P. (1987). *The Freudian metaphor: toward paradigm change in psychoanalysis*. W.W. Norton.

Spiegelman, J.M. (1996). *Psychotherapy as a mutual process*. New Falcon Publications.

Stapp, H. (2009) Quantum reality and mind. *Journal of Cosmology and Astroparticle Physics* 3, 570–579.

Stapp, H.P. (2011). *Mindful universe: quantum mechanics and the participating observer*. Springer.

Stapp, H.P. (2014). Quantum physics and philosophy of mind. In A. Corradini & U. Meixner (Eds.), *Quantum physics meets the philosophy of mind* (pp. 17–34). Walter de Gruyter.

Stapp, H.P. (2017). *Quantum theory and free will*. Springer International Publishing.

Steele, R.S. (1982). *Freud and Jung: conflicts of interpretation*. Routledge & Kegan Paul.

Stein, M. (2018). *Jung's treatment of Christianity: the psychotherapy of a religious tradition*. Chiron Publications.

Stenger, V.J. (1993). The myth of quantum consciousness. *Humanist*, 53(3), 13–15.

Stevens, A. (1982). *Archetypes: a natural history of the self*. Routledge & Kegan Paul.

Stolorow, R.D., & Atwood, G.E. (1979). *Faces in a cloud: subjectivity in personality theory*. Jason Aronson.

Stolorow, R., Brandchaft, B., & Atwood, G. (1994). *The intersubjective perspective*. Jason Aronson.

Strohminger, N., Knobe, J., & Newman, G. (2017). The true self: a psychological concept distinct from the self. *Perspectives on Psychological Science*, 12(4), 551–560.

Storm, J.F. (2020). Why does the brain-mind (consciousness) problem seem so hard? *Journal of Consciousness Studies*, 27(5–6),174–189.

Strawson, G. (1997). The self. *Journal of Consciousness Studies*, 4, 405–428.

Strawson, G. (2006). Realistic monism: why physicalism entails panpsychism. *Journal of Consciousness Studies*, 13(10–11), 3–31.

Strawson, G. (2008). *Real materialism and other essays*. Oxford University Press.

Strawson, G. (2011). The minimal subject. In S. Gallagher (Ed.), *Oxford handbook of the self* (pp. 161–208). Oxford University Press.

Strawson, G. (2016). Consciousness isn't a mystery. It's matter. *The New York Times*, May 16. www.nytimes.com/2016/05/16/opinion/consciousness-isnt-a-mystery-its-matter.html

Strupp, H.H., & Hadley, S.W. (1979). Specific versus nonspecific factors in psychotherapy. *Archives of General Psychiatry*, 36, 1125–1136.

Studstill, R. (2005). *The unity of mystical traditions: the transformation of consciousness in Tibetan and German mysticism*. Brill.

Sucharov, M.S. (1992). Quantum physics and self psychology: toward a new epistemology. *Progress in Self Psychology*, 8, 199–211.

Tallis, R. (2004). *Why the mind is not a computer: a pocket lexicon of neuromythology*. Imprint Academic.

Tart, C. (2009). *The end of materialism: how evidence of the paranormal is bringing science and spirit together*. New Harbinger.

Taylor, S. (2012). Spontaneous awakening experiences: beyond religion and spiritual practice. *Journal of Transpersonal Psychology*, 44(1), 73–91.

Taylor, C. (2012). *Sources of the self: the making of modern identity*. Harvard University Press.

Taylor, S. (2016). From philosophy to phenomenology: the argument for a "soft" perennialism. *International Journal of Transpersonal Studies*, 35(2), 17–41.

Taylor, S. (2017). The return of perennial perspectives? Why transpersonal psychology should remain open to essentialism. *International Journal of Transpersonal Studies*, 36(2), 75–92.

Tolman, C.W. (1992). *Positivism in psychology: historical and contemporary problems*. Springer Verlag.

Tononi, G., Boly, M., Massimini, M., & Koch, C. (2016). Integrated information theory: From consciousness to its physical substrate (with Supplementary Information). *Nature Reviews Neuroscience*, 17(7), 450–461.

Totton, N. (2007). Funny you should say that: paranormality, at the margins and the centre of psychotherapy. *European Journal of Psychotherapy & Counselling*, 9(4), 389–401.

Tresan, D.L. (1996). Jungian metapsychology and neurobiological theory. *Journal of Analytical Psychology*, 41, 399–436.

Trigg, R. (2015). *Beyond matter: why science needs metaphysics*. Templeton Press.

Ullman, M. (2011 [1974]). Psi and psychiatry. In E. Mitchell (Ed.), *Psychic exploration: a challenge for science*. Cosimo Books.

Van Gulick, R. (2014) Consciousness. In E.N. Zalta (Ed.), *The Stanford encyclopedia of philosophy*. Spring 2014 edition. http://plato. stanford.edu/archives/spr2014/entries/consciousness/.

Venkatasubramanian, G. (2015). Understanding schizophrenia as a disorder of consciousness: biological correlates and translational implications from quantum theory perspectives. *Clinical Psychopharmacology and Neuroscience*, 13(1), 36–47.

Vimal, R.L.P., (2009). Meanings attributed to the term "consciousness": an overview. *Journal of Consciousness Studies*, 16(5), 9–27.

von Franz, M.-L. (1974). *Number and time*. Northwestern University Press.

von Franz, M.-L. (1984). Meaning and order: concerning meeting points and differences between depth psychology and physics. In R. Papadopoulos & G. Saayman (Eds.), *Jung in modern perspective*. Wildwood House.

von Franz, M.-L. (1988). *Psyche and matter*. Shambhala.

von Lucadou, W., Römer, H., & Walach, H. (2007). Synchronistic phenomena as entanglement correlations in generalized quantum theory. *Journal of Consciousness Studies*, 14, 50–74.

von Neumann, J. (1955 [1932]). *Mathematical foundations of quantum mechanics*. Trans. R.T. Beyer. Princeton University Press.

Wackermann, J., Seiter, C., Keibel, H., & Walach, H. (2003). Correlations between brain electrical activities of two spatially separated human subjects. *Neuroscience Letters*, 336, 60–64.

Walach, H. (2014). Towards an epistemology of inner experience. In S. Schmidt & H. Walach (Eds.), *Meditation: neuroscientific approaches and philosophical implications* (pp. 7–22). Springer.

Walach, H. (2007). Mind—body—spirituality. *Mind and Matter*, 5(2), 215–240.

Walach, H. (2017). Secular spirituality—what it is, why we need it, how to proceed. *Journal for the Study of Spirituality*, 7(1), 7–20.

Waldron, W.S. (2003). *The Buddhist unconscious: the Alaya-Vijnyana in the context of Indian Buddhist thought*. Routledge Curzon.

Walsh, R.T.G., Teo, T., & Baydala, A. (2014). *A critical history and philosophy of psychology*. Cambridge University Press.

Wampold, B.E. (2015). How important are the common factors in psychotherapy? An update. *World Psychiatry*, 14, 270–277.

Wampold, B.E., & Imel, Z.E. (2015). *The great psychotherapy debate: the evidence of what makes psychotherapy work*, 2nd edition. Routledge.

Wang, Z., & Busemeyer, J. (2015). Reintroducing the concept of complementarity into psychology. *Frontiers in Psychology*, 6(27), 1–5.

Watson, J.B. (1913). Psychology as the behaviorist views it. *Psychological Review*, 20, 158–177.

Weger, U., & Herbig, K. (2019). The self as activity. *Review of General Psychology*, 23 (2), 251–262.

Weger, U., & Herbig, K. (2021). The self in the periphery. *Review of General Psychology*, 25(1), 73–84.

Weger, U., Meyer, A., & Wagemann, J. (2016). Exploring the behavioral, experiential, and conceptual dimensions of the self: Introducing a new phenomenological approach. *European Psychologist*, 21, 180–194.

Wegner, D. (2002). *The illusion of conscious will.* MIT Press.

Wehr, G. (1987). *Jung: a biography.* Shambhala.

Westen, D., Novotny, C.M., & Thompson-Brenner, H. (2004). The empirical status of empirically supported psychotherapies: assumptions, findings, and reporting in controlled clinical trials. *Psychological Bulletin*, 130(4), 631–663.

Wheeler, J.A. (1997). *At home in the universe.* The American Institute of Physics.

Wheeler, J.A., & Zurek, W.H. (1983). *Quantum theory and measurement.* Princeton University Press.

White, R. (2011). Parapsychology today. In E.D. Mitchell (Ed.), *Psychic exploration: a challenge for science* (pp. 153–169). Cosimo.

Whitehead, A.N. (1979). *Process and reality.* Free Press.

Whitfield, C. (2009). *The Jungian myth and Advaita Vedānta.* Chennai: Arsha Vidya Publications.

Whitney, L. (2017). Depth psychology through the lens of classical yoga: a reconsideration of Jung's ontic reality. *International Journal of Jungian Studies*, 9(1), 17–27.

Whitney, L. (2018). *Consciousness in Jung and Patañjali.* Routledge.

Willig, C. (2019). Ontological and epistemological reflexivity: a core skill for therapists. *Counselling & Psychotherapy Research*, 19(3), 186–194.

Wilson, C. (1984). *C.G. Jung: lord of the underworld.* Wellingborough.

Winnicott, D.W. (1964). *Memories, dreams, reflections* by C. G. Jung. *International Journal of Psycho-Analysis*, 45, 450–455.

Winnicott, D.W. (1965). *Ego distortion in terms of true and false self.* In D.W. Winnicott, *The maturational processes and the facilitating environment* (pp. 140–152). International Universities Press.

Wolf, F.A. (1981). *Taking the quantum leap: the new physics for non-scientists.* Harper and Row.

Yaden, D.B., & Anderson, D. (2021). The psychology of philosophy: associating philosophical views with psychological traits in professional philosophers. *Philosophical Psychology*, 34(5), 721–755.

Yu, S., & Nicolić, D. (2011). Quantum mechanics needs no consciousness. *Annalen der Physik*, 523(11), 931–938.

Zabriski, B. (1995). Jung and Pauli: a subtle asymmetry. *Journal of Analytical Psychology*, 40, 531–553.

Zahavi, D. (2005). Being someone. *Psyche*, 11, 1–20.

Zahavi, D. (2014). *Self & other: exploring subjectivity, empathy, and shame.* Oxford University Press.

Zukav, G. (1970). *The dancing Wu-Li masters.* HarperCollins.

Zurek, W.H. (1991). Decoherence and the transition from quantum to classical. *Physics Today*, 44(10), 36–44.

Index

Page numbers followed by "n" refer to notes.

For Product Safety Concerns and Information please contact our EU
representative GPSR@taylorandfrancis.com
Taylor & Francis Verlag GmbH, Kaufingerstraße 24, 80331 München, Germany

www.ingramcontent.com/pod-product-compliance
Lightning Source LLC
Chambersburg PA
CBHW050646280326
41932CB00015B/2804